Healing from the Trauma of Childhood Sexual Abuse

Healing from the Trauma of Childhood Sexual Abuse

The Journey for Women

KAREN A. DUNCAN

Westport, Connecticut
London

Library of Congress has cataloged the hardcover edition as follows:

Duncan, Karen A., 1955–
    Healing from the trauma of childhood sexual abuse : the journey for women /
    Karen A. Duncan.
        p.   cm.
    Includes bibliographical references and index.
    ISBN: 0-275-98084-7 (alk. paper)
    1. Child sexual abuse—Psychological aspects.   2. Adult child sexual abuse
victims—Counseling of.   I. title.
HV6570.D86 2004
362.76′4—dc22   2004040079

British Library Cataloguing in Publication Data is available

Library of Congress Catalog Card Number: 2004040079
ISBN: 978–0–313–36321–4

First published in 2004

Praeger Publishers, 88 Post Road West, Westport, CT 06881
An imprint of Greenwood Publishing Group, Inc.
www.praeger.com

Printed in the United States of America

The paper used in this book complies with the
Permanent Paper Standard issued by the National
Information Standards Organization (Z39.48–1984).

10 9 8 7 6 5 4 3 2 1

To Alice and Debbie,
thank you for believing.
And to Andy,
who inspires me with his
passion and spirit
for life!

Contents

Preface

For the past several years, I have had the privilege of working with women who wanted to heal from the trauma of childhood sexual abuse. *Healing from the Trauma of Childhood Sexual Abuse: The Journey for Women* is the outcome of these efforts and the commitment of these women.

The women who heal with this approach to recovery are a diverse group. Most are between the ages of thirty-five and fifty-five. They are married, single, with or without children. They are stay-at-home moms, volunteers, students, managers, administrators, and professionals. They work in health care services, technology, business, law, retail, and manufacturing. Their diversity did not prevent their strength of character from coming through as a common factor in their ability to heal.

While some have tried to maintain a relationship with their families in which the sexual abuse occurred, others have had to distance themselves in order for the abuse they endured in their childhood not to continue. None of the women whose stories are shared within these pages ever reported that the person who sexually abused them had personally acknowledged the trauma or the harm done without first being confronted to do so. While there are women who have the support of family or other significant people during their recovery, there are women who go through the healing process without this type of support. In the end, what both groups of women find is that it is their personal faith that sees them through and enables them to prevail.

What these women have in common is their desire to heal a trauma that devastated their lives. Each came to treatment somehow knowing beforehand that at some point in their life journey they would face what had happened to them when they were children. While healing from childhood sexual abuse is not normally considered a developmental stage in the life cycle of women, perhaps it should be, for there seems to be a stage of life that each woman enters when she is ready to heal.[1] When women find that they are at this stage, then this book will be available to guide, encourage, and support this rite of passage.

By the year 2000, the number of women in the thirty-five to fifty-four age group stood at forty-one million. One woman in three is reported to have been sexually abused during childhood. Therefore, the need is imperative for useful and relevant information about healing this trauma to be available to women and their health care providers.[2] I have often considered what percentage of the problems in women's lives is due to the impact of a trauma that occurred when they were children. At the same time, I have also questioned how well women are encouraged to seek treatment for childhood sexual abuse when, as a society, we still refuse to fully accept that this trauma occurred in past generations just as it still occurs to children today.

This approach to recovery is based on the belief that women have suffered, endured, and survived this trauma and encourages women to become active participants in their healing by becoming educated about the trauma of childhood sexual abuse in terms of how it affects women's lives. The methods described in this book can help women discover the connection between the early trauma of childhood abuse and the problems they experience today. This approach draws on the information we already have about healing and, together with new insights, provides guidance through a recovery process. The treatment approach is based on premises derived from cognitive and humanist psychology as well as feminist theory on women's development, the treatment of traumatic stress, and information from women who report being victims of this type of childhood abuse.[3]

Case studies are included to give the reader an idea of the diversity of women who experienced this trauma as children. The women whose histories are described throughout this book help explain the impact of sexual abuse for years after the original trauma ended. Shock symptoms, chronic physical and emotional pain, dissociation, reenactment behavior, repeated trauma in adulthood, and isolation from others are examples of the aspects of childhood sexual abuse that women experience for a number of years following the trauma. In her own unique way, each woman relates the dramatic and negative effects of this trauma throughout her life experience.

While women can use this book as a resource in their own self-healing, it is not meant to replace effective therapeutic intervention. I hope women will use this book and seek therapeutic support to heal. Because the victims were children, this trauma was frequently endured alone. As adults, women have the choice and the right to reach out for support and guidance during their healing. Therapists, whether they are in an individual or group practice, can use the information to guide a treatment approach with women. Physicians such as psychiatrists, family practitioners, or gynecologists who provide medical assistance to women with a history of this trauma will find this book helpful as a model for continuity of treatment with female patients since it advocates for a coordination of care among health care providers.

College professors teaching undergraduate or graduate programs and training future professionals in the fields of psychology, social work, marriage and family therapy, and women's studies can use this book as a supplement to help prepare professionals entering the field of clinical practice or health care to women. We need specific training for upcoming professionals in these fields so that they are prepared to hear, understand, and diagnosis this trauma to women. This book can also help family and friends in supporting someone who is healing from childhood sexual abuse. Within the general public, it may serve to remind individuals that although today's news often reports current child sexual abuse, there are women who live in their community who are also childhood victims of this crime. Let us all remember that women who endured this trauma also deserve our compassion when reporting and healing from childhood sexual abuse.

During the writing of this book, the disclosure of sexual abuse by priests in the Catholic Church occurred. The cardinal in Boston admitted to knowing about and concealing sexual abuse by priests for approximately twenty years. Following this admission, a similar statement was made by the cardinal in Los Angeles. Authorities in the church protected these perpetrators. This protection to perpetrators came at the cost of children's trust, safety, and well-being. As a child victim, and as a therapist, I know that the cover-up of perpetrators' behavior occurs in our families and in our society. For too long we have silenced children, protected or excused perpetrators, and allowed the trauma of childhood sexual abuse to continue. Perhaps this disclosure, as painful as it is for the adults who were victims and the families who love them, will once again remind us that we need to act on the information we have about this childhood trauma, strengthen our conviction to report this crime, prosecute perpetrators, and protect our children. Together, we can expose this crime and keep our children safe.

Any woman who has been a victim of childhood sexual abuse deserves to have information that supports her recovery. Thousands of children continue to report this crime. These reported statistics tell us that the children abused today are going to be the adults who tomorrow may seek assistance to heal. To that end, this book is a continuation of the ongoing commitment to add to the body of knowledge that exists about recovery from the trauma of childhood sexual abuse. It is a book for all women who hope someday to live free from the long-term effects of childhood sexual abuse that have devastated their lives for a number of years. It is an affirmation for people who believe that, with recovery, the legacy of childhood sexual abuse will eventually end. Victims of the past can become adults who heal, and with healing comes the hope of preventing this trauma to children in future generations.

May each woman find her path to the journey of healing.

Note about the women: The women in these stories gave their permission to share their history of childhood sexual abuse as a way to use their voice to support other women during their journey to heal. Some of the women chose to use their full names, while others chose to use their first name only or a pseudonym. I thank each of them for sharing their personal journey with each of you.

Note about women's stories: A conscious choice was made not to share explicit details about the acts of abuse committed against the women presented throughout this book. The details of the abuse are not important; rather, the real value comes from understanding what these women experienced throughout their lives because of this trauma.

Note about perpetrators: While the majority of perpetrators in this book are identified or referred to as male, my intent is not to exclude female perpetrators and the children who suffer from their abuse. While perpetrator gender is not discussed at length, since that is not the purpose of this work, the information on the belief system of perpetrators can apply to male and female offenders. The harm that sexual abuse does to a child is real regardless of a perpetrator's gender.

Acknowledgments

This book would not have been possible without the support of other people. My colleagues Linda Banayote, Anne Flood, Gina Ciremele, and Joy Preston encouraged me to write about the process of healing from childhood sexual abuse. Ted Slutz, a dedicated graduate student at Yale University, provided skillful revisions that gave clarity to my words. M. Yvonne Ramsey, my copy editor through BookComp, made the final manuscript even better—thank you! Faye Plascak-Craig, chairperson of the Psychology Department at Marian College, offered friendship, thoughtful guidance, and knowledge that eased me through the early chapter revisions and improved the quality of this work. Ron Smith, Director at the Indianapolis Counseling Center, provided information and resources on sexual offenders and, in particular, the denial system of people who sexually abuse children. To Kathy, Michelle, Jami, and Sandy, thank you for the time you gave to see that the words I wrote described what women would need to know about healing. Andrew T. Duncan researched and finalized the Internet sources so that women could use these sites for further support of their recovery—thank you! Abigail Taylor's speed at typing and attention to detail helped to finalize the manuscript, thereby decreasing my anxiety—thank you, Abbey! Debbie Carvalko, my editor at Greenwood Publishing, will always have my eternal gratitude for giving me the incredible opportunity to have this first book published. She became a coach, friend, and mentor. By putting quality before deadlines, she encouraged me to stay focused on the reason I was committed to this work. I hope all first-time authors are fortunate enough to have an editor such as Debbie. And to my husband, Tom, who made me coffee and brownies, served as my sounding board, and always believed in the girl from Jackson Street, you have my love and gratitude.

Over the years, as this treatment approach was developed, I became familiar with the work of other authors who had written about childhood sexual abuse. I felt a kinship with them because of their desire to bring information to women about the trauma of childhood sexual abuse. Their work inspired and motivated me to persist in the belief that healing this trauma was possible. In particular, Alice Miller's book, *The Drama of the Gifted Child: the Search for the True Self* (originally published as *Prisoners of Childhood*), was one of the first books to help me realize that by admitting the truth of my childhood, healing was possible.

Finally, to the women who entrusted their care to me, I will always hold each of you in the heart of this work. Your courage, honesty, and perseverance created a circle of hope for other women. All of us became sister travelers who helped one another heal. To each of you, I thank you—now and always.

Introduction

The start of my clinical practice in 1983 coincided with the increase in society's awareness that the trauma of sexual abuse was occurring to children. This awareness included the realization that a high percentage of the reported perpetrators were male. The majority of these men were family members with an established relationship of trust with either the child or the family. Attempts were being made to answer such questions as, What can be done to intervene on behalf of children? How are children being affected? How does sexual abuse correlate with other problems in a family? What can be done to prevent the sexual abuse of children? What causes a family member to sexually abuse a child? For how many years has this trauma been occurring in families? These questions, and others, brought about significant change in how we, as a society, viewed childhood and families. Within the mental health profession, the answers being proposed influenced the types of treatment offered to children and their families.

The awareness, and the changes it brought, came from several sources. Literature that described the traumatic experience of childhood sexual abuse began to be published more frequently and was more readily available. Statistics on the prevalence of this trauma to children were tabulated by agencies in the United States. Laws that specifically defined childhood sexual abuse as a crime were legislated. Courts became more involved, responding to the greater number of arrests and prosecution of abusers. Media reports were more prevalent and facilitated the public's awareness of sexual trauma to children. Schools began to offer programs to help educate children about the types of abuses. This in turn influenced the number of reports to local police of child abuse in general as well as child sexual abuse. States established child protection services to assist children who are victims of abuse and maltreatment. Television shows and movies that focused on the theme of childhood sexual abuse were produced. These multiple events assisted to expose the myths surrounding this family secret.

In conjunction with these events, women began to disclose that they, too, were victims of childhood sexual abuse. Consequently, they were also seeking answers to their questions. As a therapist, I found that the questions women asked followed some main themes: What about me, can I heal? How do I heal? Is it too late to prosecute since it happened ten, twenty, or thirty years ago? Can sexual abuse cause problems like depression, anxiety, sexual discomfort, eating disorders, chronic pain, nightmares, or addictions? How do I trust that what I remember is real? Will anyone believe me? Do I believe myself? Twenty years later, the questions asked by women who experienced childhood sexual abuse remain the same. Women still call for an appointment, walk through my door, and, when provided safety and trust, will tell how they too were victims of childhood sexual abuse. They come seeking answers. They are women who characterize what author Caroline Myss describes as "the power of the human spirit to catalyze a healing process" and reclaim their lives.[1] The indomitable spirit of these women remains alive, and it is their spirit that brings them to recovery.

The treatment approach discussed in the following chapters is a therapeutic framework that supports women's recovery from childhood sexual abuse. It is based on research, literature, clinical practice, and the female experience. Over a number of years, women helped to refine this approach through the many hours of therapy they attended. While not part of a formal research study, these women shared about how they lived through the trauma of sexual abuse in their families and how their lives changed as a result. Together, they help validate the effectiveness of this treatment approach by the improvement they reported in their lives.

This treatment approach is not meant to be an answer for all women; rather, it is a choice presented to women and advocates that healing is possible. This belief is based on the observation that when women have the opportunity to heal, they lead healthier, more fulfilled lives. From a developmental perspective, gradually identifying the connection between the trauma and specific reoccurring problems is considered integral to successful treatment. In particular is the connection of how a woman's development, identity, and self-concept have been affected by sexual abuse. What a woman accomplishes by going back to the trauma is overcoming the fear of confronting traumatic memories and regaining an involvement with life that is fulfilling and rewarding.[2]

The following premises will assist the reader in understanding the framework that formed this approach.

PREMISES OF THE TREATMENT APPROACH

1. Childhood sexual abuse is a trauma that affects the development of a woman's identity, self-concept, and belief system. Consequently, when not treated, childhood sexual abuse will affect her ability to function effectively in some aspects of her adult life.

2. An educational component early in treatment that provides information about trauma in general and childhood sexual abuse in particular can assist in stabilizing some symptoms and reinforce commitment to treatment during the initial stages of recovery.

3. Women experience traumatic memories of childhood sexual abuse in a diverse way, and this diversity needs to be understood by health care professionals if they are to treat this particular trauma.

4. Studies in neurobiology in relationship to traumatic memory continue to improve our understanding of how the processes in the structures of the brain responsible for memory are disrupted when trauma occurs.

5. Studies of somatic illness are increasing our understanding of how various traumas contribute to a variety of physical disorders. This understanding will help in the identification of health problems women suffer from that are related to the trauma of childhood sexual abuse, which in turn will improve the treatment approaches proposed to women.

6. Either a lack of treatment or ineffective treatment can cause the effects of this trauma to be prolonged.

7. A generally accepted established belief system is identified as existing in families where sexual abuse occurs. This belief system can maintain a perpetrator's control over the child victim, contribute to the family denial system, and sustain a repeated history of sexual abuse from generation to generation.

8. Negative core beliefs that arise from childhood sexual abuse can continue to affect the thought patterns of women and may contribute to a a pattern of revictimization in adulthood.

9. Understanding the specific impact of childhood sexual abuse on the individual woman is integral to establishing effective treatment programs for women based on their specific needs and the female experience of this trauma.

10. Disclosure in terms of confronting a perpetrator is a choice that some women make and identify as a benefit to their recovery.

11. Exposing the perpetrator's behavior to other people is often predicated upon a woman's desire to create an opportunity to safeguard children who are in contact with the perpetrator.

12. A coordination of care among health care providers can be especially relevant for women in the treatment of childhood sexual abuse. Models that show the benefits to women are needed within the health care community for this trauma.

13. Sharing with other women who have lived through this trauma and healed can facilitate an exchange of hope among women.

14. Programs that offer information and guidance about recovery can be beneficial to family members and friends who desire to support a woman's healing.
15. There has been a periodic backlash in the media regarding whether to believe reports by adult women about childhood sexual abuse. This backlash has had a positive effect by eliminating therapeutic methods that are not effective or appropriate to the treatment of childhood sexual abuse and evaluating those that are. It has also facilitated research and discourse that continue to aid in the understanding of how trauma affects memory. It is important to clarify that false memory syndrome does not exist as a recognizable diagnosis in the mental health field and that simulating real-life trauma in a laboratory to study the effect of trauma on memory is seldom, if ever, possible and certainly not ethical.[3]
16. The literature and research on various traumas have proposed the question as to whether it is time to expand the current diagnostic category of post-traumatic stress disorder in order to allow better differentiation of the effects of traumatic stressors.[4] Therefore, it may be time to develop a new diagnostic category that is specific to the adult female experience of childhood sexual abuse and is based on the specific female symptoms of this particular trauma. An option would simply be "Childhood Sexual Abuse Trauma, Female Specific." Diagnosis is important, as it is the basis for the development of sound treatment approaches.

Within this framework, therapeutic disclosure is advocated as a dimension of treatment protocol that facilitates the healing of childhood sexual abuse. One of the reasons for this component is that with disclosure, the complicated belief system that sustains this trauma can be exposed. In addition, as is well documented by the work of B. A. van der Kolk and others, gradually talking about the traumatic experience helps facilitate the eventual integration of it into a person's life history and eventually results in reestablishing a life of fulfillment, a life that was disrupted by the trauma. This integration occurs at an emotional and mental level as the individual relates the trauma in narrative form and reconstructs the belief system surrounding the trauma, which can help to decrease symptoms that disrupt daily functioning and increases a sense of personal control and safety. Therapeutic disclosure is even thought to facilitate integrations of the trauma biologically within the pathways of the brain where the memory can be eventually stored and recalled safely rather than as fragments of the traumatic experience.[5] Treatment with a gradual disclosure component often benefits women because of the intergenerational denial and forbid-

den openness that usually exists within the family history of this generation of women and within our culture. As women recover, their ability to
retell and reframe the traumatic experience evolves and coincides with their
disclosures.

My graduate work in women's studies with Elizabeth Poland, Ph.D., at
Ball State University, educated me on how the female experience affects
women's development, personality, self-concept, and identity. I learned
from this body of research and literature that the secrecy and silence often
surrounding the trauma of abuse can impede women from healing. It was
at this point in my life that I clearly began to understand how my personal
history of childhood sexual abuse had affected me as a woman. I am grateful to Dr. Poland for her efforts to broaden my ability to think beyond the
traditional methods and theories of the time. This background in feminist
psychology cultivated my voice as a woman and as a therapist. It gave
me an opportunity to speak about the trauma of abuse and to put into
words something that I had a difficult time describing to myself, let alone
anyone else.

While I am an advocate of therapeutic disclosure, I am also respectful that
it is an individual choice each woman makes. The decision to disclose seems
to arise from a woman's emerging self—a self who encourages a woman to
use her voice and tell the secret. I believe that the disclosure of sexual abuse
is a gift to oneself. As stated by Alice Miller in *Breaking Down the Wall of
Silence*, this gift "waits for us to summon the courage to hear its voice. It
wants to be protected and understood, and it wants us to free it from its isolation, loneliness and speechlessness."[6] Women often share that their experience of healing began when they first told about the sexual abuse to
someone who was supportive. Disclosure can assist women in understanding the specific as well as the varied problems associated with childhood
sexual abuse. Instead of disclaiming that childhood sexual abuse happened,
women can reveal it as a long-term trauma that has affected their lives over
a number of years. Eventually, women learn to integrate and view this
trauma as part of their history and not their future.

There is a freedom for women in telling the truth about their lives and the
victimization they endured by a person they trusted or were told to trust. As
put forth by Ellen Bass and Laura Davis in their book *The Courage to Heal*, disclosure is seen as an essential part of healing since it entails telling the truth
about what happened in your life.[7] Without truth, we often miss an essential opportunity for growth. With truth, we have the opportunity to change
the destructive patterns that harm our well-being.

In order for the truth to be told, women need a person they can trust to
hear what happened to them, a person who will respect their right to disclose in their own time and in their own way, without pressure or force.

Without this kind of safety, a woman can feel revictimized by the person to whom she discloses if that person responds with silence or condemnation or minimizes the traumatic experience.

Women have the right to determine for themselves when and with whom they will tell and how much of the trauma they are comfortable sharing. While I suggest that disclosure occur in a respectful and therapeutic environment, it can also take other forms. Disclosure can be enhanced by reading this book, or others, on the topic of sexual abuse; writing in a journal where remembering is done without denial or minimization; through silent prayer where confidentiality is always maintained; by writing poetry, stories, or songs or using other art forms such as painting, drawing, or sculpting; or talking to a trusted friend, family member, or minister (often identified as a frequent first disclosure). A woman's ability and decision to expose sexual abuse is guided by where she is in her life, the safety she needs, and the understanding she is offered.

Disclosure, as presented in this approach, is not a "tell all, be all" answer, nor is it discussed in the context of some of the talk shows that proliferate in the media. Rather, it is defined as a thoughtful choice that occurs gradually and only when a woman is ready. It is an essential part of healing that allows a woman to acknowledge, in a personal way, that as a child she was sexually abused. Not every woman will choose disclosure in a therapeutic process. Some women will have the need to keep the sexual abuse private. This choice is to be respected as well. What is most important is that each woman acknowledge what she knows to be the truth and to trust that she knows what is right for her.

OVERVIEW OF THE CHAPTERS

The chapters are presented as a woman would follow them within a therapeutic process. This is not to say that the order must be followed exactly, because individual differences should be allowed and not every woman will enter treatment at the same stage. Rather, the chapter order represents a sequence that, when followed, has an intuitive fit for women with the goal of healing. Each chapter builds on the other as the recovery and treatment process is presented. At the end of each chapter, there are sections titled "Supporting Your Healing." The suggestions in these sections encourage self-discovery and allow the information from each chapter to be applied by women in a flexible manner.

Additional information for women to review and choose to apply in their recovery is contained in the appendices. Women who have access to the Internet can review the sites provided in the Suggested Resources. The Selected Bibliography can be used by women for additional resources to increase their knowledge about childhood sexual abuse, its effect on women, and what works with healing. The books and articles included in this list are not exhaustive but do cover areas of relevant interest for women. I encourage women to use their libraries, contact referral sources at their local hospitals, talk to their physicians, and ask other women for resources and referrals within their communities.

The Trauma of Childhood Sexual Abuse

Silence like a cancer grows.
—Simon and Garfunkel, "The Sounds of Silence"

"It happened so long ago, I wonder if what I remember is real. I have never told anyone the secret that I have carried deep within me. I do not want to believe it is true. Yet, every day I live is another day that I deny what was done to me. It is another day that I feel I deny a part of myself. I have had such a growing need to tell someone. I do not want the secret to die with me" (Evelyn, age forty-one).

The above quote is from a woman who eight years ago healed the trauma of family sexual abuse. When she was a child, someone she trusted violated her in a way that profoundly affected her life. The violation she experienced caused her to doubt her own integrity and influenced the choices she made in her life. Women, sexually abused as children, live for years with both the memories and effects of this trauma. They struggle with feelings of ambivalence about whether to tell that they were sexually abused or to keep it a secret as they have for so many years. When they do tell, they are uncomfortable in the telling. At the same time, they also feel relieved of the burden they have carried for years. As Sandy (age thirty) described, "Telling about the sexual abuse by my dad and brother brought mixed feelings. I feel horrible about what I have told, but better because I have." Breaking the silence is a way for women to begin their journey of healing; they choose to use their voices to tell the truth about a trauma they have kept hidden for years.

As a society, we have had to acknowledge that sexual abuse happens to children today, but we struggle with accepting that it happened to children in past generations. Those children are the women who today search for answers to help them heal. Due to the underreporting of this trauma, the actual number of women who were sexually abused as children is at best an estimate. In addition, the agencies that keep current numbers on child sexual abuse reports did not necessarily keep statistics when most women of today were children.

Research conducted in the 1970s and 1980s indicated that between "15 percent and 45 percent of women were sexually traumatized as children."[1] Today, these numbers are thought to be even greater due to improved reporting methods and the willingness of adult women to speak out. Population surveys that assess for childhood sexual abuse experiences indicate that approximately one in four women report a history of some form of this childhood trauma. In addition, childhood sexual abuse is a leading cause in the development of post-traumatic stress disorder (PTSD). Bessel van der Kolk, in his essay "Posttraumatic Stress Disorder and the Nature of Trauma," cites previous research indicating "that in the U.S. at least 15% of the population is reported to have been molested, physically assaulted, raped, or involved in combat." Women report higher rates of sexual assault than men do, 7.3 percent for women versus 1.3 percent for men, and while strangers perpetrate 22 percent of the reported rapes committed toward women, husbands and boyfriends are responsible for 19 percent and other relatives account for 38 percent. Trauma that results from violence within intimate relationships is more prevalent for women and children. "Four of five assaults on children are at the hands of their own parents." Van der Kolk also points out that "sexual molestation and rape are the most common causes of PTSD in women" and that "women have twice the risk of developing PTSD following a trauma than men do."[2] The glaring realizations from this information are that it is a family member, not a stranger, who is more likely to cause the trauma of sexual abuse; that sexual assault is occurring more often to women than to men; and that child molestation and other types of abuses to children continue to be widespread problems in our society. These reports also reflect the accounts by women who have shared their firsthand experiences of family sexual abuse. The belief system that sustains this trauma and the long-term effects it has on the lives of female children has been valuable information provided by women.

Given the prevalence of sexual trauma and the increased risk of prolonged problems, the availability of information to women about treatment and recovery from sexual abuse trauma is of utmost importance. Over the past twenty years, we have begun to understand this trauma; today, we are developing treatment methods to heal it, but the research that tells us what is effective is still forthcoming. For this reason, we need a sustaining commitment in public policy to finance research and develop programs that effectively address the treatment needs of women when trauma has occurred. This policy would be similar to the one that now exists for children who are victims of abuse.[3] A policy for women would focus on research into understanding how this trauma affects the lives and health of women, identifying effective treatment programs that meet the individual needs of women, preventing revictimization, and developing outreach programs that encourage women to seek treatment. Such a commitment would diminish patterns of victimization and prevent recurring health problems related to this trauma, thus enabling women to lead healthier lives and improving the functioning of families.

Sexual abuse is traumatic mentally, physically, and emotionally to children, and it continues to affect them as they grow into adults. As a national health problem, sexual abuse affects millions of children each year. The long-term health problems can include depression, anxiety, chemical dependency and addiction, and the perpetuation of the maltreatment of children into the next generation. While child sexual abuse has finally gained national attention over the past twenty years, it continues to trouble us as a society. The safety of our children warrants our commitment and resources to intervene and prevent the effects of this trauma from occurring in order to protect future generations.

While we have helped women and children to realize that they are not responsible when someone else perpetrates this trauma, we also need to help them realize that they are not responsible for how the trauma affects their lives. Too often women feel embarrassed about the problems associated with this trauma, which can cause them not to seek help for them. For example, women will blame themselves or feel shame for such problems as sexual disinterest, lack of sexual desire, or the physical pain that results from sexual abuse. Women can blame themselves for recurring symptoms of depression and anxiety or for problems of self-harm such as eating disorders or addictions that develop from abuse. Women may not understand that these emotional states and behaviors are often reenactment of the trauma experience, expression of emotional pain, or chronic shock symptoms from abuse. The specific problems that occur from childhood sexual abuse simply, and tragically, happen. A woman is not responsible for how the abuse affected her, just as she is not responsible for the perpetrator abusing her. The responsibility a woman can take is for her own healing.

Sandy (age thirty) shares that she thought she was responsible for how the abuse affected her: "I believed I had control over how the sexual abuse affected me. I really bought into people telling me 'you cannot still be bothered by that [abuse].' Well, I am. I have struggled with emotional and physical pain throughout my life from sexual abuse." This type of self-blame and the attitude that because sexual abuse happened in the past its effects are not experienced in the present are similar to how we used to blame women when they were the victims of other traumas enacted by someone else. For example, as late as the 1980s women were blamed when they were raped or sexually assaulted by men. The established culture at the time held the view that a woman had provoked this violent behavior by such choices as how she dressed or where she was when the assault occurred. In addition, men were not always prosecuted for this crime even when physical evidence, such as damage to a woman's body, clearly indicated that there was a lack of consent. Another example of this type of blame is domestic violence. Not until the mid-1980s did states begin to enact laws that required police officers to arrest perpetrators of this violent criminal act of family aggression. However, even with the laws we have today, neither lawmakers nor the public can agree that prosecution is warranted in each case of assault and violence against women. Family violence can still be viewed as a "private matter," and we often see lower bonds set by the judicial system and repeat offenders who commit this crime against the same or a different woman released from jail.[4]

When society blames the victim for these types of violent crime, the responsibility is misplaced onto the person who is harmed rather than on the person who committed the harm. We need to reaffirm for women that they are not responsible for the impact of sexual abuse while encouraging them to seek treatment and participate in a program of healing. Recovery from the trauma of family sexual abuse is a critical decision for women to make in their lives today. We encourage women to seek treatment for such disorders as diabetes and heart disease or to have mammograms for the early detection and prevention of breast cancer; we also need to encourage them to seek treatment for childhood sexual abuse.

Information about sexual abuse assists women early in their recovery because it dispels the myths and misconceptions that can still exist for them about sexual abuse. This information can also lay the groundwork for women to begin to edit out distorted beliefs originating from the perpetrator or the family belief system that were in place at the time the abuse occurred.

The following is information provided to women during treatment. It is presented in a question-and-answer format since this information originates from questions women ask when in treatment for trauma of sexual abuse.

QUESTIONS WOMEN ASK ABOUT SEXUAL ABUSE

Why was I the one sexually abused?

Past and present reports of sexual abuse continue to substantiate that the perpetrator is often a family member or someone the family knows well and who has a relationship to the child or adolescent. While adult men are the majority of reported perpetrators of sexual abuse, adult women commit this crime as well. Adolescents, both male and female, also perpetrate child sexual abuse, often toward younger children or peers.[5] Therefore, an offender of sexual abuse is someone who has access to the child through this family relationship. It is not unusual that in a family where sexual abuse is occurring, the same perpetrator has abused other children sometimes over a number of years. Research, legal records, medical reports, data from legal services, offender treatment programs, and clinical reports document the intergenerational aspect of sexual abuse. In addition, multiple incidents of abuse to children are relatively common and are reported to occur in 50 to 75 percent of cases.[6]

How could I have been as young as I was when the abuse happened?

Sexual abuse can occur at any age. Reports of sexual abuse against children substantiates that this trauma occurs against children of various ages, even as young as infancy. Women in this treatment program reported that even as adults they have experienced the same perpetrators attempting sexual abuse in some form.

Why do I remember inappropriate behavior with other children and feel that I was a perpetrator or that I am at risk of abusing a child?

The majority of victims of childhood sexual abuse do not go on to become offenders. Children, at times, may act out the trauma of sexual abuse. For example, children may repeat words and phrases they have heard from the perpetrator. They may act out the perpetrator's abuse behavior in the presence of other children. Often, when a child displays this type of behavior, it is because she has also been, or is, a victim of sexual abuse. When this kind of behavior occurs, a child needs to be assessed in terms of how the abuse has affected her interaction with other children. Children are confused by sexual abuse. A female child who rubs her private parts against another child or who touches another child sexually may believe this behavior is appropriate for showing affection. She is reenacting the behavior she has been taught by the perpetrator.

Intervention and treatment must take place with children so that the victim does not develop offender thought patterns and behavior. This is especially important as a child gets older since juveniles are now recognized as perpetrators of this crime. A difference of two years or greater between children is one of the criteria in determining if a child would be considered an offender.[7]

Am I abnormal because it was a woman who sexually abused me?

While the majority of reported perpetrators are men, women are identified in at least 38 percent of the documented cases of sexual abuse to children reported by the U.S. Department of Justice.[8] Craig M. Allen, in *Women and Men Who Sexually Abuse Children: A Comparative Analysis,* suggests that about 1.5 million females in this country have been sexually abused by other females.[9] The female offender's relationship to the child is reported to be that of mother, sister, aunt, family friend, stepmother, cousin, neighbor, or sitter.[10] Female offenders, like male offenders, sexually abuse both girls and boys. Females are reported as acting both independent of or along with a male perpetrator, and the harm they cause to a child is no less than that of a male perpetrator. While ignored for years, sexual abuse by women is finally emerging from the shadows and being addressed by both researchers and clinicians alike. The early theories and beliefs about sexual abuse in the general population created and influenced professional attitudes toward accepting that females can, and do, commit this crime. Therefore, the attitude was that sexual abuse by females had to be extremely rare.[11] Identifying female offenders is crucial so that their victims can be heard and believed. Whether male or female, the perpetrator—not the child—is abnormal.

Are female children still reported as the majority of victims of childhood sexual abuse?

Female children have historically been the majority of reported victims of sexual abuse. Male children are considered to be underreported in the statistics from studies and agencies in the 1980s. However, while female children continue to remain the majority of reported victims, the numbers are increasing for male children. Analysis of research during the 1990s indicates that female children are three times more likely than male children to have experienced sexual abuse.[12]

Did the sexual abuse from my childhood cause other types of abuse to happen to me?

The prevalence of sexual abuse as an aspect of women's history and life experience is thought to create certain risk factors for other kinds of trauma later in life. Studies have also shown that childhood and adolescent sexual abuse poses a significantly greater risk for subsequent victimization due to beliefs acquired during the abuse, maladaptive behaviors that are learned when the abuse is occurring, and the inability to form adequate protective skills that were not taught within the family.[13]

Why do people think I would lie about this happening to me?

Children are both afraid and ashamed of disclosing sexual abuse by a family member. Adults, including professionals, need to recognize bias they may have against or for believing a child's report of sexual abuse that interferes with their objectivity. False claims represent a minority of reports made by children; these reports often result from coercion by their parents.[14] A parent will coerce a child to make a false accusation against the other parent during a volatile divorce or hostile custody proceeding. The judicial system needs to view this type of coercion as emotional and verbal abuse by parents toward their children and bring charges against the parents when coercion is known to occur. Perhaps this type of judicial action would dramatically decrease this behavior by parents, thereby decreasing false claims.

Bias against believing children and doubting the veracity of their reports also influences society's willingness or ability to believe adult women reporting sexual abuse in their childhood. This is similar to the skepticism that still exists, sometimes even within the mental health field, about believing women who report being raped.[15] The media debate in the 1990s about "false memory syndrome" also added to the skepticism that exists toward women who report childhood sexual abuse.

Why did he tell me he was teaching me about sex?

Laws exist today to protect children from harm and suffering. This legal protection includes preventing children from being sexually abused. It comes from the belief that no act of sexual abuse to a child falls under the guise of acceptable sexual behavior by adults. Perpetrators often try to justify and/or minimize their behavior and frequently refuse to take responsibility for what they have done to a child. They desire to escape accountability for exploiting their relationship of trust with a child or adolescent. Perpetrators are known to make statements such as "I was drunk when I did those things," "It is normal for children to be sexual," "I was teaching her about sex," or even "She wanted me to do those things."[16]

This type of distorted thinking by perpetrators serves to justify their behavior and avoid accountability within the family and the legal system. It is imperative to stand against the sexual abuse of children and adolescents and not accept any justification of this trauma occurring at any age to a child.

Are all perpetrators pedophiles?

Not all men who sexually abuse children are necessarily pedophiles—individuals with a fixation on young children for sexual gratification. The term "pedophilia" is the single diagnostic category used in the mental health field to classify individuals who sexually abuse children. However, a single diagnostic category may not be adequate in classifying or differentiating the known types of offenders who sexually abuse children. Perpetrators may cross several categories of existing classification that can include characteristics of antisocial sociopathy or narcissistic personality disorder.[17] Using only one classification for offenders of sexual abuse could limit the information we need about treating perpetrators who do not fit the single category of pedophilia. Just as we know that the crime of rape is an act of power, control, and physical and sexual violence, the sexual abuse of children is often about power and control, abnormal sexuality, and sometimes violence. What we are learning from clinical studies on the characteristics of sexual offenders who are in treatment programs is that not all perpetrators of this crime are pedophiles. Ron Smith, director of the Indianapolis Counseling Center, which offers specialized treatment services to sexual offenders, indicates that most of the sexual offenders he works with "do not fit the profile of the aroused pedophile with a sexual fixation on young children, whether that child is male or female."[18] In addition, a single category of defining sexual offenders of children excludes the known types of female perpetrator, and the juvenile offender is not adequately understood within a single diagnostic category either.[19] The mental health field needs to reconsider how it classifies individuals who sexually abuse children, apply the information that is now available on perpetrators, and create more than one diagnostic category for sexual perpetrators. In turn, the public needs to be informed that not all perpetrators are pedophiles and not all are adult males. With this information, parents in particular would be better educated on the characteristics of perpetrators who potentially have access to their children through the family. This information could assist the investigation and prosecution of perpetrators and serve to broaden the public's understanding of sexual perpetrators, thereby adding another level of protection for children.

Why would a man who was married sexually abuse me?

Perpetrators are both heterosexual and homosexual; they can be married or single; they are more often employed than unemployed. The men who are incarcerated for this crime are more often white males rather than a member of a minority group. They are grandfathers, fathers, stepfathers, live-in partners, brothers, cousins, uncles, and family friends. Sexual orientation, marital status, and socioeconomic or other demographic characteristics are not reliable predictors of whether an individual, male or female, will sexually abuse a child.[20]

Consistent predictors that can identify the likelihood of sexual abuse to a child are (1) whether there is a sexual offender in the family and (2) whether there is a generational history of family sexual abuse or other types of abuse. Another predictor is the family belief system that places children at risk for sexual abuse. For example, when family members minimize or ignore problems originating from abuse, when parents do not seek outside help to solve these problems, when secrecy and silence exist to protect the family and shield the perpetrator, then children are at risk. There is also the risk factor of trusting the care of a child to someone the family knows to be abusive while choosing not to act on this information. Continued research is needed so that risk factors within the family where abuse occurs along with the characteristics of known perpetrators can be effectively identified and put to use to prevent this crime.

Should a perpetrator be excused because he was abused as a child?

Society does not need to excuse a perpetrator's behavior because of possible abuse in his childhood. Abuse during a perpetrator's childhood does not entitle him to abuse another person or justify the harm he does to a child. As adults, perpetrators are responsible for their actions and legally accountable for their behavior.

We know that the safety of our children depends on keeping perpetrators away from them. Likewise, we need to stop placing guilt on a woman who chooses not to be revictimized by being around a perpetrator in her family. Otherwise, we are asking women to do what we would not consider asking of a child. When we keep known perpetrators away from children, we guarantee that children will not become victims of these perpetrators (again). This same regard needs to be extended to adult women who were abused as children. When adult women remain separated from the perpetrator who abused them, they are not at risk for revictimization by this person and neither are their children.

Did I want the abuse to happen if I felt pleasure from it or I did not actually say no?

A child does not give consent for the trauma of sexual abuse, even when her body is manipulated by the perpetrator to respond. Either the child or someone else can mislabel the manipulation by the perpetrator of a child's body and call this experience "pleasurable." Children are in emotional shock when sexual abuse happens and often feel numb, tense, and afraid. They are understandably confused by their feelings, whether physical or emotional, when sexual abuse occurs. A child is never to blame for sexual abuse. The perpetrator—not the child—caused the abuse to happen. The sense of shame and wrongness she felt when the perpetrator abused her is what most women remember long after the abuse has ended.

Mislabeling or misunderstanding physical sensations experienced from sexual abuse by a perpetrator only serves to further confuse this crime and project blame onto the child. Women, as children, were not readily able to understand what they were experiencing due to their age, inexperience of their bodies, and lack of information about human sexuality. A perpetrator takes away a child's choice of not experiencing his behavior and the physical sensations of it. As adults, women have the opportunity to understand what they experienced as well as the reason for the experience. They can choose not to blame themselves for the physical responses that occurred when the perpetrator manipulated and controlled their bodies. This source of shame is very difficult for women to speak about and share. It often confuses their sexuality and interferes with their ability to experience sexual enjoyment in their committed relationships. In addition, when a woman tries to tell others about this source of shame and the confusion she feels about what occurred at the hands of the perpetrator, she may be met with ridicule, disgust, and dismissal—"if you 'enjoyed' it, then it must have not have been abuse." The challenge is for people who have not been sexually abused to try to imagine what sexual abuse would feel like to them, then add this layer of shame on top of those feelings, and then imagine being four, eight, or twelve years old when the trauma occurred. Imagining oneself in the place of the child victim would perhaps elicit more compassion and understanding for women who were victimized by someone they were supposed to have been able to trust.

Why do I think I went along with it because he did not hit me or beat me or I did not try to get away?

Perpetrators can be violent, and when they are they cause a great deal of pain and terror to the child. We also know that perpetrators coerce, threaten, control, and manipulate children without violence. The dependence children naturally have on their caregivers and the compliance they are expected to give to adults negates the use of force and coercion for sexual abuse to occur. Threats or acts of violence by the perpetrator serve to ensure the child's silence in order to maintain secrecy about his behavior and to reinforce her helplessness.[21]

Why did I not stop the abuse or tell someone?

Children are not capable of stopping abuse. The perpetrator violates a child's right to be safe and prevents her from speaking about his behavior. Confusion, violence, pain, shock, fear of separation, loss of trust, and protecting the perpetrator so as not to cause family disruption, reprisal, and threats of separation are examples of existing vulnerabilities that cause a child's passive inability to tell about the sexual abuse. These fears, along with shame and embarrassment, also ensure her silence about the perpetrator's behavior. Sometimes, children will believe they consented to the sexual abuse because they did not tell. Remember, fear does not translate into consent.

Why am I able to remember most or some aspects of the abuse, but I do not recall all of it?

There are women who retain detailed memories of the abuse. Other women experience a loss of memory about the trauma, while some women experience fragmented memories. Recall of traumatic memories can depend upon the child's age, developmental stage, severity of the trauma, the relationship to the perpetrator, a child's emotional and mental state at the time of the trauma, and family circumstances when the abuse occurred.

Can I heal and keep my children safe from sexual abuse?

Recovery is possible. While effective treatment is still being developed, researched, and evaluated, we know that certain types of treatment such as cognitive therapy, insight and humanistic approaches, anxiety reduction, massage therapy, fear desensitization, pain management, somatic treatments, and approaches that are based on individual needs help women to heal from childhood sexual abuse. Unfortunately, while the number of children who report this crime continues to increase, these children may or may not be provided access to treatment since a majority of families still deny or justify the abuse or deny the necessity of treatment. Prevention of sexual abuse within a family system should be a recognizable outcome of treatment and recovery. Intervention without healing is not always an effective prevention of future problems, nor is it able to assure that for future generations this trauma will not occur when the family belief system has not changed.

DISCUSSION ABOUT FAMILY SEXUAL ABUSE

Documented reports and crime statistics indicate that the majority of children know the people who sexually abuse them. These adults and juveniles are family members or someone that the family trusts and knows well. Incest, as studied over the past twenty years, focused mainly on sexual abuse of daughters by fathers. In clinical practice, this definition of sexual abuse became narrow and confining because it was learned that perpetrators could be other family members as well as individuals outside the family who were trusted by the family to be with the child. Therefore, the term "incest" restricted women from fully realizing the impact of this trauma when the perpetrator was someone other than a girl's father. For example, there are cases where women minimize the trauma of sexual abuse by a stepfather, uncle, brother, or cousin regardless of the type of sexual abuse perpetrated. When the perpetrator is not a father, there are women or family members who will view the harm done by the perpetrator to the child as "less than" the harm done to a child sexually abused by her father. The impact of this restricted definition of harm is that some women may not believe they deserve treatment or may think they are exaggerating the problems they experience from childhood sexual abuse. When this view exists within the family where the abuse occurred, it translates into less support for a woman to recover and maintains a part of the family denial system that the abuse was not that bad.

Women need not compare the harm done to them with the harm done to someone else by childhood sexual abuse. There is no benefit or advantage to a woman when she or someone else makes this kind of comparison. All sexual abuse is traumatic and harmful. It affects a child's development in a multitude of ways and consequently affects her life. While women are helped by recognizing the individual differences among them regarding how they have experienced the chronic effects of this trauma, they are not helped by placing conditions that predicate whether they deserve treatment or will receive support in seeking treatment.

Since the perpetrator often knows the child, this generally means that the child was sexually abused by someone who lived with or had access to her. He was someone with some level of power, influence, or control over the child and was protected to some degree by the family's rules of silence and denial of his behavior. He was someone the child probably cared about and the child or family trusted. Therefore, the sexual abuse did not happen because of who a woman was as a child or what she did or did not do at the time the abuse occurred. The abuse happened because the perpetrator was in the child's family or trusted by the family and had access to her. Accepting this information lifts some of the responsibility women have carried for the actions of the perpetrator because it helps to challenge her misplaced blame or belief that the sexual abuse happened because of her. Challenging this false belief starts the process of transferring the responsibility of the abuse back onto the perpetrator, which is where it always belonged.

Sexual offenders abuse across the spectrum of children's ages. They abuse infants, toddlers, youngsters, and adolescents. Medical and legal reports document the age of children who are harmed by sexual abuse. Women also report that the abuse occurred before or after they entered elementary school, before puberty or during adolescence. Remembering milestones such as holidays, birthdays, school years, where they lived, or when they moved assists women in identifying when and where the abuse began or ended and the age they were at the time of the abuse. Their young age or developmental stage is another aspect of remembering that helps women stop accepting responsibility for the abuse. While women do come to appreciate the strengths they had as children to survive this trauma, they also struggle to find a way to feel grateful that they lived through the abuse and the difficult years that followed. Women have the right to feel outrage and sadness by how their lives have been affected by the acts of a perpetrator.

Some women share how the abuse by the perpetrator either began or continued during their adolescence and interfered with their ability to date, to say no to sexual advances, or caused them to fear or avoid boys their own age. Some withdrew from social activities, which limited their choices and opportunities. Most discuss how their lives were restricted, inhibited, or dominated by the impact of the sexual abuse. Many relate how the sexual abuse that happened during childhood caused them to blame themselves because they believed that somehow they had a role in their victimization.[22] The behavior of teenage girls who have been sexually abused can sometimes be mislabeled as promiscuity rather than as a reenactment of the abuse or an extension of the behavior learned from the perpetrator. E. Sue Blume, in her book *Secret Survivors,* suggests that a woman's right or ability to say no is taken from her when childhood sexual abuse occurs.[23] Blume recognizes that many adolescent girls and adult women are not able to speak up and say no to sexual advances or they are not aware that they have the right to say no. Often the perpetrator taught a child that to be accepted or loved she must behave as he taught her—passive, compliant, and nondemanding. A teenage girl's passive response to sexual advances by others along with the ease by which she can be intimidated and confused is not readily overcome without help and assistance in understanding what is occurring in relation to patterns set by the sexual abuse.

As women heal, they learn that giving or withholding their consent comes with time and that their past sexual behavior is more than likely a reflection of what they experienced during the sexual abuse. Jodi (age thirty-two) came to understand this difference:" Even if I did not say 'no,' my body was telling him not to do this to me. I felt the same way with boys, and later with men, who would try to coerce me or pressure me to be sexual." Teresa (age forty-one) shared that "Today I know when I am giving consent and when I am not or when someone is trying to force me to go along with them."

Children, too, may act out the abuse with others either directly or indirectly. Often this behavior occurs with peers or other children within the family. Sometimes she will direct it toward adults, especially men. The perpetrator has a direct affect on a child's interaction with other people and family members. Children are not naturally sexually seductive or flirtatious, nor are they sexual in their play with other children or adults. Normal child play does not include adult sexual acts or words. A child who exhibits adult behavior and knowledge, especially sexual knowledge, is repeating what has been shown to her or done to her. Intervention and treatment with children is important to decrease the risk of victims becoming perpetrators of any kind of abuse later in life and to prevent revictimization as children grow older.

Most women share that if the perpetrator is still within the family, his inappropriate behavior continues even if it is not as direct as it was when she was a child; however, such behavior is still traumatic and offensive. Women tell how perpetrators make obscene phone calls to them, mail pornography to their homes, or request sexual favors. Women describe how a perpetrator will touch them, make lewd remarks, tell obscene jokes, stare at their bodies, or make inappropriate comments about their appearance and clothing. The very fact that he can be in her presence, aware of what he has done, without ever acknowledging his abuse of her or being accountable for it, is considered a violation of the respect and consideration she deserves to be shown by him. Taylor (age seventeen) shares her experience of this kind of behavior by the person who sexually abused her: "I would hate to be in the room with him or have to sit at the dinner table with him. He knew why I was angry with him and the reasons I did not like him, but he never said a word to my parents. I would get in trouble for showing my anger towards him and he would continue to sit in silence while all the time knowing what my anger was about."

Physical penetration of children cannot occur unless forced; that is why we call this kind of sexual assault rape. Any kind of penetration that the perpetrator does to a child is harmful and painful, both emotionally and physically. The physical damage to a child's body is often permanent, and the associated pain can last into her adult life where it often serves as a constant reminder of the abuse. Health care providers need to identify and understand the original cause of physical pain when it is an outcome of sexual abuse. Gynecologists and family physicians in particular can serve as a gateway for women in the diagnosis of chronic pain, sexual disorders, and physical damage resulting from childhood sexual abuse. These physicians are often the first person with whom a woman will seek medical attention for the pain, sexual problems, and physical discomfort they experience.[24]

While currently in the minority of reported and convicted perpetrators, women do sexually abuse children. Women in this treatment approach report that a woman—their mother, sister, aunt, cousin, or babysitter—sexually abused them. Because women are seldom reported as perpetrators is only one of the reasons it is often difficult for our culture to accept that abuse by female perpetrators does occur. Part of the education about this crime that continues to need repeating is that not all sexual abuse is reported, and that simply because it is not reported to the legal system or by other means does not mean it is not occurring. Our failure to recognize this crime in families is one of the tragic reasons it continues to occur. Craig Allen, in *Women and Men Who Sexually Abuse Children: A Comparative Analysis*, reiterates this inability by our culture as it relates to female perpetrators: "Few behaviors deviate as far from cultural norms and deep-seated beliefs as those committed by women who sexually abuse children." From this observation, Allen brings to light a myth about sexual abuse in general when he states, "The possibility that sexual abuse may not require a penis is not considered." This myth is still held by professionals, the courts, and the general public when it comes to accepting that sexual abuse is not always the act of rape and that not all perpetrators are men.[25]

Another factor may have to do with the cultural myths we project upon mothers and women in general—that mothers are child protectors and have unconditional love for the child and that women are often the victims of abuse but are not perpetrators of it, especially sexual abuse. Consequently, a woman's report of a female perpetrator may be dismissed, ignored, or simply not given the validity of being real. The above reasons may contribute to and heavily influence the silence that occurs and the reluctance to disclose by women who were victims of female offenders. Whether this is due to our lack of understanding the female perpetrator, inadequate diagnosis by mental health professionals, not wanting to accept that women do exist as perpetrators, or a view of woman as incapable of sexual abuse is not altogether clear. While we accept that there are men who will perpetrate abuse, we do not want to believe that some women, especially mothers, abuse children. There also seems to be a particular kind of shame that women experience when a female perpetrator has sexually abused them. Along with this shame is the fear that they will be viewed as abnormal, psychotic, or crazy, or told that they simply misconstrued their mother's or another woman's intention. Or when they have told, the message has been conveyed that sexual abuse by a female is of little significance or that women are sexually harmless.[26] Whether male or female, perpetrators of child sexual abuse commit a crime against children. We need to understand this type of perpetration and the specific impact to children when sexual abuse occurs by a female if we are to help women heal. If we are to prevent child sexual abuse or stop it when it is occurring, we are going to have to accept that female perpetrators do exist and that they abuse both boys and girls. We will also need to challenge the belief that when women sexually abuse boys, their behavior is not harmless nor is it appropriate, and they certainly are not "helping a boy to achieve manhood." When we stop and consider that the majority of reported perpetrators of various sexual crimes including childhood sexual abuse are men, that these men often start a pattern of abuse in adolescence, that when they report being a victim of sexual abuse it occurred before puberty, and that both men and women sexually abuse boys, then it stands to reason that female and male perpetrators who sexually abuse boys have a negative influence on a boy's emotional development, moral values, and relationships with men and women.[27] Boys are not helped into manhood when they are abused by women they trust any more than female children are helped into womanhood when they are sexually abused by men they trust.

Illustration A depicts the sadness Melinda (age forty-three) feels as an adult woman and as a child because of sexual abuse by her mother. She shows her adult self crying as she told about the abuse and her child self crying as the abuse was committed by her mother. The black hole within her child self is Melinda's depiction of the emptiness left behind by her mother's abuse. Melinda disclosed the sexual abuse by her mother as she gained a level of trust with her perceptions and memories. She first disclosed the abuse by her brother within the first few weeks of her therapy. It was two years later that she disclosed the sexual abuse by her mother. Melinda stated, "I was terrified of the abuse by my brother because he was so violent, but I could at least acknowledge it happened. The abuse by my mother was something I just never wanted to believe. I refused to even think about it for many years."

Reports of sexual trauma occurring in childhood and adolescence show a high correlation to trauma in adulthood for women. A conclusion from clinical reports and research on the relationship between childhood sexual abuse and assault and rape in adulthood is that childhood sexual trauma places women at risk for victimization later in life.[28] Women in this treatment approach disclosed that they were raped or assaulted or were the object of aggression or other types of abuse at different times in their lives. Marilyn (age forty-six) related her history of adult trauma this way: "I came to believe that somehow I was destined to be a victim. I thought the abuse by my stepfather and uncle was something that allowed other men to abuse me as well."

Illustration A

The possible reasons that women who were sexually abused as children are more at risk for future sexual assault vary. Women sexually abused as children may not be able to appropriately assess situations that are not safe because they are not aware of the risks. This diminished ability to assess risk may cause a woman to perceive someone as trustworthy who is not and then prevent her from being able to protect herself from this person. Prolonged symptoms of trauma, such as depression, anxiety, or the use of alcohol or drugs, may also interfere with a woman's ability to make accurate judgments about people and situations that place her in harm's way. Difficulty setting and maintaining appropriate boundaries can also place women at risk for future trauma.[29]

What we may find out as research continues about the relationship between childhood sexual abuse and victimization later in life is that a combination of factors emerge from childhood sexual abuse that causes women to be at risk for future trauma. These factors will most likely include an absence of treatment in childhood to address the long-term developmental effects of child sexual abuse. Without treatment, reoccurring trauma symptoms such as flashbacks, dissociation, anxiety, and depression can interfere with a woman's ability to process information. Childhood trauma may lessen her ability to assess the risk in certain situations especially when they are similar to the circumstances of the childhood sexual abuse. For example, some women may display learned helplessness with certain kinds of people who have characteristics similar to the perpetrator. When this happens, she may have a diminished capacity to distance herself from this person or to ask for help and assistance.

A pattern of learned helplessness results from how the perpetrator controlled her, and what she had to accept about her limitations in regard to changing what was occurring would also seem to place women at risk for future victimization. When a woman has not experienced the control to stop bad things (sexual abuse) from happening, she can believe that being a victim is a role she is expected to maintain, and this role becomes an established pattern of behavior throughout her life. Also, not being taught as a child or not learning in adulthood that she deserves protection and safety would increase her risk for future trauma.

We also have to consider what impact occurs to a child when she is exposed to the perpetrator's belief system during the sexual abuse and to the family belief system prior to, throughout, and after the abuse. What beliefs a child acquires and how they are transferred to her adult life will most likely set the stage for victimization by other people throughout her life. Children are vulnerable to acquiring these maladaptive beliefs and developing thought patterns from them because they live within a family culture that often consents to the maltreatment of children, either directly by condoning the maltreatment or indirectly by not providing safety for the child. In addition, what the perpetrator says and does not say to the child during the abuse can also influence the acquisition of internalized beliefs that place women at risk for trauma later in life.

Finally, we do not live in a world that is safe for women. Violence against women occurs daily and places all women at risk for some kind of assault in their adult lives. Gender studies document the violence that has occurred toward children and women for generations and across cultures. A six-year study by the Centers for Disease Control and Prevention and the Justice Department's Bureau of Justice Statistics indicates that an intimate partner committed about half the reported attacks on women that cause injury. This report also shows that women were more likely to be attacked and injured by someone they know than by a stranger.[30] When society stops tolerating violence, we will see this pattern of continued violence toward women

Illustration B

begin to change. In addition, when men change their beliefs that sustain violence and dominance toward women and when nonviolent men speak out against violence toward women to other men, we will see positive changes for the lives of women. The freedom to live in a safe world is a right for all of us. Breaking any cycle of violence or abuse begins with taking a stand against the beliefs that maintain it.

Illustration B diagrams the possible risk factors from childhood sexual abuse that may cause or contribute to future trauma. When harmful patterns are changed, vulnerability is decreased and future victimization can be prevented. The idea that women can change patterns of victimization is what may be most useful from studies on victimization in adulthood linked to childhood sexual abuse. When women heal, they can disrupt and stop the pattern of victimization started by the perpetrator and reinforced in the family where it occurred. Just as women increase the likelihood of preventing breast cancer with self-examination and annual mammograms, perhaps encouraging women to examine the effects of childhood sexual abuse on their lives and then supporting them in changing identifiable victimization patterns would prevent future trauma. The belief system of a woman changes when recovery and healing occur. She is reenergized to make life choices that lead her away from abuse or other types of damaging relationships and situations. Healing as an approach to preventing future trauma offers another means to change the future lives of women in a profound and meaningful way.

Believing children about sexual abuse when it occurs can prevent it from continuing; when adult women are believed, revictimization to them can be prevented as well. We need to consider that when adult women are encouraged to protect themselves from a known perpetrator, they are also protecting their children by keeping them away from this person. By applying the information we have about known offenders, we are taking an important step toward decreasing this trauma to children in families today.

While treatment programs for male perpetrators are in place today, the validity of their effectiveness is still in question and needs continual study. An approach with perpetrators that may have the potential of preventing these men from revictimizing children is to challenge and change their beliefs that sustain the offending behavior and to require proof of the change to these beliefs and behaviors. Among these beliefs is a denial system in which the perpetrator tends to justify, rationalize, and blame the victim for his abusive behavior. The following are examples of the types of denial identified and accepted by professionals working with the offender:

Denial of facts. The offender attempts to convince himself that the sexual abuse he perpetrated was not actually abuse or that the abuse never occurred. Examples of the distorted thinking that accompanies this type of denial are "It was not abuse because she wanted to" or "She is lying, I never abused her."

Denial of awareness. The offender reports that he was not informed, conscious, or aware that what he was doing was abusive. He might say, "I may have abused her but I do not remember what I did" or "I was drunk or high on drugs."

Denial of impact. The offender lacks victim empathy and is either not able to or refuses to empathize with the victim. In other words, the offender does not acknowledge, accept, or feel the negative effects of his abuse on the child and later the adult woman. Statements such as "This is/was no big deal," "It only happened once," or even "This has not affected her life" are common with an offender who has this type of ingrained belief that leads to distorted thinking about his behavior.

Denial of accountability. The offender attempts to justify his abuse by placing
the responsibility of the abuse on someone or something else as he
attempts to make an excuse for his behavior. His thinking is similar to
the other types of denial, such as "She wanted me to" or "I was teaching her about sex."[31]

For women, identifying where they have internalized these beliefs by
perpetrators and mistakenly taken responsibility for the abuse is helpful in
recovering from the trauma of childhood sexual abuse. Appendix B provides a list of internalized beliefs that can originate from childhood sexual
abuse and are influenced in their development by the perpetrator.

Labeling all perpetrators as pedophiles has the potential of restricting
what we are able to learn about offenders that could help prevent this
trauma to children. We should also not assume that certain demographic
characteristics indicate the profile of perpetrators as a group. The growing
body of literature and research on offenders indicates that not all perpetrators are pedophiles, just as we know that not all child molesters are serial
killers, rapists, or child pornographers. Demographic characteristics of men
who sexually abuse children represent a range of characteristics rather than
a narrow profile.[32] In addition, diagnostic categories presently used in the
mental health system exclude the types of female and juvenile perpetrators.[33] The only consistent means we have right now to prevent the sexual
abuse of children is to not allow known perpetrators around them.

Women can experience feelings of betrayal by their bodies because of
childhood sexual abuse. Lois (age forty-seven) recalls experiencing physical sensations she labeled as "pleasure" that always confused her and
caused her to feel intense shame. She describes her father as a "seducer of
children." "He did not use force or physical intimidation during the abuse;
in fact it was just the opposite. It was as if he was trying to seduce me into
what he called 'the ritual of sex.' He thought if he treated me 'nice' then he
was not harming me. Can you imagine? Here he is, doing these horrible
things to me when I am nine years old, and he thinks that he is not harming
me and that he is being nice. I remember how my body responded while my
skin crawled and my mind went blank. I felt such shame. I really struggled
to understand and talk about this part of the abuse."

Lois typifies how some women blame themselves for the abuse by
wrongly believing their body's response meant that they consented to the
abuse or that what they felt caused the abuse to continue. A child's body can
respond to physical manipulation by the perpetrator. As adults, women
can fail to realize that the perpetrator knew ways to force the child's body
to respond. This violation of her body is another way he controlled the child,
caused her to feel ashamed, and guaranteed her silence.[34] William Prendergast, in *Treating Sex Offenders: A Guide to Clinical Practice with Adults,*

Clerics, Children, and Adolescents, explains that the seductive perpetrator's ability to manipulate a child is based on "tak[ing] care to first form a trusting and caring relationship with the intended victim" in order to initiate the cycle of sexual abuse. Prendergast describes perpetrators as "cunning" and "seductive"; they "prefer to manipulate their victims rather than use force of any kind."[35]

As Lois goes on to explain, "I accept that my father manipulated my body in much the same way he manipulated me. He was always good at blaming somebody else for his mistakes. He thought it made sense when he would tell me, 'I would not have abused you if you did not enjoy it.' I feel such anger toward him that when I was nine years old he abused me in so many ways and takes no responsibility for what he did to me."

Women describe their confusion, embarrassment, and feelings of shame as "the bad touch [that] felt good," as one woman put it. This source of and kind of shame is difficult for a woman to share due to misplaced thoughts of responsibility as well as harsh self-judgment about the sexual abuse and a fear that other people, even her therapist, will blame her for the sexual abuse. Women need to be aware that in maintaining this distorted and negative belief, they are in some ways mirroring the distorted beliefs held by perpetrators and thus continuing to take the blame rather than holding the offender accountable.

Women need to become educated about childhood sexual abuse. In doing so, they can understand the variety of ways a perpetrator manipulates and controls a child. The child who was sexually abused can experience physical sensations without the woman labeling herself as enjoying the sexual abuse. Human beings respond to touch, whether pain or pleasure. A woman can block the emotional pain of childhood sexual abuse and in doing so create a fragmented memory. This fragmented memory may hold feelings labeled by the child as pleasure and influence a woman to think that she (as a child) did not stop the abuse because it "felt good." Children are as powerless to stop the feelings of the abuse as they are to stop the abuse by the perpetrator.[36]

The belief that if children are sexually abused the perpetrator must have used violence to get the child to participate is not always true. Research and reports by women and children tell a different story. Perpetrators seduce, coerce, threaten, control, isolate, and manipulate children before and during acts of abuse. Perpetrators use violence or the threat of violence to maintain a child's silence, not necessarily her acceptance of the sexual abuse. Since children are dependent on adult caretakers, a perpetrator seldom needs to resort to violence to guarantee a child's obedience to abuse. However, lack of violence by the perpetrator does not mean that the child consented to the sexual abuse. This message needs to be very clear to women who did not experience a violent perpetrator or women whose natural curiosity as children was manipulated and played on by a perpetrator.

Children are not capable of stopping abuse. The position of power that the perpetrator has over the child and his use of contrived manipulation or intimidation are how he entraps her in the cycle of abuse. Such manipulation exists even after the abusive episode. A paradox of child sexual abuse is that adult women blame themselves as children for not stopping a perpetrator but would never blame a child they know today who is a victim of a perpetrator. Some women even blame themselves for not knowing the abuse was going to happen or because they were sexually curious. Children are never to blame for any aspect of the abuse; responsibility always lies with the perpetrator.

A lack of power, small body size, neglect, a family belief system of denial and secrecy, and the needs, fears, and dependency of children combine to create a complete picture of the true helplessness women experienced as children during the cycle of family sexual abuse. As women learn about the trauma of sexual abuse, they come to accept that the abuse was not something they could stop. Even if as a child she was sometimes able to hide or get away from the perpetrator, she was not stopping the abuse but rather only preventing it from happening that one time. Averting one incident of abuse does not mean that a child could have stopped the perpetrator at any other time or prevented the abuse from occurring.

Women retain memories of the trauma and find their truth within these memories. Even so, they have developed various ways to inhibit memories that help them live with the experience of the trauma in their adult lives. When women recall the trauma, their memories are vivid, detailed, consistent, and intense. Some women experience their memories as fragments or flashbacks. During recovery, women work at putting their memories together so that they can make sense of what they recall and understand how they were affected by the trauma of childhood sexual abuse. The women who report a loss of memory have inhibited recall until, at some point in their lives, remembering occurs. Research that focuses on understanding how trauma affects memory is more frequent today than twenty years ago when women were disclosing childhood sexual abuse.

Sexual abuse has multiple effects that occur over a number of years. For some women the longer the trauma is untreated the more severe or chronic their problems become. Reporting and documenting the sexual abuse of children has occurred more frequently over the past thirty years. The application of this information to treatment has been more gradual. Studies, clinical reports, statistics, criminal records, and medical reports have provided valuable information about this childhood trauma. We need the same kind of documented information on women who suffered childhood sexual abuse. Information on the *adult female experience* of this trauma will enhance what we know about the long-term effects of childhood sexual abuse. This kind of focused information will improve our ability to provide effective therapeutic interventions and medical treatment that support women in their healing and recovery today.

The most important information for women about the trauma of sexual abuse is that recovery is possible. A woman can regain and restore a healthy life. Recovery diminishes the multiplicity of problems that have occurred over the course of a woman's development. Positive and lasting changes occur for women when the trauma of family sexual abuse is healed. Recovery is a commitment that will improve the lives of women for generations to come.

SUPPORTING YOUR HEALING

1. Write your personal history. Begin with, for example, "My name is Sally Jones. I was born July 15, 1955, in Sacramento, California. I was the youngest of three children." Write with honesty. Write a little at a time. Gradually tell your story.
2. Make time for your recovery and be consistent with a daily commitment to your healing. Practice saying no to requests or demands from others that are nonessential to your life and would prevent you from keeping this commitment. The time to heal the past is in the present.
3. Write down what you think regarding the questions and answers in the section "Questions Women Ask about Sexual Abuse" earlier in this chapter. If you have questions, write them down; as you continue to read you will find answers to your questions. Identify what you are confused about or have difficulty accepting. Ask yourself these questions: Does what I struggle with cause a barrier to my healing? Does my resistance to accepting information about sexual abuse maintain my self-blame for the trauma?
4. If you are in therapy, talk to your therapist. If you are not in therapy, do you have someone you trust to confide in, a person who will understand both your questions and the answers you seek? If so, consider sharing with this person.
5. Ask questions that help you heal. As an adult woman, you are now free to discuss what the child never could. Just as we encourage children today to tell, we need to encourage women to tell as well. An affirmation for women is, "I will never again allow anyone to silence me."

2

Remembering the Trauma

It is the gift of truth, which can free us.
—Alice Miller, *Breaking Down the Wall of Silence*

Memory matters. The past matters. One of the major effects to women's lives from childhood sexual abuse is the disruption this trauma causes to their memory and the resulting confusion about what underlies problems they experience today—problems for which there seems to be no explainable cause and for which medical treatment does not appear to help. For example, women are not sure what causes them to experience such problems as anxiety, depression, intense fears, sleep disturbances, eating disorders, chronic pain, sexual discomfort, and a lack of intimacy in their relationships. Some women report that these problems subside for a while only to continually return and disrupt their lives. What women and those who treat them often do not understand, or may not readily accept, is that from the time of the trauma to the time of the treatment of its symptoms, the connection between the true cause of a problem and its present-day expression may not be obvious. The past does matter when assessing the problems of today, but because of the nature of this trauma, memory—the expression of the past in the present—is disrupted. When women are not willing to trust their memory or their memory is not fully available to them, they are either not able to believe their past or do not comprehend it within the context of their lives today. Therefore, they are not likely to associate the current problems they are having with the abuse in their past.

Women need to have appropriate support and steady guidance in order to experience their memories without being overwhelmed by them. Recalling memories of childhood sexual abuse can be frightening since traumatic events tend to consist of intense emotions and disconnected images that are vivid impressions of the trauma imprinted within a woman's historical memory. These imprints of the trauma can include touch and smell as well as physical sensations of trembling, gagging, crying, and numbing. Because remembering includes reexperiencing the trauma mentally, emotionally, and physically, women need to take this process slowly, maintaining a pace that does not overwhelm their capacity to cope in the present. By discussing what occurred during the episodes of abuse, women can then understand the symptoms they are experiencing in their lives today and aid their ability to heal.

Association to the traumatic experience is therefore central to realizing the connection between the sexual abuse and its present-day effects. Without this association, recalling details, answering questions, and providing information about the trauma experience is not possible, and diagnosis of symptoms will be limited or prevented altogether. When women do not have access to their memory as a base of information, identifying and understanding the specific problems that originate from childhood sexual abuse is impeded because assessment of present problems is obstructed. Without accurate diagnosis, women are at risk of experiencing ineffective treatment approaches and recurring problems that can intensify and continue to disrupt their daily lives. By understanding the cause of their symptoms, discussing what occurred during the abuse, and allowing themselves to reconnect to the traumatic experience safely, women aid their ability to heal this trauma via the experience of remembering.[1]

As women recall what happened to them during the abuse and remember how they coped afterward, much of what they have never understood about themselves finally becomes clear. For example, women come to understand why they experience their bodies a certain way, what their chronic fears and anxieties have been associated with, how addictions or compulsions developed, and why they respond so intensely to certain smells, sounds, or touch. This gradual realization between the past and present is what women have needed to make sense of what they experience in their lives. While this process of regaining a connection to the trauma is difficult in the beginning, eventually it brings a sense of relief. Women find that they are less confused about the underlying cause of their problems. They realize what has disrupted their lives, affected their adult development, and interrupted the formation of a positive self-identity.

Memories of sexual abuse are confusing at times. They often have a quality to them that makes them seem unreal, but they are real—as real as the perpetrator and what he did. These surreal feelings, which are quite common, can cause women to question whether what they remember about the abuse is real. The reasons women experience this type of doubt are multiple: the nature of the trauma, the number of years that have passed since the abuse occurred, and the dissociated experience during the traumatic episode(s).

The nature of the trauma has to do with her age at the time of the sexual abuse, her relationship to the perpetrator, the acts and severity of the sexual abuse, and whether there was more than one perpetrator abusing her. The number of years since the trauma and the dissociated experience also help to break the connection between thoughts, feelings, sensations, behaviors, and images of the sexual abuse. This disruption can cause aspects of traumatic events to be isolated from each other or fragmented and split off from non-traumatic memory.[2] To survive each incident of abuse, the child had to emotionally separate from the trauma. After the abusive episode, this type of emotional and mental detachment allowed the child distance from the abusive episode. She could either pretend that the abuse did not happen or forget that it occurred by pushing down and putting aside the memories. The factors that disrupt memory during and after trauma help explain how incidences of sexual abuse are not fully stored in memory, how traumatic memories can become fragmented, and why some women do not recall the abuse until years later.

RECALLING MEMORIES OF SEXUAL ABUSE

How traumatic memories are stored, recalled, and experienced is better understood today than in the past when women were first reporting memories of childhood sexual abuse in their families. In this treatment approach, women report experiencing memories supported by research and clinical observations.[3] They report delayed memories, complete memories, intrusive memories, selective or fragmented memories, emotional and sensory memories, body or somatic memories, and dream memories.

Information on how trauma affects memory is based on research of the structures of the brain that store, recall, and assimilate experience into memory. Three areas of this research are structures within the limbic system, the right and left hemispheres and prefrontal cortex of the brain. These areas of the brain play a central role in taking experience, turning it into memory, storing the memory for later recall, and assimilating memory as it occurs throughout a person's life experience. When an experience is received through the five senses (touch, taste, smell, feel, and vision), it is processed and stored for possible recall later. What is thought to occur with traumatic memory is that the areas of the brain responsible for memory development and integration are not able to process traumatic experience the same as ordinary (nontraumatic) experience. For example, certain structures of the limbic system are not able to receive the traumatic memory in the same way as ordinary memory, therefore traumatic experience is not processed in the same manner as nontraumatic experience. Another example is the prefrontal cortex of the brain, which integrates social, emotional, physical, and autobiographical aspects of an individual's life. This function of the prefrontal cortex may also be disrupted, and this disruption prevents integration of traumatic memory with existing memory and hinders a narrative account of the event.[4] Appendix A offers an overview of possible affects that trauma has on memory.

Documented research on the neurological effects of trauma within the structural functions of the brain is ongoing. Theories of how trauma effects memory date back to 1889 with neurologist Pierre Janet, who was one of the first individuals to differentiate ordinary memory from traumatic memory. Through his work and clinical observations, Janet proposed a theoretical understanding of the relationship between trauma, dissociation, and memory. He viewed memory as central to organizing the human experience, and he viewed the function of remembering as integral to healthy psychological well-being.[5] Since Janet's time, traumatic memory has been denied, debated, analyzed, researched, observed, and periodically accepted. What women can find relevant from today's research is that it is the trauma that affects their ability to remember and recall the abuse, and not that the individual is purposely creating a loss of memory or making false memories. Women of past generations who were among the first to disclose memories of sexual abuse can feel vindicated that current research is substantiating that what they remember is relevant and that remembering the past is a part of their healing.

Delay in recalling sexual abuse memories can continue for years and then begin to emerge at some point in a woman's life.[6] Age may be a factor in the recall of traumatic memories for some women. Joan Borysenko, author of *A Woman's Book of Life*, explains that "therapists have noted that women who were abused in childhood, and who have coped reasonably well throughout their twenties and early thirties, suddenly 'crash' in their late thirties and early forties and begin a cycle of healing."[7] This observation by therapists supports the idea that a woman will enter a stage of life significant to her adult development that will bring about a desire to heal the trauma of childhood sexual abuse. Perhaps this stage of life influences a woman to stop denying that the sexual abuse occurred, whereby she becomes motivated to pursue recovery.

Recalling memories of the trauma seems to be an involuntary process for women. A particular woman may not necessarily try to recall memories of the abuse. Rather, she has little control over the sudden experience of these memories. While some women report having complete recall of the abuse, they develop ways of blocking thoughts of the abuse. Other women discuss experiencing selective memory where they remember only parts of the abuse, and these parts are often fragmented. Women also report experiencing intrusive memories where images of the abuse are constant. Although they may not last long, women are unable to block the images from their thoughts. Women also report dream memories in which images of the abuse are recalled or reenacted in their sleep. For example, a woman might wake up screaming, trembling, and crying, and these experiences are similar to how she felt or reacted as a child to the abuse. Dream memories can be characteristic of nightmares because they are often frightening, increase anxiety, and feel confusing. They can also cause sleep disturbances because a woman may want to avoid sleep in order to avoid the dream memories or because she is awakened by them and not able to return to sleep.

There are women who recall and experience the abuse as sensory or emotional memories. A sensory memory is the response to a particular experience whereby women do not recall visual memories but have retained the feelings and emotional sensations connected to the abuse. These sensations are experienced as intense responses to a particular place, person, act, phrase, or smell. Body memories, also referred to as somatic memories, can be experienced in response to trauma. Our bodies react to everything that happens to us, whether good or bad. When we are frightened and scared, our skin prickles, our blood pressure rises, flushes occur, we feel nauseous, and our adrenalin is activated. These types of sensations accompany somatic memories of the sexual abuse. These memories are thought to relate to where the trauma has been stored physically in a woman's body or possibly portray physical responses such as gagging, nausea, muscle tension, trembling, and pain in her genitals that she experienced during the abuse.[8]

Emotional and body memories are associated with repression due to dissociation in terms of the loss of concrete memory about the abuse, and they can occur in conjunction with other types of memory experiences. They are perplexing for women since they experience what seem to be unexplainable emotions, feelings, and physical responses in the absence of identifiable causes. Maryanna Eckberg, who worked therapeutically with people in healing trauma, provided bodywork to help people recall traumatic memories via their somatic experience of the trauma. Eckberg explains that somatization rarely occurs in the absence of a severe history of trauma. She cites one study where more than ninety percent of women with somatization reported histories of abuse.[9]

CASE STUDIES: HOW WOMEN RECALL MEMORIES

The following case studies illustrate how women can experience disruption in their memory, how they might recall the traumatic experience, and how they can make a connection between sexual abuse in childhood and problems throughout life. Each case is presented and discussed to assist women in examining their own experience at recalling memories of sexual abuse. The women described in these case studies agreed to have their histories shared. Names were changed to protect anonymity.

Delayed Memory

The following case study is an example of how delayed memories of sexual abuse are recalled. Delayed memory, also referred to as repression or loss of memory, seems to be the least understood type of memory in terms of how it occurs in response to trauma in childhood and how it later emerges with adult women. Consequently, it also seems to be the most controversial and difficult type of recall for people to accept. Delayed memory received media attention in the 1990s, creating a vigorous debate and backlash about the believability of women's disclosures of sexual abuse during childhood. These media reports brought into question the reliability of some practices by mental health professionals in the diagnosis and treatment of this trauma. They also created skepticism about believing women who reported that someone in their family sexually abused them as children. The individuals who do not believe memories of sexual abuse are in the minority, not the majority.[10] While anyone who makes a false report of sexual abuse needs to be exposed, equally important is skepticism toward individuals who claim that false reports are prevalent when they are not able to substantiate these statements with sound research and clinical observation.[11] False reports do invalidate the credibility of substantiated reports of child sexual abuse, and they need to be differentiated from substantiated reports.

Case Study: Linda's Story

Linda (age forty-three) is representative of some women who experience a delay in the recall of memories of childhood sexual abuse. She told the truth about abuse by her father when it was safe for her to do so and came to understand that the anxiety she was experiencing came in response to remembering childhood sexual abuse.

Linda was referred by her family physician for an assessment. She was having daily panic attacks that were increasing in intensity and frequency. Neither she nor her doctor could explain the reason. When Linda walked into my office, I observed an elegant woman in her early forties. She spoke softly, her speech was hesitant, and she described herself as "shy." "My doctor says I am having panic attacks," she explained. "They started after my father died." She discussed her father's death and how the family had dealt with his illness; she talked more about his death than his life. As part of her social and family history, I asked what her relationship was like as a child with her parents. She described both parents as "unapproachable" and her father as "distant and stern, the supreme ruler in the family." As we discussed the panic attacks in conjunction with her history, Linda referred to "strange pictures." I listened to her share the "pictures" and asked her to explain what she thought they meant. "I am not sure what they mean because they do not make sense. The first one happened while I was standing at my kitchen sink, doing dishes, and it was like this film strip started running in front of my eyes. My father was doing things to me that frightened and confused me." This was Linda's first reported memory of sexual abuse by her father.

Why was Linda remembering now? After her father's death, memories of the sexual abuse by him began to return. As they did, she started having panic attacks. She was not only remembering the abuse, she was experiencing the shock and consequent anxiety of the trauma. At first, her memories were fragmented. As she began to relate these memories, by writing in her journal when they occurred and disclosing them in session, she gradually started to remember more details of the abuse. Her panic attacks increased in frequency and intensity as her memories emerged. She experienced flashbacks, which frightened her due to their suddenness and the vividness of what she was remembering. For Linda, it was as if she was living through the trauma for the first time. The abuse, hidden for more than thirty years, was being experienced as an adult. By not recalling the memories of the abuse by her father, Linda survived the trauma while living in her parents' home. Her father was also physically abusive, and his physical abuse seemed to reinforce the disruption of memory. A particularly painful recollection was when her mother walked in while her father was sexually abusing Linda in the living room. From this memory, she learned that her mother knew about the abuse. She met with her mother to talk about this memory, and her mother told Linda the truth—her father had sexually abused her, and her mother had known about it but did not know how to stop him.

Linda began to find her voice and the ability to talk about the trauma in the process of recalling her memories. As she progressed through recovery, she became less passive and timid and more confident and assertive. In a family session, she talked to her brothers about the abuse. They confirmed that their father was also physically and emotionally abusive. Each of her siblings could recall some aspect of abuse by their father throughout their lives.

When I met Linda, I saw the frightened, anxious, and overwhelmed child who went into shock and dissociated when the abuse happened. She stayed in this emotional and mental state of chronic shock throughout the duration of the abuse, which occurred over a number of years. When she began to remember her childhood experience of trauma and disclose to others in her family who were supportive, she began the remarkable journey of healing. No longer afraid, she found the freedom to recover not only her memories but also her life. Linda eventually joined a women's recovery group and contributed to other women's understanding of delayed memory and family sexual abuse.

Women who have disrupted memories may have symptoms of sexual abuse that seem unexplainable or manifest as problems without an identifiable cause. They may have periods of depression, daily anxieties, poor communication skills, and forgetfulness; they may withdraw from social activities and isolate from other people. Women who experience delayed memories may begin to recall the abuse when the perpetrator has died or when other stressors occur in their life: a serious illness, divorce, a major loss, the birth of a child, or some kind of significant change. These stressful times (whether negative or positive) can trigger memories of the abuse. When the memories begin, they are often frightening and confusing. Like Linda, women are unsure what to believe and disturbed about what they are experiencing. Increased depression and/or anxiety are common for women to experience when the memories of sexual abuse begin to emerge and organize in their memory.

This is how depression, anxiety, and memories of the abuse coincide. These symptoms are often experienced as they were in childhood when the abuse happened. A woman's anxiety is the emotional shock experienced from the abuse and now experienced from the memories. Depression is the hopelessness and helplessness she felt as a child when she could not stop the perpetrator's abuse of her. Now she cannot stop the memories either. I find that most women who have delayed memory, if given a choice, would stop the memories of abuse from occurring. None of them seem to want to recall the abuse or believe that it happened. However, they find that when they accept the reality of what they are experiencing, the anxiety lifts and the depression soon passes. If they try to suppress the memories, anxiety increases and depression returns.

Memory loss resulting from trauma is not a new medical or psychological phenomenon. The intense emotions evoked by painful situations can cause memories of trauma to be disrupted at the physiological level. Furthermore, individuals who have been in automobile or motorcycle accidents and suffered emotional trauma and physical trauma to their brain can have memory loss. Individuals who have strokes and seizures often incur memory loss. Soldiers who are prisoners of war have suffered loss of memory about their traumatic experiences. If trauma is known to affect memory in these human experiences and situations, why then are women, who were sexually abused as children, not accepted as credible when they suffer memory loss due to trauma? What bias does society hold against believing women when they report sexual trauma? Perhaps it is the societal theme discussed in the work of such feminist authors as Susan Faludi, Carol Gilligan, Anne Wilson Schaef, and Elizabeth Wurtzel whereby when the life experiences of women are excluded or discounted, the voices of women are silenced and certain truths about their lives can be ignored.[12] Today, women have refused to be silent. Their voices are heard and their experiences are validated, and disturbing however unpleasant these experiences may be for other people to hear.

I do not practice interventions such as hypnosis to recall memories. I advocate that women will remember what they need to remember, and what they do not remember is either not integral to their recovery or the mind's way of protecting them. Women need to honor that they may not remember all aspects of the abuse or acts too traumatic and painful to recall. I try to assure women that this is a way of protecting themselves in the present just as they protected themselves as children, and I urge them to respect their ability to self-protect. Women need to connect with their historical memories to understand how the abuse has affected their lives today, but they also need to trust that what they truly need to remember they will, and that is enough for anyone.

Intrusive Memories

Intrusive memory is the more common type of memory women in this treatment approach disclose. Women with these types of memories have always known about the abuse, but they practice pushing the memories down in order to keep them from their thoughts. Most women share that while they live daily with the knowledge of the memories, they have never told anyone about them. If women state that they did tell as children, they also share that seldom did anything happen to the perpetrator and that the abuse did not necessarily end. Women remember feeling an overwhelming sense of disappointment and helplessness that telling someone in their family did not stop the perpetrator.

In a recovery group, when women who told as children share with the women who did not tell it helps the latter to reconcile that telling as a child may not have stopped the perpetrator. Women of an older generation often say, "If only I had told," when they hear reports of child sexual abuse today. When many women of an older age group were children, there was not a police officer or child-welfare worker available to tell. It was a different time and a different culture. While there are families today who believe children about this trauma, children of the past report that when they told they were not necessarily believed. These children paid the price for the protection of family secrets or for a family's inability to stop the perpetrator. Often, even when the abuse ended, treatment was not forthcoming.

Women with intrusive memories live their lives afraid that they will be blamed for the sexual abuse. Some women avoid telling because they do not trust that their family, especially parents and siblings, will be supportive of exposing this family secret. These reasons cause women to avoid telling about the abuse or the perpetrator. Even though they know the abuse happened, they try not to think about it. Some describe how they want to quit their jobs or move someplace else so they can "escape." Others have physical problems such as migraines, high blood pressure, irritable bowel syndrome, fibromyalgia, and other stress-related disorders. Some are just ready to tell and hope that the person they tell will listen, believe them, help them, and show them the way to solve what is wrong in their lives.

Intrusive memory is often linked to anxiety disorders or a chronic history of depression. Consequently, these women live in a recurring state of hopelessness while feeling helpless to change. They report compulsions and often have a need for total order in their lives while feeling they live in a constant state of chaos and crisis. They are often so busy taking care of others that they ignore their own needs. They overfunction, doing as much as they can for others to put aside the memories, hide the shame, and mask the worthlessness they feel about themselves. These women turn to therapy as a final hope for making their lives less stressful. If life does not get better, then life does not seem worth living. These women lived through the abuse but doubt they have the confidence to go on living with the memories. Some are at risk for suicide due to the isolation, loneliness, and chronic stress induced by the incessant feelings and memories of childhood sexual abuse.

Case Study: Sally's Story

When I met Sally (age twenty-six), she was a young woman who looked and sounded exhausted. I was not sure whether she would make it through our appointment. As we discussed what brought her to therapy, she shared that she wanted to get out of her marriage. She had been feeling suicidal and also thought she could "physically hurt someone." She described herself as the main caretaker of her two young children and perceived herself as the responsible adult in her marriage. She related how she had always taken care of those around her. Demands at work were difficult to cope with, and she viewed her supervisor and coworkers as "insensitive and uncaring."

She had been experiencing chronic pain in her lower back and pelvis for the past three months. Migraines were occurring more frequently, and she had a one-year history of chronic bladder infections for which her doctor could not identify a cause. She could not talk with her husband, and there was very little emotional intimacy in the marriage. She viewed him as only caring about sex and not about her. A friend had suggested that she try therapy to reduce her stress. Sally found talking and sharing openly difficult. I asked very specific questions in order for her to provide information about her life. She responded with brief answers and volunteered no information spontaneously. When I asked if she noticed that she had a difficult time opening up she stated, "I learned a long time ago to guard what I say, to speak only when spoken to, and to tell others only what I think is safe."

We began completing a social and family history. During the social history, Sally began relating that she was abused as a child. She told about the physical abuse first and eventually disclosed about the sexual abuse by her brother. She had "been able to block the memories of the sexual abuse by my brother until the death of my father." She recalled, "It was when I was at my father's funeral and saw my brother standing a certain way that I accepted the sexual abuse had happened. I had always thought about the physical abuse by him because of the scars on my body. I never wanted to think about the sexual abuse."

Her memories of the abuse by her brother had begun to intrude within the past year. She could not block them the way she had in the past by keeping busy or, to stay in control, by having other people depend on her. Her coping methods were no longer working, and she did not know what to do. She experienced uncertainty and self-doubt on a daily basis. She felt that her family would never believe her, and consequently she wanted to escape her life.

As Sally continued in her recovery from the physical and sexual abuse by her brother, she began to recall sexual abuse by her father as well. The abuse by her father began around age five and continued until she was fifteen years old. She remembered the abuse perpetrated by him as "sadistic" and accompanied by "severe physical pain" that often left her small body battered and bruised. These memories overwhelmed her, and eventually she had to take a medical leave from work. This medical leave affirmed that she was healing. She was making choices to take better care of herself in the present than she had in the past.

Her journey of remembering has been painful. The emotional scars are apparent even with her healing. Sally is a young woman who struggles every day with the physical pain that she endured as a child and suffers with as a woman. While at times she has wanted to give up, she has not. She continues to heal from the trauma that ravaged her body and her life. Today the memories are not as intrusive, but they still occur. She is better able to experience them and less affected by them than she was three years ago. She knows to talk about the memories and not to keep them a secret, and she heals with each memory that she shares. She is able to distance from the trauma and place it in the past as she talks about what she remembers.

Women who have complete or intrusive memories live daily with the traumatic memories of the abuse. As they block the memories, they seem to forget how the abuse affected them and may not readily associate the problems they are having today with the abuse from the past. What they do know is that they have problems that feel overwhelming and cause them not to function consistently. Women need to know that their problems originated from the sexual abuse. Sally did not just happen to become a woman who wanted to escape from her life; she wanted to escape the emotional and physical pain she experienced as she remembered the abuse and could no longer deny what her father and brother had done to her as a child.

As the above case study illustrates, sexual abuse continues to affect women years after the abuse has ended. The trauma, the memories, and the impact do not simply disappear because the abuse ends. The occurrence of long-term problems is what makes sexual abuse so pervasive in a woman's life.

Selective Memories

Women with selective memories report remembering aspects of the abuse but have not retained full recollection of it, and some of what they do remember is fragmented. Women seem to be able to protect themselves from some aspect of the abuse with this selective recall. However, a lack of total recollection can create questions regarding why they remember some of the abuse but not all of it. Women will wonder what happened when they were abused that they are not able to recall.

For example, one woman recalled being forced into a sexually abusive act by her older cousin but did not remember what happened after he abused her. Another woman remembered how she felt before the abuse by her stepbrother, but could not recall specifically what happened during the abuse. She then remembered being physically sick afterward. Cindy (age forty-eight) recalled that her brother-in-law "woke me up in the middle of the night and took me to the living room, where he sexually abused me. I am not able to remember exactly what he did or how I got back to my bed in the morning." Another woman shared, "I awoke and found I was in my father's bed. He was touching me and I pretended I was asleep." She could not recall how she came to be in his bed or what happened afterward. These selective recollections of the experiences of abuse suggest that perhaps certain memories of the abuse were filtered when women, as children, dissociated, and what they recall are the least traumatic memories of the abuse. As one woman said, "I remember the bed where the abuse happened more than I remember the abuse. While that bed can still give me the creeps, I wonder what happened that I do not remember."

Case Study: Joan's Story

Joan (age thirty-one) came to my office because of ringing in her ears. She explained that she had been in counseling a year earlier. Her diagnosis was depression, with no specific cause. She stated that she began to feel somewhat better with medication. As she stopped taking the medication, she said, "I began to feel more anxious, and then the ringing started." She reported being more irritable, experiencing a loss of sexual desire, and drinking more than she normally would have in the past. Her symptoms of anxiety were prominent and evident in her rapid speech. As therapy continued and Joan completed the assessment process, she disclosed sexual abuse by a close and trusted family friend of her parents. "He was at our house every week, since he and my parents were very close friends. He was like an uncle to me and my siblings." From some of her memories, Joan could determine her age at the time of the sexual abuse but was unsure when it began or ended.

She knew the abuse involved certain sexual acts, but her memories were incomplete and fragmented. The fragmentation of memories caused uncertainty about the time and place where the sexual abuse occurred. She was distressed because she did not know how long the sexual abuse went on in her life. Over a six-month period, Joan recalled more about the abuse. She learned that the abuse occurred in her parents' home and an apartment the perpetrator lived in after his divorce. She recalled what he was wearing and that her younger sister was sometimes present. Her younger sister, who had complete recall of the abuse, verified that the abuse had happened and was able to fill in some of the memories for Joan. Before Joan's disclosure, she and her sister had never talked to each other about the sexual trauma.

Joan lived with uncertainty about the abuse for most of her life. Because her memories were selective, she doubted herself when she first began disclosing. Her fragments of memories made her think that perhaps it did not happen. She had used drugs and alcohol throughout adolescence to block when memories intruded and to calm the anxiety that accompanied thoughts of the abuse. She now understood why she experienced anxiety and thought that the "ringing in her ears" was a noise that blocked what she did not want to hear herself tell. As the memories became more intrusive, her anxiety increased and she would drink more to forget.

As Joan went through the process of recalling and telling about the sexual abuse, understanding the vulnerabilities of her childhood, and disclosing the abuse to her family, her anxiety decreased. The ringing in her ears started subsiding and gradually ended. She was eventually able to confront the perpetrator and tell him that she remembered what he did to her. The outcome of confronting the perpetrator was that he admitted responsibility for what he did and how it affected Joan, both as a child and as an adult.

Though she never gained complete memory of the abuse, what she did remember validated the cause of her identified problems. Additionally, accepting that she was not responsible for what someone had done to her also helped Joan to reduce the stress in her daily life and diminish her use of alcohol. She took responsibility for her healing and allowed herself to complete a journey of recovery. By confronting the perpetrator, she overcame her fear that what she remembered was not real. In putting her memories together, Joan answered questions about the problems that had brought her to therapy. As she learned to trust her memories, she learned to trust herself.

Emotional and Body Memories

Women who experience emotional and body memories of sexual abuse are probably the ones filled with persistent self-doubt. They wonder why they are experiencing seemingly strange behavior, unwarranted intense feelings, or painful and uncomfortable body sensations. When these women seek therapy, their reasons seem to focus on the fear that they are "going crazy." Sometimes they seek therapy because a family member is worried about them or they are encouraged by their physician, who is not able to explain their symptoms. An emotional memory of abuse is one where the woman experiences intense emotional or physical sensations but cannot recall or pinpoint anything that explains them. Such sensations occur more often than not, are variable as to when they occur, and can be inconsistent in the intensity of the experience. While skeptics once scoffed at the belief that the body is an organ of memory, researchers are beginning to document how trauma is stored in the body and expressed as changes in the biological stress response.[13]

Clinicians who have worked directly with women in the field of treatment and recovery from childhood sexual abuse have long reported what the research is now documenting: women experience uncomfortable and at times intense emotional sensations as well as physical problems in relation to childhood sexual abuse. These experiences can include chronic headaches and migraines, pelvic pain, spontaneous vaginal bleeding, constriction within the vaginal walls, sexual discomfort, throat constrictions, difficulty swallowing, numbness on the surface of the skin, shallow breathing and gasping for breath, stammering speech, muscle tension, and body tightness. While the above can be caused by other types of trauma as well as by experiences that are not traumatic, they are frequently associated (based on reports by women) as occurring with and because of childhood sexual abuse. Physicians are often baffled by these symptoms, especially since they seem to be continuous in spite of medical treatment. Women who have these types of experiences feel strongly that something traumatic has happened to them, but they do not know what. They have no visual memories of the abuse while experiencing sensory flashbacks that cause emotional and physical responses. These traumatic responses occur without a woman being able to understand them.

Case Study: Allison's Story

When I met Allison (age twenty-three), she had been in therapy for three years with two other therapists. During her previous treatment, she learned that two family members had sexually abused her younger sister. Allison began to wonder whether the problems she too was having could have resulted from sexual abuse. She had vague memories of these family members that were always associated with emotional distress. She remembered one individual as "touchy" and recalled feeling uncomfortable around him. The other family member she described as "threatening, intimidating, and controlling." Certain members of her family knew that these men were perpetrators of abuse.

Allison found speaking difficult; her throat would constrict whenever she tried to talk about the possibility of abuse. She would often gag, feel nauseated, and experience feelings of disorientation. She doubted her abilities to succeed in the world. She experienced more severe anxiety during her premenstrual cycle when she felt uterine pain. While she was seldom comfortable around people, she was extremely uncomfortable around men and would often avoid being around them. The few male relationships she had experienced were sexualized. Even when she did not want to be sexual, she felt pressured to go along rather than disappoint her partner or provoke his anger.

Due to Allison's symptoms, a previous therapist had discussed with her the possibility that she had been sexually abused. Allison was never sure because she could not visually recall sexual abuse. She felt within her body that something had happened, but she did not know what. We worked together to understand how memories of sexual abuse are inhibited—how trauma is stored in the body and felt by women who have been sexually abused. The following were identified as indicators and risk factors for Allison: (1) there was a history of sexual abuse in her family; (2) there were two perpetrators who had access to her as a child; (3) until recently the family had kept the behavior of these perpetrators a secret; (4) her emotional and physical responses were similar to women who vividly recall childhood sexual abuse; (5) she was likely experiencing somatic memories of the abuse as documented by research in this area of trauma; (6) there was a reason she was experiencing problems; and (7) her physical reactions (gagging, disorientation, throat constrictions, freezing, nausea, and feeling numb) were the same responses as women who had experienced specific abusive acts associated with these responses.

Allison began to accept that more than likely one or both of these men had sexually abused her when she was younger than age six. Her acceptance of the possibility of sexual abuse and the idea that she had developed multiple problems as a result helped calm Allison's fears rather than escalate them. She had lived for seventeen years not knowing why she experienced these recurring emotional and physical problems. Her family's support in believing her and acknowledging that perpetrators exist within the family also helped validate Allison's experience. Her younger sister's report of abuse gave Allison the confidence to come forward and discuss her own problems.

Together, Allison and her family were able to discuss the history of family sexual abuse. As she told her story she began to understand her problems, and with understanding came self-healing.

Dream Memories

There are women who report dreaming about the abuse, and these dreams sometimes increase during disclosure. E. Sue Blume, in her book *Secret Survivors*, uses the term "night terrors" to describe nightmares of sexual abuse and the terror, anxiety, and intense fear women experience with this kind of remembering.[14] Women recall dreams that are reminiscent of the abuse, that reenact it, or that are a symbolic recollection of its memory. These memories of the abuse can occur once as a single episode or as a recurring dream. In my own case, I recall a recurring dream in which someone was chasing me and I was terrified of being caught. I would sense a presence behind me, ready to grab me, and then I would escape whatever was chasing me. This dream came to symbolize being trapped in a room with the perpetrator, the fear I experienced of being alone with him, and my need to escape. While in my dream I was able to escape, I still felt the terror I had as a child. Once I understood what the dream was about, the fear diminished and eventually the dream stopped occurring.

Another example is Mickey (age forty-two), who came to recall explicit memories of the abuse by her maternal cousin by first remembering repeated sexual assault and rape by a friend of her cousin's family. Through her dreams of recalling details of the rape by this adult male when she was a teenage girl, she began to remember the sexual abuse by her male cousin that occurred when she was a young child. The sexual assault by the adult was superimposed upon her recurring dreams of the sexual abuse by her cousin. Eventually, through these repeated dreams, Mickey came to understand that she was recalling sexual abuse by her cousin as well as details of the rape by the family friend. These dreams were frightening and caused her to avoid sleep due to the fear of reliving these traumas. When this type of remembering occurs, it can cause sleep disturbances in much the same way the trauma did when it originally happened.

Women often disclose dreams that involve vivid memories of the abuse. These nightmares help some women recall aspects of the abuse that they had forgotten. Dream memories can also help women understand an emotional dimension of the abuse, such as the anxiety they experienced before and after the abuse occurred. Women begin to realize how the sexual abuse by the perpetrator disrupted and changed their sleep pattern. Sometimes dreams are reenactments of the abuse in which the woman is able to stop the perpetrator. Taylor (age seventeen) disclosed a reoccurring dream in which she was fighting the person who sexually abused her. In each episode of the dream, she became stronger and taller. In the last dream she had, he was reduced to a small size and she no longer felt afraid of him, and her anxiety when thinking about the abuse diminished.

Almost all women sexually abused as children report being terrified of the dark and of being alone. This is due to the circumstances when the abuse occurred; more often than not, the perpetrator abused her when she was alone or when everyone else was asleep. Therefore, women do not feel safe when they are asleep, in the dark, or alone. Some women experience these fears at a certain time of the day or evening that is reminiscent of when the perpetrator would arrive home or come to her house. As one woman explained, "If you are asleep, you are not safe. If you are in the dark, you are not safe. If you are alone, you are not safe. If you are in his presence, you are not safe. For at these times, the perpetrator could get to you. For at these times, the child was most vulnerable to his abuse."

Flashbacks

As women recall the trauma of childhood sexual abuse, they experience flashbacks. Women can feel, think, and behave as if past incidences of sexual abuse are occurring in the present. While flashbacks are temporary and do eventually subside, they can occur rather suddenly and catch a woman off-guard in a way that is similar to how she felt when the perpetrator abused her. Because they can occur so quickly and the sensations are so intense, flashbacks often cause anxiety to increase temporarily. They might even cause a woman to reexperience the physical sensations of the sexual abuse. Women need to give themselves time, with rest and relaxation, to recover from a flashback.

Women are encouraged not to allow the experience of a flashback to become a barrier to recovery. Rather, they need to focus their strength and energy on getting through a flashback. An affirmation for women to use during this time is, "What the child survived, the adult can heal." Eventually, women gain control over these sensations and feel less anxious and afraid when they happen. Usually after the first flashback, women are more prepared and with support can manage recurring ones. Appendix E offers suggestions to help women manage anxiety; these suggestions can also assist with the experience of flashbacks.

Often, experiencing some kind of an association to the sexual abuse is what triggers a flashback. Examples of triggers are being in proximity to the perpetrator or visiting at the location where the abuse occurred or a place that is similar. Sometimes being with family will cause flashbacks to occur. Experiencing a certain smell, seeing a picture, or hearing a certain phrase the perpetrator used that was associated with the sexual abuse can cause flashbacks. What triggers a flashback can be conscious or unconscious. If possible, women should identify what causes a flashback to be experienced, because identifying causes can help a woman be prepared for flashbacks and gain more control over her response to them. This sense of control helps diminish the fear that normally accompanies these sensations. Women may also be able to approach a situation differently or let someone she trusts know that she is experiencing a flashback. She can also remove herself from the situation that is causing the flashback.

Case Study: Mary's Experience

Mary (age forty-six) was sexually abused on several occasions while growing up by an older cousin. She talks about how flashbacks affected her and what she did to overcome them. "When I began to have flashbacks, it was during the first six months of therapy. What I found difficult was that they would come suddenly, even when I was not thinking about the abuse. I knew what was happening because I had learned about flashbacks in my therapy sessions. I was struck by the intensity. I could feel the perpetrator touching me. I could smell him, and it was as though he was right there with me. I learned that I could get through it by telling myself 'it isn't really happening now,' by slowing down my breathing, and walking. Sometimes I needed to leave work and go home early, but that was okay. I needed to take care of me. Journaling afterwards or sometimes even during the flashback would help. The abuse was becoming real to me. I realized how profoundly terrified I had been when it happened.

Eventually, by making this connection, I realized that I could never have stopped him. He was bigger, more powerful and had the control. I thought, 'How unbelievable that I could have survived something this devastating at such a young age.' I also came to accept how vulnerable I really was. Eventually, the flashbacks stopped. I have not had them for quite a while. I am sometimes amazed that when I do think about the abuse, my feelings are not the same. I am still sad at times, and I still get angry, but not for very long. It does not take me a whole day to be okay with myself again. I actually enjoy my life."

Remembering as Healing

Understanding how memory is disrupted and connecting trauma symptoms to current and past problems is a continual yet gradual process in healing. While this process does temporarily escalate certain symptoms, such as anxiety, eventually women learn that remembering is a key part of their recovery. Women should remind themselves that as children they survived the abuse and that as adults they can survive the remembering of it as well. They can focus their thinking with verbal and mental reminders that help them to affirm daily that the abuse is over. What women remember will help them heal. So much of what women feel confused about and think is wrong with their lives originated from the abuse. Women are helped when they reframe the difficult experience of remembering as freeing themselves from the trauma versus staying trapped in the cycle of abuse. This reframing can remove the avoidance patterns and other barriers women have molded to defend themselves against the fear of their memories and to keep the sexual abuse a secret. While childhood sexual abuse harms every victim, the memories can no longer harm anyone. As women understand, accept, and verbalize how the trauma affected them, they move closer to regaining their true self and preventing the reenactment of the trauma in their daily lives. By learning new responses to situations and people, women gain confidence that their lives can be restored with healing.

SUPPORTING YOUR HEALING

1. Write your memories of the abuse in a notebook. When you no longer need them, you can destroy it. In your own time and in your own way, remember what will help you to heal. Acknowledging what you went through because of childhood sexual abuse will be a relief.
2. Recall how the abuse made you feel so that you can begin the process of learning to trust not only your memory but your emotional experiences as well. Write down how the abuse affected your memory. If you are in therapy, share these effects with your therapist. You can tell her directly or allow her to read from your journal.
3. As you continue to read, consider sharing some of your memories with people you trust and with whom you feel comfortable sharing. You do not have to tell everything; you are entitled to your privacy. Privacy is not the same as secrecy. You have a right to choose what you will tell.
4. You can learn constructive ways to release your feelings. When you allow yourself to express what you went through as a child, you will find that you pass through many of the emotions that have been locked within you for so many years. Understanding and expressing feelings of outrage, shame, and fear about the abuse is an important step. The appendices in the back of the book offer suggestions on how women can express as adults feelings about the abuse in a safe manner.
5. Retelling the same memory without a purpose for retelling can sabotage recovery. If you need to discuss some part of a memory to understand yourself better, then certainly do so. Eventually you will be ready to let go of each memory that you disclose as you move forward with your healing.
6. Have you experienced flashbacks? What can you identify that causes flashbacks to occur? What helps you to get through a flashback? How do you restore yourself after a flashback?

7. Make a collage of the effects from your experience of childhood sexual abuse. Put them together on a board as you would a puzzle. As you heal from them, you can remove them one at a time. Underneath the effects write down healthy and positive characteristics about yourself that are being restored to you. For example, under the effect of "shame," you might write personal attributes such as "caring," "intelligent," "sensitive," and "funny." As you discover who you are as a person, you can reveal the woman you are becoming. Think of her as the woman you were meant to be all along.

A Family Legacy

I look in the mirror
Through the eyes of the child that was me
—Judy Collins, "Secret Gardens"

The trauma of sexual abuse is often hidden within a family's history and can span generations. Children are vulnerable to becoming victims of sexual abuse when certain risk factors exist within their family.[1] For example, children are endangered when a known perpetrator exists within the family and his behavior is not exposed directly by the family or he is not reported for prosecution. When parents have been abused as children and their ability to form secure attachments and emotional bonds with their own children has been affected, then their children are placed at risk. Parents who are not emotionally connected to their children are less likely to nurture or may neglect their children's personal safety. Such parents may not be consciously aware that certain individuals could harm their children, thus placing the children at risk of being vulnerable to a perpetrator's behavior. When mothers have a history of repeated victimization due to childhood sexual abuse, they are at risk of marrying or living with a partner who is a perpetrator of abuse, then their children are at risk as well.[2] A general belief system also seems to exist within some families that maintains denial about sexual abuse and places children at risk. While not all of the beliefs exist within a given family, at least some of them do.

REPEATED PATTERNS OF RISK

These risk factors seem to have a central connection: a history of sexual abuse that is hidden by the family members and/or a family history of not recognizing sexual abuse that inhibits seeking help to heal from its long-term effects. This central connection results in continuous trauma within the family and to specific family members. Mickey (age forty-two) recognizes this continuous trauma within her family. "My mother has been victimized all her life—a minister exposed himself to her when she was a child, her brother made repeated attempts to sexually abuse her, and my father verbally abuses her. In her own way the 'dirt and dust' that infiltrate her life on a daily basis has never been a compulsion that could rid her of any of the bad feelings associated with these abuses. I too am a statistic of this pattern and my daughter as well."

Sharon (age fifty-eight) recalled how her grandmother told her and her siblings to "stay away from Grandpa." While Sharon never knew exactly what her grandmother meant, she did as she was told, even though "Grandpa was allowed around us kids." When Sharon became an adult and had children of her own, she came to understand exactly what her grandmother meant by her warning; Sharon learned that her grandfather had sexually abused one of her daughters. Because Sharon's family had never directly exposed the grandfather's behavior, Sharon's children were placed at risk of becoming his victims. If the family had directly exposed the grandfather as a perpetrator, Sharon's daughter could have been protected. Sharon's three marriages were also indications of a family history of abuse and a repeated pattern of victimization. Her first marriage was to a man who was an alcoholic. Her second husband was physically abusive, and her third husband was a man with a sexual addiction. All three marriages indicate a pattern of neglect and the effects of abuse repeated within her family history. Today she is single, living on her own, and happier than she has ever been. She has confronted the abuse in her family, exposed the perpetrators, and challenged the beliefs that allowed the family's silence about a trauma that continued to affect Sharon's life and the lives of her daughters.

Brenda (age forty-eight) shared that both she and her brother had been sexually abused as children. Her grandmother's boyfriend sexually abused Brenda as a child; this boyfriend had also abused Brenda's mother when she was a teenager. A Boy Scout leader sexually abused Brenda's brother. As an adult, her brother was prosecuted and convicted for sexually abusing his girlfriend's children. Brenda married a man who was verbally abusive toward her and physically abusive toward their children. Brenda's family has never acknowledged that these perpetrators exist within the family. "For my family, abuse just does not happen. It does not matter that they know I was abused, that my brother is in prison as a perpetrator, and that I divorced my husband because of his abusive behavior. To my mother and father 'the family is perfect,' which is what they like to say when we are together. It amazes me that they can continue to deny what is right in front of them."

Children are at risk when there has been a history of abuse in the family, when family members are unwilling to expose a perpetrator, when specific steps are not taken to keep children away from known perpetrators, and when treatment has not occurred within the family. Some mothers learn about these risk factors when they find out that their children have been sexually abused either by the same perpetrator who sexually abused them as children or by another perpetrator in the family. Women often maintain contact with a perpetrator because the family belief system denies the possibility that this man will abuse other children, misleading women into thinking that their children are safe around a known perpetrator and that as mothers they are not continuing a history of sexual abuse. What these mothers come to face is that when the family history of sexual abuse has been hidden and the perpetrator has not been exposed, their children are at risk for sexual abuse.

For some women learning that they have been at risk for a repeated pattern of abuse comes as a surprise. Either they do not realize the risk or they refuse to believe that it exists and can continue to influence their lives, thereby influencing the lives of their children. One of the ways this lack of realization or refusal of acceptance occurs is that women who are not perpetrators believe that if they are not abusing their children, then their children are not at risk. Tragically, women who are either not aware or who deny the repeated risk factors for sexual abuse learn that their children have been sexually abused. The following case study is a clear example of how the trauma of child sexual abuse can continue into the next generation when perpetrators are not exposed, the pattern of abuse is not stopped within a family, and treatment does not occur.

Case Study: Lilly's Story

Lilly was eleven years old when I met her. She and her mother came for help after Lilly disclosed that her father had sexually abused her. Lilly's mother knew that this trauma could happen in a family because her own father had sexually abused her. Lilly soon revealed the rest of her story: her grandfather had also been sexually abusing her. Her mother's father—the same man who had sexually abused his daughter—had continued his history of abuse with the next generation by sexually abusing his granddaughter. In some ways, Lilly's mother found the abuse of her daughter by her own father harder to accept than the abuse by Lilly's father. As this mother said, "I cannot believe my father would abuse my child. I never thought he would do this again." Lilly's mother had never told anyone that her father had sexually abused her. She believed that keeping the secret about the abuse by her father would keep her daughter safe. She said, "I really thought if I did not tell, my father would not do this again."

This mother also had to accept that the perpetrators were sexually abusing her daughter during the same period. When Lilly was at home, her father was sexually abusing her; when she visited her grandparents, her grandfather was sexually abusing her. Lilly described her grandfather as a seductive perpetrator who would "try to make it a game." He began the sexual abuse in stages as he gradually brought Lilly into his abusive behavior. Lilly described her father as a violent perpetrator. "He would force me to do things to him when he came into my bedroom at night. He would yell at me and threaten to hit me if I did not do what he told me to. I was afraid he would punish me the next day if I did not do what he said." Both men started sexually abusing Lilly when she was five years old. For six years, Lilly endured betrayal and trauma by the two most important men in her life. Her mother had already endured the betrayal of sexual abuse as a child; now she had to experience the betrayal by her husband and once again by her father.

Eventually, the perpetrators were prosecuted and found guilty. Lilly testified in court about the sexual abuse by her father. Her parents divorced, and her father was sentenced to several years in prison. He was court-ordered to participate in probation upon his release and to pay for half of Lilly's medical treatment and therapy. During the legal proceedings, her father admitted to some of the sexual abuse he perpetrated but consistently minimized his behavior. He never showed remorse for the harm he had done to his daughter and wife, and he was often angry and blaming toward them because he was prosecuted.

The grandfather voluntarily turned himself in to legal authorities. He told the police and the prosecutor that he had sexually abused both his daughter and his granddaughter. He readily admitted to each act of abuse and did not minimize or blame anyone else for his behavior. He stated in court that he was relieved he had been exposed. Whether his words were true or not, he showed more responsibility for the sexual abuse than Lilly's father did. He was sentenced to five years' probation and court-ordered to pay for the total cost of Lilly's treatment until her father was released from prison, after which he would pay half. Lilly's grandfather also agreed to seek treatment. His actions may have helped him avoid prison. Lilly and her grandfather eventually had therapy sessions together. Her mother also had sessions with Lilly and later on with the grandparents and Lilly. This family began healing when Lilly disclosed the sexual abuse, her mother admitted to the sexual abuse by her own father, and the grandfather admitted to being a perpetrator without minimizing or trying to justify his abusive behavior. Lilly does have a relationship with her grandfather today; this relationship has very specific boundaries that Lilly insists her grandfather follow. She knows what he is capable of and does not spend time alone with him. The history of family abuse is not hidden as it had been for at least four generations. Through the course of her family therapy, Lilly learned that an older male cousin had sexually abused her grandfather when he was a child. She learned that her father's parents emotionally and physically abused him as a child. Lilly's mother eventually discussed the sexual abuse she had experienced as a child at the hands of Lilly's grandfather and shared her reasons for not disclosing and admitting the sexual abuse from her childhood. For this mother and daughter, forgiveness became possible by their willingness to understand the shared history of abuse within their family. At age eleven, Lilly showed the adults in her family the path to healing.

A MOTHER'S ROLE

Lilly's mother came to understand her role in the sexual abuse to her daughter, even though acceptance of this role was difficult. What she had learned from her father—to keep the abuse a secret—was taught to her as a means of protecting him, not her or her child. However, Lilly's mother was not responsible for what her husband or her father did to Lilly. Working through the process of forgiving herself because she did not tell about her father and did not keep her daughter away from a known perpetrator took some time. While she knew about her husband's childhood abuse, she thought that since he was not sexually abused as a child he would not sexually abuse their child. She recognized that he was verbally abusive in their marriage, but she did not recognize the emotional abuse he directed toward Lilly because that type of abuse as well as sexual abuse had been a part of her own childhood history. She did not deny the sexual abuse to her daughter when it was exposed. Prior to this exposure, Lilly's mother had denied that her father was likely to sexually abuse again; her father and the belief system in her family taught this denial to her, and his behavior of never admitting to the sexual abuse reinforced the denial.

As she participated in therapy with Lilly, Lilly's mother came to realize that as a child of abuse who did not have treatment she was at risk of a pattern of abuse continuing in her life and that as a mother she had not learned how to keep her child safe from perpetrators. She had learned as a child to maintain the silence of the perpetrator and the family belief system of denial. She was not taught how to keep herself safe or that she deserved to be protected. She lacked confidence in her own beliefs, perceptions, and convictions about sexual abuse and thus continued what the family believed was appropriate. As an adult woman, she learned that disclosing sexual abuse, exposing the perpetrator, and challenging the family belief system is what will keep children safe and assure that a family history of abuse is stopped.

At times, our society can too quickly judge the mother of a child who is a victim of sexual abuse without considering that the mother may have also been sexually abused as a child. A mother who is not a perpetrator does not give permission for her child to be sexually abused. When a mother is not the perpetrator, she is not responsible for the perpetrator's behavior. The perpetrator is always responsible for his behavior. Yes, sometimes a mother will know about the sexual abuse, but most of the time she does not. Mothers, and fathers, are responsible for protecting their children. They are also responsible for their own healing when they too have been children of abuse. Children are placed at risk when treatment for sexual abuse is withheld either for the child or for the family.

Women often learn that their mothers are victims of childhood sexual abuse. Other women come to recognize that their fathers or grandfathers are perpetrators of emotional, verbal, or physical abuse. Mothers of this generation of women did not have the information we have today; they did not readily have the opportunity to seek help or talk to someone about what was happening to them as children. Their trauma occurred before there were effective laws to prosecute abuse, shelters for victims, therapy programs in their community, and media exposure on the topic of abuse. Our mothers were, and in some ways still are, one of the most silent generations about this trauma. Women across generations can continue a pattern of victimization into their adult lives. Their lives as well as the lives of their daughters and granddaughters can be affected by a history of family sexual abuse. From my observations and review of the literature and clinical work with women, children, and families, I am not convinced that women sexually abused as children make conscious choices and decisions; rather, they repeat destructive patterns that began in childhood. This is not to excuse or relieve any mother of the responsibilities she has toward her child. However, I do believe it is important to recognize that the impact of sexual abuse can, and does, continue to affect a woman's life. We need to remember that the impact of abuse does not end because at some point in time the abuse did.

Mothers, daughters, and granddaughters share a history. Understanding this shared female history can help women to forgive not only their mothers but themselves as well for sexual abuse that continues into the next generation. From understanding, women can begin to acknowledge that they are not to blame for what was done to them and that they do not have to repeat the past by remaining a victim—they have the right to change destructive patterns. When this understanding is put into action, women learn to change their present and thereby change their future. Daughters often find that they are changing the beliefs their mothers accepted as true, beliefs their mothers never considered changing within their own lives. In doing so, women have a greater opportunity to keep their children safe and prevent this trauma from happening in future generations.

IDENTIFYING CORE BELIEFS OF ABUSE

Over the past thirty years, a substantial body of literature has identified the beliefs that create and support a climate for sexual abuse and other traumas within a family. Family members, whether offenders or not, often propagate and defend these beliefs even when children are harmed as an outcome. The beliefs operate within a family in a covert, nonconspicuous manner that is not always seen by people on the outside. Families in which abuse occurs can seem to typify any American family—the parents work, the kids go to school, and they all blend into the community as they go about the activities of "being a family." They have an everyday life of watching television, going to the movies, having dinner, and being together just as other families do; they do not always fit the stereotype that society has about the family in which sexual abuse occurs. This stereotype may, in fact, reinforce not only the belief system within a family but also the perpetrator's ability to mask his sexual abuse of children.

The difference between a family in which sexual abuse does not occur and a family in which it does occur is that underneath the layers of normalcy exists a secret not to be revealed. In the outward behavior of the family in which sexual abuse occurs, the image of the family is maintained; underneath this facade is where the abuse occurs and where the beliefs form that sustain it. Somehow, the family members know when not to talk, not to hear, and not to see what is going on around them. This conspiracy of silence can sustain abusive beliefs and behavior for years. When these beliefs are identified and steps are taken to change them, intervention can take place at a core level within the family to prevent this trauma from reoccurring and to help the family heal.

This treatment approach identifies core beliefs in families that continue to maintain abusive behavior across generations. Women help to identify these beliefs by evaluating when possible their family belief system prior to, during, and after the time of the sexual abuse. When women consistently report a belief as existing within their family, this belief is then identified as a core belief. These core beliefs are compared to the traits of families where abuse and trauma occur as identified and discussed in the literature over the past several years. When there is a similarity or when women or the literature consistently report a belief, it is identified as a maladaptive belief that contributes to a history of abuse and places children at risk. As shared by Charlotte Kasl in *Women, Sex, and Addiction,* "Genuine recovery necessitates going back to the core beliefs and reexperiencing the events that set them in place" because "the horror of having negative core beliefs lodged in the unconscious is that they are like inner bondage, controlling and sometimes ruining our lives."[3] Since they are acquired within the family during childhood, negative core beliefs can underlie the risk factors that cause women to blame themselves for the abuse, contribute to a pattern of continuing abuse, prevent the abuse from being exposed, and disrupt integration of the trauma that is necessary for healing.

CHANGING MALADAPTIVE BELIEFS

In treatment, women work to identify and change maladaptive beliefs that continue to interfere with their adult lives and contribute to a pattern of self-blame, shame, and revictimization. By challenging these beliefs, women can prevent them from continuing and exerting a negative influence on their lives because of the thoughts, behaviors, and emotions that accompany them. Women can then develop an enriching, self-accepting belief system that enables them to more easily acknowledge their lack of responsibility for the abuse, withdraw from a continuing pattern of victimization, and make steady progress toward a recovery that supports healing and restores their lives.

CORE BELIEFS OF FAMILIES WHERE SEXUAL ABUSE OCCURS

The following eleven beliefs are identified from an ongoing process of isolating the specific maladaptive beliefs that exist in families where sexual abuse occurs. If maladaptive beliefs can be identified, they can serve as part of a parent and family education program on how to prevent child sexual abuse:

1. The rules that exist in the family and govern behavior are arbitrary and rigid; they are not based on mutual respect.
2. One (or more) of the adults has absolute power and control over children. These powerful adults are seldom questioned about their behavior, and this can be especially true about a perpetrator's behavior.
3. Family secrets are pervasive, and a distorted loyalty is demanded. Therefore, talking about known or suspected problems in the family is viewed as being disloyal.
4. The perpetrator's behavior is kept a secret within the family; it is not to be talked about or exposed. The three little monkeys who hear no evil, see no evil, and speak no evil have come to symbolize this belief within families where abuse and other childhood traumas occur. The secret is rarely revealed even within the family and never outside the family.
5. Inconsistencies and contradictions are a part of daily life and prevent children from experiencing a sense of security that comes from predictability. Chaos and uncertainty in turn cause a great deal of emotional instability within the family.
6. The phrase "it is for your own good" is often stated to children to justify maltreatment. Such words reinforce a child's silence and influences what she believes is good for her.
7. Love and trust are confused in families where abuse exists. Love is conditional: "I will love you if you meet this condition." Trust is modeled as unconditional: "Trust me no matter what I do or say to you."

8. Adults expressing feelings and communicating emotions in a healthy manner to children seldom exists. Therefore, children have few, if any, family role models to help them learn healthy ways to understand and express emotions, needs, and expectations. The expression of anger, loss, or sadness can be particularly problematic in families where abuse exists.

9. Adults deny or minimize problems in the family, leaving few, if any, solutions available for solving problems or understanding how they occur. This denial or minimization increases the likelihood of problems being repeated.

10. Patterns of other kinds of abuse can exist within the family. Within these abusive patterns, children's boundaries are violated, often repeatedly. This violation of boundaries causes children to experience degrees of anxiety, fear, helplessness, and confusion and can also create offenders who violate other people's boundaries.

11. Children are powerless to effect change within the family system. Consequently, they are not able to influence or change the family belief system and, in turn, will often propagate it in one form or another.

DISCUSSION OF THE CORE BELIEFS

The rules in an abusive family are arbitrary and rigid. They cannot be changed, negotiated, or compromised. There is seldom discussion, questioning, talking, or listening among family members. The rules are given, and the rules are obeyed. When the rules are not obeyed, negative consequences follow. Disrespectful behavior, especially toward children, is common in a family with such rigid and arbitrary rules. Some children grow up learning a passive response to the rules—that is, they go along in order to keep the peace. Other children rebel but do not necessarily adopt a more flexible belief system; their thinking is still rigid but in the opposite direction of the family rules. Because abusive families are authoritarian rather than consistent, fair, and reasonable, children from abusive families have trust issues with authority figures outside the family. These trust issues are displayed by either not trusting authority or by wanting to please someone in authority. Adolescent females can reflect these trust issues with criminal behavior such as drug and alcohol use or shoplifting or with sexual passivity in their relationships with adolescent boys.

Abuse involves absolute power and control over another human being. Children are not allowed to question this power and control; if they do question it, they are labeled as "back talking." Adults who were children of abuse have a similar attitude. They believe that adults should have power and control over children. Adults are viewed as never wrong; their opinion is the only one that matters, and their decisions are final. A common phrase that adult women remember hearing as children is that "children should be seen and not heard." If a child is heard, then she is not seen; not only does her voice hold no value, but her thoughts and opinions have no value either. These beliefs reinforce feelings and thoughts that she is not important, not intelligent, or not able to reason effectively.

This belief system leads to confused thinking. For example, outwardly the family is viewed as caring for the child, but within the family the child is harmed repeatedly through the abuse. The idea of family tells us that family members will keep a child safe, but the reality is that she is not protected from the perpetrator. The frequency with which children doubt their experiences, blame themselves for the abuse, carry guilt about exposing the perpetrator, and fear family retribution are examples of the confusion they experience within the family's maladaptive belief system. Women have shared that rather than feeling it is their right to expose the trauma of childhood sexual abuse, they feel disloyal to the family if they do. Although they have done something right, they think they have done something wrong by talking about the perpetrator, the abuse, and what happened within the family. This thought of wrongness reflects a maladaptive belief that truthfulness, which reveals the family problem of sexual abuse and exposes a perpetrator, is not considered a right action for the family.

Another example of the confusion that exists in families is perpetrators who believe they have a justified right to abuse a child. As discussed earlier, the maladaptive beliefs exhibited by perpetrators play a part in their continual abuse of a child. The nonoffending adult who denies the abuse or knows about it yet does not stop it reinforces the perpetrator's beliefs. This aspect of the belief system can also be relayed to the child indirectly by family members when they are either unaware of the abuse or minimize its harm to the child. The continual secrecy and denial of sexual abuse maintains this belief by the perpetrator as well as his demand for loyalty from the child in keeping his behavior a secret.

Maladaptive beliefs are one reason abusive families do not often support women when they enter a recovery program. Women share comments that family members make to them when they learn a woman is in therapy to recover from sexual abuse. Examples of these statements are, "I hope you are not talking about what Dad did," or "All of that happened a long time ago. Why bring it up now?" And even, "That [sexual abuse] is not still bothering you, is it?" Just as a healthy family protects itself, so does an abusive family. The difference is that a healthy family protects itself through openness and honesty that promote and support discussion of problems. Consideration and compassion are given to family members to show concern for their experiences and needs. An abusive family protects itself through secrecy, denial, and silence. Openness and honesty are deterred because of fear of what might be revealed. An abusive family feels threatened when a family member breaks the no-talk rule. Family members often minimize, if not outright deny, the trauma of abuse or their role in it. They may not readily agree or accept that it is a woman's right to share and discuss what occurred to her in the family or that her sharing is a step in her healing.

Because this belief system is maladaptive, neglect and mistreatment of children can occur with little or no awareness by the adults. Neglect often precedes sexual abuse—neglecting to protect a child from a perpetrator by not paying attention to her safety. Minimal and careless supervision of a child or not listening to or observing a child's behavior are some of the ways that families can ignore children and neglect their basic needs of safety and security. Contradictions and inconsistencies are a part of children's daily life when abuse is occurring. The rules, even though rigid, can change often. When rules are arbitrarily established, those in power can contradict them. Confusion follows contradiction, and unpredictability follows inconsistency. When these characteristics dominate a child's life, she does not know who to depend on or trust on any given day or who to rely on for protection. Because she is not taught about personal safety, she grows up not knowing when she is safe and when she isn't.

Harsh punishment even for minor infractions of the rules is an example of mistreatment of children. Condemnation, criticism, ridicule, belittling, teasing, and other forms of emotional and verbal harassment can also occur in families where children are sexually abused. These children grow up feeling devalued or not worthy of being loved, and they question their sense of worth. When love is conditional, it can cause children to question what they need to do to earn love. A perpetrator of sexual abuse has a pivotal role in teaching his victim this distortion of love. Women recall ways the perpetrator taught them conditional love: "I will love you in a sexual way, and I will love you if you do not tell what I am doing to you, and I will love you if you protect me, and I will love you if you let me do these things to you and not cry." From this imposed condition of what is labeled love, the child learned that she had to trade herself for the feeling of being loved by someone who made her believe she was unlovable. Her confusion about love causes a deep sense of distrust for others who say they love her. She can also experience self-doubt about how to show and give love to her partner or her children.

Unconditional trust is taught repeatedly to children when they are sexually abused. One woman remembered her father telling her, "Trust me no matter what I do to you, and you are never to question what I do." Like this woman, children often find that if they question an adult's behavior, they are punished. A child perceives that the perpetrator can do whatever he wants to whomever he wants and nothing will happen to him. On the other hand, she is punished for whatever she does, however minor, or so it feels. When trust is taught as being unconditional, women become unsure of who to trust in their lives. They will question their judgment about when to trust, or they tend to trust people who are not trustworthy. This confusion contributes to establishing relationships with people who are similar to the perpetrator or other unhealthy family members and can be one of the factors that place women at risk of continuing a pattern of abusive or neglectful relationships in adulthood.

Honest and thoughtful expression of feelings seldom occurs in abusive families. Instead, feelings are expressed to manipulate the child to meet the needs of the perpetrator or other adults. Guilt is a common emotional experience for a child who has been sexually abused, and the result of this imposed guilt is shame. She carries both into her adult life as emotional burdens distorting and skewing her self-image. She grows up feeling guilt because of someone else's behavior, shame from the misuse and violation of her body, and blame for not stopping or exposing the abuse. As a child, she was not allowed the expression of her feelings, so she buries them along with the memories of the abuse. These repressed emotions are experienced later as problems that manifest in various ways throughout her adult life. They can also disrupt her relationships when they are displaced onto people in the present although they are really about the people from her past.

Anger, sadness, and loss can be especially problematic emotions in families where sexual abuse occurs. Women often fear anger—their own and others—because the anger they experienced as children became rage. Therefore, they suppress the healthy anger that they all need to experience. Each time their boundaries were violated, they felt anger. After years of suppression, a child's anger can turn into adult outrage. When some women suppress anger, it is often focused inward and becomes depression; for other women, it is focused outward toward other people. Anger, although felt repeatedly, was not allowed expression during all the years it was experienced. The same is true for feelings of sadness and loss. A child's sadness over the trauma of abuse and the losses throughout her life are often experienced as reoccurring depression, helplessness, and hopelessness. She may not know why she seems to be depressed and views her life as never turning out the way she had hoped. These suppressed emotions of anger can drain a woman's energy and enthusiasm.

Women identify denial and minimization of problems as prevalent in their families. This denial goes hand in hand with the no-talk rule. The thought pattern that sustains this belief seems to be expressed in the following way: "If we do not talk about the problem, it is not real; and if it is not real, then it is not happening; and if it is not happening, then we do not have to deal with it; and if we do not have to deal with it, then we can go on as we are; and if we go on as we are, then no one will know that we have problems." It is an endless circle of denial. The old adage "what you do not know cannot hurt you" could never be more wrong than in a family where children are sexually abused.

Children also learn denial firsthand from the perpetrator; he teaches her the behaviors of denial during and after the sexual abuse. During the abuse, he neither admits nor acknowledges the wrongness of his acts or the pain to the child. After he abuses her, he leaves the room, wakes up the next day, sits at the breakfast table with her, and behaves as though nothing happened to her the night before. A child thus learns to mimic the perpetrator's denial behavior. His behavior teaches her to keep his secret, remain silent, and pretend he is a good person and that nothing he does is wrong. In therapy sessions, perpetrators often explain that their denial reinforced their lack of remorse for what they did to the child as well as enabled them to continue the abuse. While offenders may show discomfort at being exposed, they seldom express remorse for what they did or the harm they caused.

When the family learns of the sexual abuse, they may minimize the trauma with statements such as, "It was not that bad," or "You are exaggerating," or "I do not remember that happening." This type of minimizing allows the family to continue the denial of both the sexual abuse and its effects. They also deny the need for treatment when they minimize how the perpetrator affected the child emotionally, physically, mentally, and spiritually. Minimizing also has a role in maintaining the power a perpetrator has over a child and keeping the sexual abuse hidden. When a woman breaks her silence about the abuse, she also breaks free of the denial system of the family members and the perpetrator; family members may not be supportive of this decision, because not only is the perpetrator exposed, but so is the family's belief system.

When women are aware of the maladaptive beliefs acquired within their families prior to and when the sexual abuse was occurring, identify the impact of these beliefs on their thought patterns, and then change them to more enriching and life-adaptive beliefs, their healing becomes more stable. What a woman believes about herself in relation to the sexual abuse she experienced is profoundly affected by the beliefs that existed, or still exist, within her family. A woman's recovery necessitates the modification of these acquired beliefs from the family system of abuse if she is to thrive and not merely survive the trauma of childhood sexual abuse. Self-determination requires moving beyond the control of maladaptive family beliefs in order to move into healthy adult living.

SUPPORTING YOUR HEALING

1. Make a diagram of your family and place the names of your family members in boxes. Under their names, write down what you honestly know about them; list the characteristics of each family member. If you can, go back a generation and write down what you know about your parents' families. What characteristics do you identify in your family that created an environment for sexual abuse?

2. If there is information for you to gain about your family that would help you answer questions or understand your family better, then contact family members with whom you can talk. Write down the questions you want to ask each person regarding your family's history.
3. Review the list of core beliefs in this chapter and write down the ones you know were or still are operating in your family where the abuse happened. Be specific about the ways your family expresses these beliefs. How do the beliefs affect your thoughts, feelings, and behavior?
4. Write down your beliefs about family and children. Which ones do you want to keep? Which ones are important to change if you are to stop the history of abuse from continuing in your life today? What beliefs have you kept from childhood that distort your life today? What beliefs from childhood maintain the secrecy, shame, guilt, and self-blame about the sexual abuse? What beliefs have you instilled today that help you live healthy?
5. Look at the characteristics of a healthy family in Appendix C. Which of these characteristics do you instill in your family today? Which ones does your family need to develop? Note: The definition of family for this question is the family you have established for yourself in the present, not the family where the abuse happened.

4

Chronic Shock Symptoms
and Dissociation

As you pass through my life, look, but not too close,
for I fear I will expose the vulnerable me.
—Deidra Sarault, from *Each Day a New Beginning:*
Daily Meditations for Women

Understanding the impact of sexual abuse is a cornerstone of recovery for women. Two of the long-term consequences of child sexual abuse are chronic shock symptoms (CSS) and dissociation. CSS and dissociation are intense mental, emotional, and physical responses that flood a child at the time of the assault.[1] Indications of CSS and dissociation include lost time, constricted breathing, flashbacks, heart palpitations, numbing, and confusion. These symptoms can occur whether the abuse is a single episode or a repeated pattern and do not necessarily stop being experienced once the sexual abuse ends. They are among the symptoms of trauma that disrupt memory and contribute to specific problems in adulthood.

Mickey (age forty-two) said that her "experience with chronic shock and dissociation occurred for a long time. I physically feel my breathing shut down and that I am holding my breath until my body tells me this will not work anymore, and I start to breathe again. I feel the muscles in my body tighten, especially my jaw. I know at this time I am in what I call the 'zone.' I really do not see anything around me and I do not hear what is being said to me, and if I do, I only hear bits and pieces. Nothing in the present seems important and I am consumed by the vision and feelings of the past abuse." As Colleen (age twenty-seven) shared, "My throat tightens and I find it difficult to speak. I also cannot breathe and I feel every muscle in my body tighten. There is also the feeling of leaving the present and of just not being here."

The historical context in which the sexual abuse took place is the reason most women did not receive treatment at the time the abuse occurred. This lapse in treatment can prolong symptoms of chronic shock and dissociation. On her own, a child developed ways to live through the trauma in order to survive and reach adulthood; after the trauma ended, she used what internal resources she had to shelter some part of her personal integrity. The coping methods each child found adaptable and beneficial to her survival did not always prevent chronic shock symptoms from enduring once the abuse stopped. Coping methods alone cannot prevent the traumatic effects of sexual abuse from extending into adulthood because they are not meant to be used as a long-term way of living. Therefore, women can continue to experience symptoms of chronic shock and dissociation years after the trauma has ended. Women are helped when these symptoms are identified as prolonged effects of sexual abuse so the disruption they cause to women's lives can be addressed. Consequently, the specific set of symptoms related to chronic shock and dissociation along with the problems they create for women need to be better understood by health care providers who offer treatment to women for this trauma. When not diagnosed and treated as an outcome of childhood sexual abuse, CSS and dissociation cause periodic and, at times, prolonged disruption to a woman's life. When treated they can be stabilized so that eventually they subside and, in turn, so do the myriad of problems they cause to women's lives.[2]

IDENTIFYING CHRONIC SHOCK SYMPTOMS

A child simply does not have the resources available to handle the traumatic effects of sexual abuse. Today, much literature exists to help women identify symptoms of chronic shock and understand the extent and variety of symptoms that stem from sexual abuse. The work of Maryanna Eckberg, Wayne Kritsberg, Richard Lazarus, and Hans Seyle, among others, can also explain how the coping methods that are used to defend against ordinary stress do not adequately deal with traumatic stress.[3] Their work, adapted for use with this treatment approach, explains certain aspects of what women experienced as children when the sexual abuse occurred. This information also helps women to understand that the reason they are affected by sexual abuse is not due to some inadequacy or weakness in their ability to cope with the trauma of sexual abuse; rather, the trauma was too overwhelming for them to deal with on their own. As Alexander McFarlane and Giovanni de Girolamo state, "Traumatic stressors are events that violate our existing ways of making sense of our reactions, structuring our perceptions of other people's behavior, and creating a framework for interacting with the world at large." Traumatic stressors are "uniquely destabilizing," according to McFarlane and Girolamo, because they "demand more than adaptation and

Illustration C

coping." They also "necessitate a confrontation of the threat of helpless-ness." The nature of childhood sexual abuse violates and changes the child's world—namely, the family, which is where she is supposed to learn that she is protected. The family thus becomes a world that she can never return to again in order to feel safe and secure.[4]

Wayne Kritsberg describes the effects of traumatic shock on breathing. Restriction in the chest disrupts the normal flow of breathing, causing a child's breathing to be shallow and ragged rather than an even and steady flow. Kritsberg also identifies an increase in heart rate, an elevation in blood pressure, and cold sweats on the skin. A look of vacancy and distance appears in the eyes of the child as she disconnects to what is occurring, and her face and skin lose color and then appear flushed. Kritsberg notes that these symptoms indicate the child is experiencing extreme reactions brought on by trauma.[5] Illustration C is the self-portrait of a child who depicts these symptoms of shock. She drew this picture to help convey the symptoms she experienced during the trauma.

Maryanna Eckberg states that a victim responds to trauma by going directly into a state of immobility, where she is frozen in place and unable to move. The person is not able to resolve the trauma on her own or with available coping methods because it is too overwhelming. Eckberg explains that a victim of severe trauma is likely to suffer debilitating symptoms of post-trauma as well. These symptoms include chronic hypervigilance expressed as a constant scanning of the environment for danger, chronic hyperarousal where intense emotional or physical responses related to the original trauma are felt more often than not, and debilitating physical symptoms, such as pain and muscle aches, that are expressions of how the trauma has been stored in the body. Intrusive images, where details of the abuse are seen repeatedly in a victim's mind, are also identified as the result of trauma, as is intense and overwhelming anxiety that is felt when these images occur. The person experiences disorientation in which there is confusion as to time and place, and short-term memory is disrupted.[6]

Put in the context of the above descriptions, sexual abuse is life-threatening and overwhelming to a child; it dramatically changes the perception she has of the world around her and the people in it. Through his abusive acts, the perpetrator transforms her world into a place that is now unsafe. He is perceived as a threat to her personal safety and well-being, and in reality he is a threat to both. When the abuse occurred, the child was caught off guard and unprepared; she became immobile, frozen in place and unable to escape. A child simply does not have the resources available to her that would help her to escape or prevent the trauma. If the perpetrator repeats the trauma, shock symptoms reoccur.

Hans Seyle studied the body's response to chronic stress. His work provides further understanding of the potential symptoms of shock experienced during sexual abuse. He defined chronic stress as life-threatening because when a stressful event is unrelenting and there is little time in between to recover, the individual is going to deplete the resources she employs to defend against the stress and reduce its impact. Seyle identifies three phases of responses that individuals go through as they try to cope with chronic stress. He first describes the biological response to sustained and unrelenting stress, which he terms as the alarm reaction—the stress activates the body's nervous system and places it on alert status. This is also known as the flight-or-fight stage of stress response, when the body and mind are getting prepared for what is about to occur so that action—either fleeing from the stress or fighting against it—can take place. Seyle identifies the next phase of stress response as the resistance phase—if the stress cannot be prevented, then an individual attempts adaptation to the stress by employing coping methods. When the stress persists and the individual is unable to adapt by use of available coping methods or she is not able to end the stress, the third phase of stress response, the exhaustion phase, occurs. Seyle describes the exhaustion phase as life-threatening because the individual's psychological and biolog-ical systems are going to shut down due to depletion.[7]

The work of Richard Lazarus on the use of coping methods further adds to the understanding of how chronic and overwhelming stress give rise to the shock symptoms women experience from the trauma of sexual abuse. As Lazarus indicates, when a person determines that the demand of a situation exceeds her resources, she experiences stress. Sexual abuse is a demand placed by the perpetrator on the child that exceeds her resources. Lazarus proposes that the concept of coping is also relevant because depending on how the individual copes with the event, the effects of stress will vary. One dimension of coping explained by Lazarus is problem-focused coping involving direct action to solve the problem. A child is unable to take direct action to stop the abuse by the perpetrator. The perpe-trator controls the child; the child does not control the perpetrator. The sec-ond dimension of coping, as identified by Lazarus, is for the individual to seek information that is relevant to developing a solution.[8] The solution would be for an adult to intervene on behalf of the child and stop the perpe-trator or for the perpetrator to stop abusing the child. Neither of these solu-tions is readily available to the child at the time of the abuse.

The work of these authors helps in understanding child sexual abuse as a major life-threatening and life-changing traumatic event. Their work also helps to explain how symptoms of shock occur and are prolonged because a child cannot stop the problem of sexual abuse on her own or seek treat-ment for it without adult assistance. She is limited in her ability to deal with the assault or prevent the sexual abuse by the perpetrator simply because she is a child; the perpetrator's silence—not admitting to the abuse—prevents intervention, also causing symptoms to reoccur. Without effective adult intervention, the pattern of CSS will likely occur as long as the perpe-trator has access to the child. Without effective treatment, the child, and later the woman, is at risk of continuing to suffer from symptoms of shock and other effects of the abuse on either an intermittent or a continuous basis. The aftershock symptoms of sexual abuse also inhibit her ability to return to a state of prior being. All of the above contribute to the potential of prolonged problems related to the effects of chronic shock from childhood sexual abuse. The traumatic experience of child sexual abuse is unique, necessitat-ing intervention rather than adaptation and coping to prevent both present and future problems to the child.

In healthy families, when events or situations occur that provoke anxiety, fear, or trauma to children, adults take the opportunity to help by supporting children through the traumatic event and resulting crisis. The family members will acknowledge that the event occurred and then inquire about a child's feel-ings and thoughts in order to understand her experience of the event. She is provided comfort, and her sense of safety and security is gradually restored.

If needed, the family will seek outside help to prevent any future impact to the child from the trauma. Throughout these steps, the child receives support and the trauma is acknowledged rather than denied. Because the family discusses the trauma, she is able to process the traumatic experience and is given a context by which to understand it. More than likely, the experience of the trauma will become a part of, rather than fragmented from, her ordinary memory. When this healthy process occurs, a child has the confidence and assurance that her family can be called upon for comfort, support, and guidance. The outcome is that the family uses its resources to help the child through the trauma rather than to keep it a secret. This process is an example of how integration of traumatic experience can occur at an emotional, mental, and physical level when a child receives support and assistance within the family.

In families where women experienced childhood sexual abuse, the above process did not occur. The resources in the family were either limited or not available to help her through the trauma. Alone, she had to try to understand the abusive behavior of the perpetrator and the reason the abuse was occurring; her context of understanding was limited because she was a child who did not have adult intervention to assist her. With only herself to count on, she developed a means of surviving and going on with her daily life. Intervention was not possible since the only person who knew about the sexual abuse was the perpetrator, and he did not expose his behavior to anyone but the child. Her injuries, whether emotional, physical, or mental, were not attended. Only she and the perpetrator were aware of what he had done to harm her, and he protected himself at the cost of the child. Her well-being was not important to him, and he did not alert anyone else in the family that the child needed help. The belief system within the family is a contributing factor to her symptoms not being identified or being ignored.

When the abusive episode was over, the aftershock of the abuse was still felt as her body, emotions, and thoughts continued to experience the impact of the trauma. What does a child think, feel, or experience after sexual abuse has occurred? Women share common memories of the aftershock: "I laid there immobile, but I do not know how long." "I could barely breathe or move. I think I pulled a blanket over me." "After a while, I got up. I do not know how I was able to make it to the bathroom." "I think I passed out so I would not see it happening. I do not remember how long it was before I came to." "It took a long time to be able to breathe." "I curled up and went to sleep. I did not feel anything." "I cried until my eyes burned." "I think I threw up." "I remember shaking."

Most women share that the physical, mental, and emotional symptoms of the abuse continued for hours or days. None are sure that they have ever fully returned to their emotional, physical, or mental state of being before the trauma. Maryanna Eckberg concurs that severe trauma overwhelms a person beyond her capacity to cope, and her system of perceiving, thinking, and behaving changes.[9] Shock symptoms originating from childhood sexual abuse can endure into adulthood as extended and prolonged states. When women are provided with information on symptoms of chronic shock, they readily identify with and recognize these effects of sexual trauma experienced then and now.

CSS AND THE CYCLE OF SEXUAL ABUSE

Through continued research and clinical observation, we are learning how sexual abuse occurs. As perpetrators are prosecuted and ordered by courts into treatment programs, the opportunity exists to understand how they create a cycle of abuse, first by drawing children into the abuse and then by controlling them. What we are learning is that this cycle occurs whether the sexual abuse is a single episode, a repeated pattern of short duration over a few days or a few months, or a prolonged pattern over a number of years.[10] Some women can describe how perpetrators brought them into the abuse in stages by progressing toward more severe acts of abuse and gaining control over them. A perpetrator may begin the cycle of abuse with the use of intimidation, inappropriate touch, forced physical closeness, bribes, guilt, or isolation of the child. The cycle begins the moment the perpetrator decides he is going to sexually abuse the child.

Stage One: Symptoms of Chronic Shock Begin

A child experiences the first episode of sexual abuse by the perpetrator as emotional, physical, and mental shock. She does not want to acknowledge that the abuse has happened or believe that someone she was supposed to be able to trust has committed these acts against her. She numbs her painful emotions and actively tries not to remember or think about the abuse. She may try to pretend it did not happen and disguise the fear she now feels about the perpetrator. She feels helpless and unsure of what she might have done to cause the perpetrator to abuse her. Nightmares, refusal to go to bed, and resistance to sleep often occur. These effects disrupt her sleep pattern and cause fatigue; they will likely continue to some degree as a prolonged effect into adulthood. In this initial stage of the trauma, she may or may not reenact the abuse in her behavior. She is afraid of being alone and may cling to other adults, refuse to leave the house, or not want to go to school. At other times, she may want to escape being in the presence of the perpetrator. Fantasy and daydreaming are common coping methods to escape thoughts of the sexual abuse.

Stage Two: The Perpetrator Repeats the Sexual Abuse

After the first episode, the child worries that the perpetrator will repeat the abuse. When he does repeat it, her worry becomes real fear. She has

increased feelings of helplessness. Nothing she says or does stops the perpetrator's abuse. At an internal level, she acknowledges that she is powerless to stop the abuse and feels it is hopeless to believe that the perpetrator
will stop since he has abused her again. The impact of the trauma is affecting her sense of self, and changes to her developing identity are occurring.
Denial of the trauma and its effects on the child are often reinforced by the
family belief system. The child is unable to speak about the trauma; the perpetrator reinforces her silence by keeping his behavior hidden. The thought
process of blaming herself for both the trauma and its effects is beginning.
She feels bad about the abuse and therefore feels bad about herself. This is
the first phase in which she begins to internalize acquired beliefs from the
perpetrator and his abuse. This internalization of a negative self-concept
includes the belief that she, rather than the perpetrator, is responsible for the
abuse. Self-blame becomes a part of her internal dialogue about her self-
worth. Dissociation during the trauma replaces pretending that the abuse
either is not happening or did not happen as the child strives to cope on her
own and somehow defend her integrity against the abuse.

Stage Three: A Pattern of Sexual Abuse Is Established

The type and frequency of abuse and the severity of symptoms will influence the emotional, mental, and physical effects of the trauma. Chronic
shock symptoms combined with the trauma to a child's body can cause her
to experience psychosomatic disorders such as headaches, stomachaches,
shortness of breath, rapid or delayed speech, fatigue, self-harm behavior,
mood fluctuations, and appetite and sleep disturbances. Emotional numbing, in response to chronic shock symptoms and as an outcome of dissociation, is experienced.

The child is learning to maintain the perpetrator's denial system, which in
turn reinforces her isolation and silence about the abuse. He may be assuring
the child's obedience with threats, intimidation, bribes, acts of violence, elic-
itation of sympathy, or verbal aggression. Shame, fear, guilt, and embarrassment will also cause her to conceal the abuse. If other types of stressors are
occurring within the family, the child may perceive other adult caregivers as
not available for protection, ineffective to provide safe haven, or aggressive
themselves. She may also fear getting the perpetrator in trouble or having
someone in the family be angry with her. She also senses that she could be
blamed for the abuse. As the abuse goes unnoticed, she continues to lose faith
and trust that she will be protected or comforted within the family.

Loss of safety, intense helplessness, and early stages of depression and
anxiety are common. The child continues to develop coping strategies on
her own to somehow live through the trauma and survive. The continual
effects of the trauma may shift, change, and increase in severity as the abuse

escalates and becomes a constant pattern in the child's life. Dissociation and inhibition of memories occur frequently in order for the child to get through the day. The internalized shame she experiences will harm her self-concept and negatively affect her female identity.

Stage Four: The Perpetrator Is in Control

The child cycles in and out of the abusive pattern with the perpetrator. She has no sense of control over her life because the perpetrator has taken control. She experiences more volatile and unstable emotions as the cycle continues. Self-blaming thought patterns are formed and reinforced by statements made by the perpetrator or other family members. She is unable to tell anyone about the sexual abuse; this contributes later on to her loss of connection between the trauma and her behaviors, emotions, thoughts, and perceptions.

Stage Five: The Cycle Continues

She is most likely inhibiting memories of the abuse on a daily basis; spontaneous flashbacks interrupt her ability to function naturally and with ease. Coping methods become defense strategies that enable her to survive within the cycle of abuse created by the perpetrator. Her identity that was emerging before the trauma is profoundly changed. She is most likely not aware of problems resulting from the abuse, and she will tend to blame herself for the problems she does experience. Because of the perpetrator's and the family's secrecy, silence, control, and denial, there has been no intervention to stop the abuse or provide treatment for the child. She will grow into adulthood with memories of the abuse most likely dissociated from the effects of the trauma. She questions her ability to make thoughtful choices and trust her judgment. Intense fear and anxiety are experienced. Feelings and thoughts of shame permeate her self-concept and impede her healthy identity development.[11] The multiple effects of sexual abuse can accumulate over time. They can also become more pronounced during times of stress. A woman is at risk for the effects of sexual abuse to transfer into her adult life and cause recurring problems such as depression, loss of sexual desire, and anxiety. Because she is viewed as an extension of those around her, she struggles to differentiate her sense of self from others' expectations of her. Challenging the family is difficult, if attempted at all, and her ability to develop separately from the family and the perpetrator is impeded.

THE EFFECTS OF DISSOCIATION IN ADULTHOOD

Dissociation is accepted as a means of coping with trauma even though it is not fully understood. It is identified in this treatment approach as occurring with chronic shock symptoms and is a contributing factor in the disruption of women's memory. While dissociation is viewed as an initial adaptive response to childhood sexual abuse, it becomes maladaptive because it can inhibit a woman's awareness of the abuse experience. When awareness is inhibited, a woman is limited in her knowledge of the content and details of the abuse, which in turn disrupts the connection to her feelings and emotional state at the time of the abuse. Dissociation can cause recurring emotional states that hinder recovery, especially when it becomes a coping mechanism for current stress or is associated with self-injury.

Episodic dissociation is not abnormal for women who have experienced childhood sexual abuse. In the late 1800s, Pierre Janet proposed that dissociative states occur in response to trauma. These states become an underlying cause of pathology when they are prolonged without corrective intervention. Dissociative states disrupt memory and prevent integration of the trauma into the woman's life experience, and if not treated as responses to trauma they can trigger a variety of problems, such as physical sensations of the trauma, intense emotional reactions to current stresses, and behavioral reenactments of the trauma.[12] Women need help to recognize how the dissociative response from childhood continues after the abuse by the perpetrator has ended so that they can address these problems in treatment and learn to disrupt the dissociative state when it occurs in the present.

In relation to childhood sexual abuse, dissociation serves as a primary defense strategy to protect the child from the overwhelming and helpless experience of the perpetrator's behavior. Most women relate that dissociation in childhood was not necessarily a conscious process; rather, it simply began at some time during the trauma. Some women engaged in dissociation at a more conscious level as they became familiar with its survival value. Therefore, since dissociation worked to help some children live through the sexual abuse, some could initiate it for continual use while for others it remained an unconscious process that simply occurred in response to the trauma as an automatic coping method. I have observed both of these behaviors in therapy sessions—women who automatically dissociate when discussing memories of the abuse, and women who describe to me how they just chose to "blank out" so as not to feel what they were discussing about the sexual abuse. Both groups of women describe experiencing dissociation in a similar manner throughout the time of the abuse and afterward. The women who choose to dissociate also seem to be the women who reenact the abuse through self-harm types of behavior. Dissociation may also be part of the explanation as to how a child is able to go on with life, even temporarily, while being sexually abused. If through dissociation she did not have to remember the sexual abuse experience on a daily basis, then she did not have the conscious experience of it throughout her day. This dissociative response is an answer for women who question how they ever survived the abuse for as long as they did.

Women describe dissociation as including emotional numbing, shutting down mentally and emotionally during and after the trauma, and distancing from the trauma by mentally moving out of or away from the trauma when it was being perpetrated. Other aspects of the dissociative experience include little to no emotional response when the trauma is recalled. This loss of emotion is observed in therapy as women relate the traumatic experience but do not exhibit emotions about the abuse even when they are describing their feelings about it. Women also share how their minds went blank or how they would block out some aspect of the trauma and view it as unreal or occurring to someone else. The sensation of being frozen in place and unable to speak is often described by women as a dissociative response to the abuse. Women report intense reactions to certain triggers such as places, smells, or behaviors. Women seem to have no explanation as to why these reactions are felt until certain remnants of the abuse are recalled and connected. For example, one woman became numb and speechless when she smelled roses; she later recalled that roses were frequently in the room where her stepfather abused her because her mother grew roses in the yard. Innocuous objects thus become triggers of the trauma because they became associated with the perpetrator and the abuse, even when a woman is not immediately aware of the association.

Dissociation can even cause women not to recognize the traumatic event as harmful. Even though they remember it, they do not know how to express what they feel about it or their knowledge of how they were affected is inhibited. Another aspect of dissociation is tunnel vision, where the focus is on a visual image rather than the abuse and this image is what is remembered more vividly. Some women share that they used, or the perpetrator may have forced them to use, alcohol or drugs, which can induce dissociative-like states. Some women share that they consciously created another name for the abused self who stayed in the trauma so that they could distance from being the victim.

DISSOCIATION IN ADULTHOOD

Women in this treatment approach report the experience of dissociation when they reenact some aspect of the abuse in their present-day life or when they experience associations related to the abuse. Dusty Miller, in her book *Women Who Hurt Themselves*, describes trauma reenactment syndrome (TRS) as behaviors reminiscent of the trauma. "The key to recognizing TRS is the connection between an adult woman's symptomatic behavior and her own unique story of childhood trauma; TRS women do to their bodies something that represents what was done to them in childhood." Miller goes on to explain that "for all TRS women the self-inflicted harm resonates the pain that was inflicted upon them as children. Their self-destructive behavior tells the story of their childhood experience over and over again."[13]

Examples of reenactment behaviors include vomiting to remove feelings of the abuse; exercising or running to escape thoughts, feelings, and sensations of the abuse; or self-abusing with alcohol and drugs to numb feelings and avoid memories of the abuse. TRS-related self-harm may also include a woman cutting on her body where the perpetrator held her down or scrubbing parts of her body where she feels the violation of the abuse or believes that her body is unclean. Reenactment of the shame a woman felt during the abuse can cause her to burn or scratch areas of her body that she blames for causing the abuse to occur. Some women gain weight in an attempt to alter their appearance because they believe if they had looked different or the perpetrator found them "less attractive," then he would not have abused them. A woman recalls a perpetrator stating that certain aspects of her appearance caused him to abuse her; women then come to loathe these attributes and desire to eradicate them. Other women injure a part of their bodies that the perpetrator belittled and criticized during or after the abuse.

One woman related how her numerous treatments of liposuction were "to remove the feelings of how my father told me he liked my legs while he was abusing me." Numerous diets, surgeries, and cosmetic treatments and alterations are not always recognized as harmful ways that some women hurt themselves after sexual abuse. As Miller indicates, "Some of these women engage diet specialists who collude with them in dangerous or at least seriously unhealthy weight loss programs. There are also women who undergo numerous elective surgeries. Their bodies become like clay—shaped, distorted, and worn-out by surgeons for whom they're medical objects and sources of revenue."[14] As a therapist, I have sometimes pointed out to women who have cosmetic surgeries and who have been sexually abused that instead of cutting on themselves, they pay expensive surgeons to do it for them, thus allowing them to mask their self-injurious behavior in a way that other women who cut on themselves are not able to do.

Whatever way the reenactment is played out, women enter into a dissociative state so that intense feelings and images associated with the pain of the abuse are not experienced but rather avoided. This avoidance is similar to the way women, as children, experienced the dissociative state in order not to feel, remember, or acknowledge the perpetrator's abuse. Not all women engage in reenactment behavior, and those who do may not do so on a continuous basis. As Miller explains, "Some women seem to have at least superficially successful lives that are suddenly disrupted by an unexpected outbreak of self-destructive behavior" that is "often triggered by the awakening of memories of previously forgotten abuse."[15] Miller's therapeutic observations correlate with research on how traumatic memories and dissociation are closely linked to the replaying of traumatic events through specific yet personalized behavior when memories start to be recalled.

Women use dissociation as a memory inhibitor and an emotional anesthesia to block thoughts, feelings, and physical sensations of past abuse.[16] They describe this use of dissociation as a response to external events and internal feelings that trigger thoughts of the abuse. These stressful episodes cause a woman to perceive herself as being out-of-control or events as being beyond her capacity to cope, which in turn triggers heightened feelings of anxiety. This intense level of anxiety often leads to panic attacks, and because women want to prevent this reaction they dissociate from what is causing their feelings of intense anxiety by shutting down, distancing, or numbing. In some way, these episodes seem to mirror the abuse experience. For example, when stress occurs and a woman perceives her life as no longer in her control, she becomes overwhelmed and experiences a mirror response of the abuse that can include dissociation. While other people may experience a mild or slight form of dissociation for a short time under similar circumstances, for a woman who was sexually abused as a child the current stress triggers an emotional response the same as or similar to what occurred during the time of the abuse. Therefore, she experiences not only the present stress but also the stress of the past abuse. One woman called this the "double jeopardy," and it is one way dissociation becomes a maladaptive response in the present. When not addressed, it will create a barrier to healing by interfering with learning more adaptive responses to stress that occurs in the present.[17]

TREATMENT OF CHRONIC SHOCK SYMPTOMS AND DISSOCIATION

When CSS and dissociation are identified as present symptoms of childhood sexual abuse that are contributing to specific problems in adulthood, they can be understood and diminished with treatment. When women experience a stabilization of these two symptoms at an early stage of treatment, they may become more committed to a recovery program because of the relief they experience from these problematic states. Gradually, women no longer experience continual symptoms of shock and manage their life better on a daily basis. When women come to accept that if they continue to use the maladaptive coping response of dissociation they will impede their recovery, they have a substantial reason to work at diminishing the use of it in the present. Treatment of trauma symptoms, and chronic shock and dissociation in particular, requires a flexible approach by a knowledgeable therapist who can individualize the treatment plan based on a woman's particular experience of sexual abuse and the symptoms she presents. Coordination with physicians is sometimes necessary due to the relationship of anxiety and depression to both chronic shock and dissociation. However, medication alone will not heal the trauma of childhood sexual abuse.[18]

This framework promotes an approach to healing that suggests treatment for the complete trauma and not just the isolated symptoms. We know that women experience specific problems related to childhood sexual abuse such as eating disorders, anxiety, depression, or chronic pain. While we have treatment approaches that work to heal these specific problems, the treatment of a specific problem that is an isolated effect does not necessarily heal the traumatic experience as a whole. We need to understand the total impact of childhood sexual abuse that women experience as a diverse group and then develop proven and effective treatment programs that meet the individual needs of women. In doing so, we increase the likelihood of ending the long-term disruption this trauma causes to women's lives. Women deserve a framework to understand the specific impact that sexual abuse, as a chronic trauma, has had on their thoughts, feelings, behavior, bodies, and identity. The more we understand the total long-term impact of this trauma on women and the better able we are to offer a variety of effective treatment approaches, the more women we will be able to help heal.

"The treatment of the depression, anxiety, and dependency that I had experienced from the abuse was like a domino effect to some of my other problems," said Teresa (age forty-one). "By taking care of the anxiety and depression, I no longer felt so afraid or so hopeless about my life. I felt encouraged to solve more immediate problems facing me and more willing to try different approaches. I began to feel better about myself and less dependent on others to feel good about me."

Summary of CSS and Dissociation

When women experience prolonged problems from childhood sexual abuse, continual symptoms of shock and dissociation may be contributing factors. If these symptoms and the behaviors that accompany them are diagnosed, they can be treated effectively. Women can then make informed choices that support their recovery in order to discontinue the use of ineffective coping methods and to approach present-day problems more effectively. They can discuss information about their symptoms, ask questions about treatment, and receive information about approaches that are recommended. In turn, women gain a sense of control over their lives because they are actively participating in decisions about their recovery and treatment. If a woman is not currently experiencing abuse, she will likely find that with treatment the specific long-term problems resulting from childhood sexual abuse can be healed. As life becomes more manageable, a woman's sense of well-being increases. With increased well-being, a healthy identity is restored and a woman's life improves.

SUPPORTING YOUR HEALING

1. Review Appendix D to identify what continual symptoms of chronic shock you have been experiencing from childhood sexual abuse.
2. Do you currently experience dissociation? If so, what will cause it to occur? Are there triggers you have identified that cause dissociation?
3. How do you respond to stress when it occurs in your life today? Do you have adaptive responses or maladaptive responses?
4. Do you experience trauma reenactment behavior? If so, what will cause it to occur? What thoughts or feelings of the abuse do you experience when reenactment occurs?
5. Do you inflict harm to your body? How do you inflict harm? How is this behavior related to the abuse?
6. Have you talked to anyone about this behavior? If not, what are your reasons for keeping it a secret?

The Stages of Treatment and Healing

When we start at the center of ourselves, we discover something worthwhile extending toward the periphery of the circle.
                                   —Anne Morrow Lindbergh, *Gift from the Sea*

The decision to heal from the trauma of childhood sexual abuse is life-
changing. The change that women experience occurs gradually and in stages
as it becomes a permanent part of their lives. One significant change is the
diminishing of destructive patterns. Sexual abuse profoundly affects the
thoughts and emotions of women that in turn create patterns of behavior
that have the potential to cause problems throughout their lives. This
interconnection of how a woman's thoughts, feelings, and behaviors were
influenced by the sexual abuse is what underlies the destructive patterns
that women have lived with and the problems they cause.[1] As women experience internal changes during recovery, their thoughts, feelings, and
behaviors change and destructive patterns diminish. These changes occur
because the past trauma of sexual abuse is no longer a dominant force in
their lives. Examples of the outcome of these internal changes are a greater
degree of self-confidence, improvement in decision-making and problem-
solving skills, feeling safe when alone or with others, decreased feelings of
tension, and increased feelings of relaxation. Women experience a greater
comfort with and acceptance of their bodies and find that intrusive thoughts
of the abuse fade, harmful behaviors diminish, fears are resolved, and optimism toward life occurs more frequently.

Women report that external changes also unfold from personal growth
and healing. Examples of external changes that women experience are a
redefining of relationships with others, a decrease in problematic and disruptive behaviors, and the ability to establish clear and congruent boundaries. Life becomes more consistent and predictable as setting limits
becomes easier, and they feel physically better in terms of the energy level

and motivation they experience. Women report that they manage better on a day-to-day basis and have resources available to them that prevent issues from escalating into reoccurring problems. For most women, healing that brings growth and change is the first time since before the trauma that they have experienced themselves as healthy, functioning, and capable individuals. Women describe these experiences of wellness as being "felt on the inside, before they are experienced on the outside."

A woman's identity and self-concept are affected in a profound way by the trauma of childhood sexual abuse. How she came to think about herself, perceive her life, and behave toward others have been influenced by the abuse; therefore, how she has viewed herself within the world was influenced as well. As women move through a process of healing, they identify how the trauma of family sexual abuse affected their development. Negative beliefs formed during the abuse (see Chapter 3) underlie and sustain the prolonged effects of this childhood trauma on a woman's identity. The relationship between symptomatic behavior and a woman's unique experience of the sexual abuse suggest that these negative beliefs are maintained as thoughts that women have about themselves that have influenced their identity.[2] A woman feels these negative beliefs emotionally and then acts on them through her behavior. This is another way destructive patterns are set in place by the sexual abuse and one of the reasons women reenact this trauma in various ways throughout their lives.

For example, some women view their bodies in a way that represents what the perpetrator did to them during the abuse. Other women exemplify the loss of power they felt during the abuse by continuing to experience self-blame for not being able to stop the perpetrator or for how the abuse has affected them. There are women who exhibit a cycle of depression throughout their lives, causing them to experience an extended sense of hopelessness and apathy and to doubt that their lives will ever improve. As Eileen (age forty-two) stated, "I viewed my choice to be in a loveless marriage as a decision I had made when I was twenty years old and one that I could never change. The man I married had characteristics similar to the perpetrator who abused me. He was domineering, controlling, and manipulative. As I changed how I viewed myself, I changed how I viewed my choice to remain in this marriage. The day I filed for divorce was a week after I had disclosed the abuse to my family and exposed the perpetrator. I no longer felt bound to a marriage that I would not choose to have today."

Women actively work at identifying the negative beliefs and destructive patterns associated with the trauma of childhood sexual abuse that continue to influence their lives today. In doing so, they are then able to develop their own beliefs about the trauma based on new information and the knowledge they have gained from their life experiences. As women challenge the thought distortions brought about by the perpetrator and his behavior, they find they have lived much of their life based on the way in which he treated her. In addition, they discover that they no longer have to continue the maladaptive beliefs of the family—a family that avoided discussion of the trauma and prevented new information from reaching them. This change in destructive patterns is an outcome of healing that causes the thoughts, emotions, and behaviors arising from the sexual abuse to diminish. A new identity begins to emerge based on meaningful information about a woman's strengths, abilities, and developing sense of self. This emerging identity is, in some ways, reminiscent of the person she was developing into before the trauma of sexual abuse occurred. Women describe this emerging identity to be the essence of the person they were before the sexual abuse became a part of their lives. A woman can integrate this former sense of self into her emerging female identity that is forming in the present. This identity is absent of negative beliefs that were acquired from the abuse or the family's belief system and prevents self-destructive behavior from continuing unnoticed.

As women identify their new beliefs and form an identity based on their strengths and individual character, they separate from the trauma in a healthy, conscious way. This conscious separation, which occurs emotionally and mentally, is reflected in their behavior and is another step that promotes the eventual integration of the trauma into a woman's life history. One of the outcomes of this healthy separation is that the responsibility for the trauma is externalized and placed with the perpetrator, where it always belonged. Women can then acknowledge that the trauma occurred without blaming themselves. Once the blame for the sexual abuse is shifted, they can more readily accept how the abuse affected them. Separation from the negative beliefs of abuse and the internalized blame that resulted from them is a part of the healing process. Appendix B identifies thought patterns that women with this treatment approach recognized as affecting their identity as women.

THE STAGES OF HEALING

The following stages of healing were adapted from the work of Wayne Kritsberg with Adult Children of Alcoholics (ACOA)[3] and the work of Bessel A. van der Kolk on the diagnosis and treatment of traumatic stress.[4] Kritsberg's proposed stages of healing were redefined within this framework for treatment of sexual abuse. Van der Kolk's research and clinical approaches were reviewed to assure a sound clinical structure of diagnosis and treatment as applied to trauma. Ideas were then assimilated and applied in the recovery and treatment of sexual abuse as a traumatic and chronic stress to women. The proposed stages of healing are meant to serve as a guide for women, answer questions they may have about the recovery process, and provide a touchstone to help them identify where they are in their recovery. Women can then assess where healing for them has occurred and what stages of healing might still need to be completed. Therapists and other health care professionals can use these stages as a framework for treatment at an individual level with women.

Initial Stage: Assessment

During the assessment stage, a woman, along with her therapist, needs to do the following:

1. Determine what symptoms of shock occurred during the cycle of abuse and which of these symptoms are being experienced today.
2. Determine what testing will be given to obtain information on depression, anxiety, self-esteem, adult development, relationship patterns, assertiveness skills, and boundary issues. Sexuality is assessed in terms of sexual comfort, sexual behavior, sexual identity and orientation, and how sexuality is currently affected or not.
3. Assess other problems that are also identified. Other problems might include personality functioning, existence of an eating disorder, or specific stresses such as parenting and the marital relationship.
4. Identify if reenactment thoughts, feelings, or behaviors are occurring and, if they are, when they occur and what triggers them, and if there is a history of trauma reenactment behavior.
5. Determine how dissociation is experienced and what functional purpose it serves in a woman's life as well as the maladaptive use of it.
6. Complete a social and family history; obtain preliminary social and family information about the partner as well if she is in a committed relationship.
7. Obtain medical information on physical disorders such as migraines, irritable bowel syndrome, or chronic vaginal infection related to this trauma; obtain information on current and past medications prescribed and their effectiveness at alleviating the symptoms of chronic shock, especially depression, anxiety, intrusive images, and sleep disturbances; determine if somatization exists within this cluster of symptoms.
8. Identify what physical pain a woman has experienced or is experiencing, how it has been treated, and to what level of success the pain has been relieved.
9. Provide information to women on the ways sexual abuse affects women, and answer specific questions a woman might have about the trauma of family sexual abuse in her life.
10. Provide information and answer questions that women have about the recovery process and, if agreed upon, how treatment will be coordinated with other health care providers.

11. Develop a plan for the first six months to a year of treatment. This treatment plan should be reviewed with a woman to explain recommendations and answer her questions and should be reviewed and updated at least every six months.

This assessment process helps women to discuss their symptoms of the trauma, which in turn allows their gradual disclosure about the trauma of childhood sexual abuse they experienced in their family. Providing information to women about childhood sexual abuse and recovery can be facilitated during assessment, which can decrease some of the emotional distress women experience upon entering treatment. Assessment identifies what specific problems are most likely reenactments of the trauma while seeking to understand where coping methods are maladaptive and contribute to current problems. In addition, assessment gives treatment focus during the first six months of therapy and navigates the treatment process.

The treatment plan provides information to physicians and other health care professionals who are involved with a woman's health care. This approach to recovery advocates coordinated services for women in the treatment of this trauma. Monthly status reports that summarize how a woman is progressing in treatment can be provided to other health care professionals. These status reports can also address issues of medication, pain management, or other relevant treatments that are occurring elsewhere with women. For example, I will provide, with the written permission of women, reports to physicians, craniosacral therapists, massage therapists, surgeons, and others who are a part of a woman's health team for recovery. These status reports are reviewed with women beforehand so they know what information is being shared with other providers. However, at all times, the woman determines if information is shared, what information is shared, and with whom.

First Stage of Recovery: Making the Connection

Disclosure. Women entering treatment need a gradual disclosure process that occurs at their individual pace. The importance of carefully and slowly allowing the memories and experience of sexual abuse to be told cannot be overstated. Throughout this stage, there is a gradual shift from denial or minimization of the sexual abuse as traumatic to realization of its damaging effects. This gradual shift is achieved by working from the premise that disclosure of the trauma is healing only when it occurs within the context of a noncoercive, carefully constructed therapeutic relationship. A therapist who allows women to feel protected and safe within the treatment process gives assurance that their traumatic experience of childhood sexual abuse will be understood at an individual level. Because the beliefs attached to the secrecy of family sexual abuse are complex and tenacious, the therapeutic process has to support the gradual disclosure of trauma. This is also the time when the underlying family belief system begins to be identified.

Disclosure occurs throughout the recovery process since women recall and share their memories at various times during treatment. This means that disclosure can occur over several weeks, several months, or longer. For disclosure to be healing, the therapeutic relationship needs to be one of respectful listening and posing thoughtful questions, a few at a time. Women determine the pace of this gradual noncoercive disclosure. A therapist working within this process provides an environment that is respectful of a woman's tolerance for sharing so as not to overwhelm her. The reassurance of emotional safety is provided in part when boundaries are discussed and respected throughout the therapeutic process, but especially at the beginning stages. A therapist needs to be mindful of the individual differences among women regarding both their desire and ability to disclose at any given time during this stage. A knowledgeable therapist who is skilled, empathetic, and willing to learn about each woman's unique experience and has an attitude of mutual respect can represent the respect, safety, care, and trust that was missing in childhood. An experienced therapist can provide validation as to how the abuse was traumatic for an individual woman while affirming that healing is possible.

Acute Crisis. A woman often comes to treatment because she is experiencing the effects of abuse as ongoing or recurring problems in her life. She may enter treatment acknowledging that she has become less able to function in her daily life or that she is suffering from multiple health problems. She may have recently experienced marriage or the birth of a child; perhaps she has a child who just reached the age when the abuse in her childhood began. Sometimes this crisis state occurs when the perpetrator has died. This state of stress may have started because she has been experiencing intense flashback sensations, more frequent and vivid memories of the abuse, a loss of appetite, sleep disturbances, or a greater degree of depression and anxiety. Whatever her reason, she is seeking relief.

Awareness. While women may or may not be prepared to talk about the abuse, they are most likely ready to acknowledge that it happened. Once abuse is acknowledged, they begin the process of actively thinking about it with less ability to block it from their consciousness. This active thinking signals a first stage of connection: admitting the possibility that childhood sexual abuse has caused problems in her adult life. Since this is an emotionally vulnerable time, a woman needs to know that she can trust the therapeutic process to provide her a safe environment in which to gradually begin to connect the abuse to other problems she has experienced. This is often a good time to review the questions and answers presented in Chapter 1 and for her to share her thoughts or questions about this information. A dialogue about the trauma of sexual abuse is beginning in therapy.

Safety and Trust in Therapy. A woman needs to know that the therapist is a safe person who can be trusted with her experience and the memories of the trauma. She needs confidence in the therapist's ability to understand the shame and embarrassment she feels surrounding the sexual abuse and to help her understand which of the problems that she experiences today are a result of the trauma. The opportunity to share her story one memory at a time and have it understood is crucial. A therapist does need to ask specific questions about the abuse: Who is the perpetrator, what was his relationship to the child, when did the abuse occur, how old was she at the time of the abuse, where and how often did it occur, what does she remember about how she felt, and how she coped during and after the abuse? There should be no probing of memories and no attempts to induce memories since these types of intrusions tend to cause inhibition of expression rather than facilitate discussion. Information about flashbacks, how trauma affects memory, and the types of memory related to sexual abuse will help her to move through this stage. Questions about how she coped with and survived throughout the abuse will help a woman understand and identify which coping methods she uses today that are related to the trauma as well as what her strengths might be.

Discussing the Cycle of Abuse. The age at which the abuse began, the severity, whether there was early treatment, and the identity of the perpetrator will underlie the degree of impact to a woman.[5] Whether the perpetrator was violent or seductive will need to be determined. A woman may go through periods of wanting to talk about the abuse, then a period of minimizing it or its effects; at the same time, she is also experiencing the desire to continue her healing. While this variability is a normal part of moving toward acceptance and recognition of the trauma, she will also feel that the pain of remembering is overwhelming. During these times, a woman can feel emotionally exhausted and want to give up, or at least want to take a break from treatment. These thoughts and feelings are expected throughout the early stages of recovery. Women may use some of their previous strategies of coping such as numbing, distancing, minimizing, and forgetting to help them get through this stage. By pacing discussions and providing coaching, modeling, and support, therapists help women learn how to discuss the sexual abuse and learn new ways of managing the memories of the trauma.

Second Stage of Recovery: Experiencing Emotions

Emotions of Outrage and Grief. During this stage, women often experience a profound sense of loss and sadness about the abuse and what it took from her as well as intense outrage about what the perpetrator did to her. Some women may experience an increase in depression due to the grief and loss, while others experience more intense anxiety due to the outrage. These increased, and at times intense, emotional states are temporary. Women may cry at various times or for several days while feeling the sadness that they were unable to express as children; this is natural. A woman needs to feel her losses and allow them to be real without being viewed as abnormal. Trusting one other person to share her feelings with will help open the emotional silence she has kept about the trauma. Being held by someone she trusts is comforting. She has the right to grieve. There will be times when she needs to be alone with her grief but not isolated. Cocooning—being by herself where she can feel what she needs to feel that words cannot explain—can be helpful. She will share when and if she is ready. Gradual disclosure, nonintrusive questions, respectful listening, and safe physical touch are important therapeutic approaches for women at this stage. This is another stage in which boundaries within the therapeutic relationship should be discussed and defined.

The outrage a woman experiences can be deep and intense. This is the prolonged anger that she was never allowed to voice. Just as the perpetrator suppressed his behavior with secrecy, he also suppressed her emotions of outrage. Over the years, she may have directed this outrage at herself or others. Women need help in releasing this outrage in ways that are healthy and nondestructive. There are creative and controlled ways of expressing outrage from trauma. Verbalizing her outrage about the perpetrator or family members will also help alleviate some of the intensity of CSS; it can also lift degrees of depression, decrease self-blame, and increase her energy.

Women will need to let go of the myth that "nice girls do not get angry" or that the only way to release their outrage is to "let it all come out." Neither is true. A woman needs to work with her therapist to find what will work best for her in releasing the outrage, a little at a time. Most women realize that their ability to feel and express anger has always been affected by the abuse and other family dynamics. For example, a woman may have used the outrage as a means to protect herself and to keep others at a distance. One woman describes using her outrage in this manner: "I was an outrager. My fierce anger kept people away from me. I could hold my outrage close, like a shield. I was saying, 'Get back. You will not get a chance to hurt me!' My outrage caused people to avoid me, while giving me a sense of safety. I used it as a wall against feeling vulnerable and unprotected. I gradually came to realize the cause of my intense anger and that I had used it as a way to protect myself for many years. Eventually, I became ready and able to release the outrage in a healthy and focused manner. As I did, I could allow others into my life as a trusting person once again. As someone once said: 'Walls not only keep us in, they keep others out,' which is what I did with my anger."

By acknowledging and expressing sadness, outrage, and other emotions related to the abuse, women begin to feel a range of feelings. An emotional thawing begins. A woman who passes through this stage is ready to accept that the abuse happened. She can admit that she did not cause the adult to abuse her and begin to realize that she is not responsible for how the trauma has affected her. Through the expression of grief and outrage and by letting go of self-blame, women reconnect with how powerless they were as children. This reconnection helps to dissolve the resistance they have had about admitting their inability to stop the abuse or its effects. Women put a voice to their traumatic experience as they relate what they went through both during and after the abuse. This emotional connection to the child's lack of control over the perpetrator allows the adult woman to move through another stage of resolution as a step toward integration of the trauma. By admitting her helplessness as a child, she is acknowledging her lack of responsibility for the trauma. At the same time, she is acknowledging her ability to heal.

Third Stage of Recovery: Identifying Chronic Problems

Healing Prolonged Problems. By this stage, a woman's thinking is less negative and critical, and she is experiencing a greater sense of hope and optimism. Women find that they are ready to trust their opinions more often than not as they regain the value of their own perceptions. They are no longer alone and isolated because they have reestablished trust in their lives. Women communicate better and are more open, honest, and direct with themselves and other people. Their anxiety lessens, and they are more committed to continuing recovery. Negative core beliefs become a primary focus for identification and change. This is the stage when a woman's sense of identity is being renewed and reformed.

An area of treatment that women will focus on within this stage is resolving reenactment thoughts, emotions, and behaviors. As women identify the negative beliefs that formed during the cycle of abuse and within the family belief system, they will continue to experience a diminishing of dissociation and CSS. Their ability to set age-appropriate boundaries in relationships improves as they develop a style of assertive communication with others. This assertive style replaces a passive or aggressive style of relating and interacting within her significant relationships and everyday interactions. The ability to solve problems, identify a range of feelings, and establish a self-actualized belief system is an outcome of this stage. Women are encouraged to create opportunities that will nurture their personal growth and self-awareness and enhance their self-esteem and self-worth. Another area of healing is sexual enjoyment. This aspect of a woman's recovery comes from sharing questions that they have about human sexuality and learning about female sexuality specifically. They can explore their own sexual preferences within an established, trusting relationship with a partner. Women's groups and workshops are a good source of information and sharing on the topic of sexuality. Women need to work through understanding and accepting that the sexual acts forced upon them as well as their responses to those acts were not choices they were given as children, and they need to realize that today, as adults, they have a choice about their sexual behavior.

Other important areas of healing for women have to do with their role within the family, the emotional nurturing of their children, and effective parenting skills and attitudes. Their family relationships start to change in a positive way, but these changes will often challenge other family members in terms of redefining and reworking relationships with them. Women make progress in continuing to diminish and change destructive patterns, relinquish childhood coping methods, and address dual-treatment issues such as addictions and eating disorders. There are a variety of prolonged effects that result from childhood sexual abuse, so what women will need to focus on at this stage of healing is individualized. Chapter 6 discusses the prolonged problems from childhood sexual abuse that women in this treatment approach frequently present for healing.

Decisions about Disclosure. This stage is where women make decisions about whether to disclose the history of the abuse to other people. Their first step may be to attend a women's recovery and support group. A recovery group also allows women to learn even more about healing. Through individual therapy, she has gained confidence that what she knows and remembers about the abuse is real, and she is now ready to share this confidence with other women. This decision is based on a woman feeling, and believing, that for her it is time to build another level of trust. In a women's group, she can disclose as little or as much about the abuse as she thinks is appropriate. Focusing on the developmental impact the abuse has had on her identity, rather than on the actual acts of abuse by the perpetrator, is helpful at this stage. By placing the focus primarily on how the trauma has affected her, the trauma experience recedes into the past without her denying that it happened.

Another decision women will make is whether to disclose the perpetrator's abuse to partners, parents, siblings, family members, or friends. Women need to give careful consideration to the people they choose to disclose to as well as when to disclose. If possible, these disclosures take place in a therapy session where a woman is given the support of her therapist to answer questions that might be posed by the people she chooses to tell. These sessions need to be planned between her and the therapist.

A woman's decision to disclose to a partner has to be based on trust. If a woman does not trust her partner, then disclosure is not recommended. Frequently, a woman has told her partner about the sexual abuse at some time during their relationship but then never discussed it again. The therapist can meet with a woman and her partner to answer questions and provide information about recovery. Partners do benefit from understanding what has caused problems in the relationship, what healing from childhood sexual abuse involves, and what changes he may need to make in the relationship. How the relationship has been affected by the abuse as well as the boundaries a woman has established during her recovery can also be discussed. Unfortunately, a woman does not always have a partner who is trustworthy, respectful of her right to privacy, or supportive of her recovery. Other significant issues that can prevent a woman from disclosing to her partner are past or present abuse by the partner, whether the partner shares characteristics of the perpetrator, or whether he manipulates her in order to have control of the relationship.

A critical issue regarding children is whether the perpetrator has had access to them over the years. A mother needs to ask her child, in general, about the perpetrator's behavior; if she then suspects that abuse has occurred, she will need to ask her child specifically about the perpetrator's behavior. A family history of sexual abuse will not end if her children are not protected from the perpetrator who abused her or from others within the family. A decision about reporting the abuse, if it has occurred, will also need to be made. Her therapist can work with her and child protective services to ensure that she and the child are protected and supported. If a mother decides after talking to her children that abuse by the perpetrator has not occurred, then she will need to discuss how the relationship with the perpetrator will change.

Disclosure to the Perpetrator. Deciding whether to safely confront the perpetrator is an important decision for women. This decision can be controversial within recovery programs and within her family. Confronting the perpetrator is disclosure to the person who sexually abused her; it is not permission to be abusive. Women should never confront a violent perpetrator; disclosure is always decided with a woman's safety as the first priority. Chapter 7 discusses this decision in detail. In general, the focus of this disclosure is about telling the perpetrator that she remembers what he did to her and letting him know firsthand how the abuse by him has affected her life. If a woman still has contact with the perpetrator, then she also communicates how the relationship will change. Once a woman decides to confront the perpetrator, it needs to be planned with attention given to her level of readiness and how it pertains to her recovery.

Fourth Stage of Recovery: Integration

Resolution. At each stage, a woman has been actively, yet gradually, integrating the trauma of family sexual abuse as part of her history, rather than her destiny. In passing through each previous stage, she feels both emotionally and mentally free of the abuse. She has likely healed the CSS and is no longer experiencing dissociation. While she may still be healing the developmental impact, she can acknowledge the past trauma without being overwhelmed. Most women describe the experience of resolution and the passage into integration as speaking about the trauma or having thoughts of it that are not intrusive—resolution does not cause flashbacks to occur, depression and anxiety are not experienced, and dissociation or CSS are not present.

While women still have feelings about the abuse, their feelings are intact, coherent, and relevant. Their identity as a congruent adult, rather than a victim of trauma, is forming. At this stage, a woman is neither victim nor survivor since she no longer feels, thinks, or behaves as though she is. Rather, she views herself as a woman who can continue her life free of the trauma of childhood abuse. In reaching this stage, a woman has disclosed and talked about the abuse and understood its impact to her; internal and external changes have occurred within her life, her self-concept and identity are renewed, and she is ready to embrace and move forward with her life.

Building Confidence. At this stage of the journey women practice living their recovery as they experience day-to-day life. Relationships continue to be defined and negotiated according to her current needs as a woman. She may decide to have supportive family sessions or sessions with her partner and children for help with particular issues. She views herself as capable of making new and meaningful decisions about her life. During this stage, she integrates her emerged identity as she continues to grow and develop as a woman. This follow-up period in therapy is a time of building confidence and may last for at least a year or two. Afterward, women are encouraged to schedule an annual session to discuss how they are doing, share their continued successes, and review relapse prevention where needed.

COMPLETING THE STAGES OF HEALING

Some stages of healing will take longer. "However long it takes," as one woman said, "is how long it takes!" Healing is not about finding a quick fix. Rather, it is about permanent recovery. Recovery is always moving forward as long as women are committed to their healing. They may need to rest along the way, slow down their life, and take care of themselves. When they do, they find that they are ready to move on to the next stage; they do not have to force their readiness or make it happen. The process will flow as steady as a stream as long as they remain willing to do the work, are open to healing, and practice patience with themselves. Women are encouraged not to allow other people to determine their willingness or personal commitment to healing. Sometimes, even those who love us are threatened by and afraid of the changes our healing will bring to our relationships with them and to their lives.

At times, a woman may remain in one stage longer than she did a previous stage or she may need to go back through a stage. For example, if a woman is having recurring memories or begins to remember more about the abuse than she did in an earlier stage, she may remain longer in the stage of recall and need more time to work through these new memories of the abuse. Other times a woman may come back through feelings of outrage and grief as she experiences disappointment or disloyalty from her family where the abuse occurred. If she decides to confront the perpetrator, after earlier deciding not to, she will return to this stage. Some women return to a stage when they become married or when they go through a divorce. Healing is an individual process experienced in a unique way by each woman.

Women also enter recovery at different stages. While some women enter treatment at the crisis stage, others might enter at the safety and trust stage. Where treatment begins will depend upon where a woman is in the process of healing, the recovery work she has already accomplished, and her willingness to work through each of the stages. There will also be times when a woman needs to focus on a specific problem or a decision related to her partner, children, or work. Women need to respect their individual needs in recovery just as they would in any stage of life.

Honoring and respecting her unique history as she comes to understand how this trauma affected her life is what remains important for each woman. With her own voice, each woman tells her story of what another did to her. As women heal, they grow; no longer victims or survivors, they become women who have healed.

SUPPORTING YOUR HEALING

1. Review the stages of healing and write down your thoughts on what stage of recovery you are in or would be in if you committed to a treatment program.
2. If you are in therapy, talk with your therapist about taping therapy sessions; taping sessions can help women review what they discuss and what they learn about themselves. Listening to session tapes at least once or twice a week will help a woman stay focused on her recovery and provide her ongoing support during the time between appointments. Another benefit of taping sessions is that it helps a woman identify how negative beliefs distort her thinking.
3. Keep a recovery journal; write down questions, thoughts, and feelings to share with your therapist. Journaling and taping sessions are two ways to keep your recovery congruent. Women tell me that taping their sessions and keeping a journal supports their recovery in a meaningful way.
4. Read other recovery books on specific topics that you want to learn about regarding this trauma; actively participate in your recovery.

Educate yourself about specific developmental impacts, trauma reenactment behavior, and chronic shock. Use your local library to check
out books; the Suggested Resources and Selected Bibliography in the
back of this book will give you some direction.

5. Buy yourself a daily affirmation book. Go to a bookstore, look through
   some of the affirmation books, turn to the day of your birthday, and
   read what is there. If you feel a connection to the passage, buy the book.
   As you read a daily affirmation, write about it in your journal. Use one
   quote a week from what you read to challenge negative beliefs.

6. Write down what you remember about how the sexual abuse affected
   you as a child. Look over the cycle of abuse in Chapter 4. Allow yourself gradual remembrance of your experience of the trauma. Identify
   your losses in terms of what the perpetrator took from you; be specific.

7. Are you fearful of expressing anger? What have you learned and been
   told about anger and women? How do you define assertiveness? Do
   you hold anger in? Do you explode in anger? Are you able to speak
   your outrage and anger about the abuse, the perpetrator, or your family where the abuse occurred? Are you able to express anger in your
   life today? Are you able to accept other people's anger? In what area is
   anger problematic for you? Appendix F contains information on how
   to express the outrage of sexual abuse.

8. Be honest in your assessment about how you have been affected by
   this trauma. Make a list of how the trauma continues to disrupt your
   life and the confusion it causes you about your identity and self-
   concept. Once you have made this list, write down a description of
   how each effect is specifically evident in your life today. Choose one to
   three of these problem areas that you want to focus on in recovery;
   once these are healed, identify two more, and so on, until you have
   worked your way through your list. Women are often surprised about
   the domino effect of healing—as one area heals, so do others.

9. Answer the following questions: Have you admitted that you
   were sexually abused? Have you told someone who believes you?
   What do you experience emotionally when you remember the abuse?
   What is difficult for you to think about regarding the abuse? Have
   you accepted that you were not responsible for the abuse or how it
   affected you?

10. How does your body indicate that the trauma has been stored?
    Where does your body hurt? What do you experience physically
    when you think about the abuse? What part of your body seems most
    affected? What are your physical symptoms of childhood sexual
    abuse?

11. Review the distorted thought patterns identified in Appendix B.
    Which of these relate to your way of thinking about yourself? How do

they relate to your thoughts about the abuse? How do they relate to how you think about your life? Which ones maintain a negative self-concept? Which ones lower your self-esteem? Which ones devalue you as a woman? Which ones prevent you from healing?

Answer the above questions a few at a time. Write them down along with your responses in your journal. In three months, six months, and twelve months review them again. Go through these questions until you have completed them at least three times during your recovery. Pay attention to what you are discovering each time you review them.

6

Prolonged Problems from Childhood Sexual Abuse

You must do the thing you think you cannot do.
—Eleanor Roosevelt, *Each Day a New Beginning*

When the effects of sexual abuse persist, they become prolonged problems that disrupt women's lives.[1] Throughout the years of living with these problems women develop ways to mask them just as they developed ways to mask the sexual abuse; they keep the effects a secret not unlike they kept the abuse a secret. For example, they may believe "I cannot tell anybody about the problems I am having" or "There is no one to tell how I feel." This is similar to the child not being able to tell or believing that she could not tell about the abuse. They can avoid acknowledging a problem such as sleep disturbances by convincing themselves "It is just a nightmare; tomorrow I will sleep better"—even when sleep is not better the next night or the next week or month because details of the abuse keep showing up in their dreams. Sometimes women mislabel problems arising from the abuse, such as "I must be one of those frigid women since I do not like sex," instead of either understanding or being able to acknowledge that the abuse has affected their sexuality. The strategies of masking, avoiding, and mislabeling are reminiscent of how they blamed themselves for the abuse, how they tried as children to convince themselves that the perpetrator would not abuse them again, or how they coped with the confusion experienced during and after the sexual abuse. Some women's strategies are a way to convince themselves that what happened to them was not abuse at all but an act by the perpetrator that they "misunderstood." There are other reasons women give for the delay in seeking help, such as fear that they will not be believed or understood by health care providers, that they will be stigmatized for having problems, or that they will be viewed as not being strong enough to overcome their problems on their own. There is also the belief by some women that acknowledging the problems will not help, and yet others are overly concerned about the impact to their family if the cause of their problems is revealed.[2]

The strategies and reasons that women develop to convince themselves not to disclose their problems and seek help occur over time. They serve the purpose of giving women a layer of protection to shield themselves from acknowledging that the trauma occurred or admitting to the devastation the trauma has caused in their lives, and they also sustain the avoidance pattern of the sexual abuse being brought into the open that was embedded in childhood. When they remain in place, they prevent women from understanding the cause of the problems they experience and present internal barriers that inhibit women from seeking help. Sadly, the strategies that women develop to protect themselves can also contribute to their inability to protect their children from sexual abuse. These means of self-protection can endure for years until at some point in time they start to crumble. This crumbling is a precursor to healing—when women understand the connection between the sexual abuse during childhood and the problems they are having today, they can begin to heal these problems and prevent their lives and their relationships from being further disrupted by them.

UNDERSTANDING AND IDENTIFYING PROBLEMS RELATED TO CHILDHOOD SEXUAL ABUSE

The problems related to childhood sexual abuse for both children and adults have been well documented in the literature for the past twenty years.[3] Short-term effects, those that occur during and immediately following the trauma such as initial shock symptoms and dissociation, and long-term effects, those that persist after the trauma has presumably ended such as depression, eating disorders, and chronic pain, are sometimes used to differentiate problems associated with childhood sexual abuse. Differentiating the problems women experience from childhood sexual abuse in terms of short- or long-term effects, while of interest, may not be as important as identifying which ones persist and occur in relation to the abuse so that the context in which they develop can be understood, what has caused them to persist can be identified, and individual treatment strategies can be developed to facilitate healing.

The diagnosis of post-traumatic stress disorder (PTSD) is used in the mental health system to describe and diagnose symptoms of traumatic stress.[4] While not specifically developed for the diagnosis of childhood sexual abuse, PTSD can help women (see Appendix J) to understand some of the problems they experienced when the trauma occurred; problems they may be experiencing since starting treatment such as flashbacks, avoidance of associated triggers, and nightmares; and some of the problems that have occurred periodically due to the trauma of abuse. However, women need to keep in mind that PTSD does not differentiate among the various groups of people who experience sexual abuse trauma (children, adolescents, men, women, boys, girls), nor does it differentiate specific symptoms based on a specific trauma or the context or nature of the trauma.[5] We have learned a great deal since some of the first books and research findings were published about the trauma of childhood sexual abuse and about what the process of healing might entail, and we will continue to learn from ongoing research, clinicians who work in the field, and the women, men, and children who seek help to heal.

SPECIFIC PROBLEMS IN ADULTHOOD ASSOCIATED WITH CHILDHOOD SEXUAL ABUSE

The following list of problems associated with childhood sexual abuse are identified here to give women a reference point to ascertain if the problems they are experiencing are related to childhood sexual abuse. These problems are among the most prominent that women in this treatment approach confirm as occurring in their lives. Some of the problems persist due to the developmental stage when the sexual abuse occurred. These problems create difficulties that disrupt relationships, prevent the development of appropriate ways of expressing affection or other emotions in intimate relationships, and interfere with the development and establishment of a positive identity and self-concept.[6] Some women experience these problems at different times in their lives, while other women experience only a few of these problems. However, these problems can also be persistent and sometimes intensely experienced. The prolonged problems related to childhood sexual abuse can also be specific in regard to how an individual person is affected. For example, some women experience an absence of emotions (numbness), while other women experience difficulty controlling their emotions (intense emotions impulsively released). These differences can indicate how a woman responded to the sexual abuse at the time it occurred in childhood. In addition, these problems seldom occur in isolation; rather, they seem to be experienced by women as persistent patterns appearing over time and often together.

Addictions
- The use of alcohol or other substances to numb emotional or physical pain resulting from sexual abuse.
- The use of alcohol or other substances to engage in reenactment behavior or assist in dissociation.
- The overuse of prescription drugs or not taking medication as prescribed.

- Sexual behavior is sometimes a reenactment behavior, and the use of substances accompanies this behavior as well.
- Compulsive behaviors and obsessive thoughts have an individual quality to them in terms of developing as long-term strategies to live with the reality that the sexual abuse occurred. Some examples are excessive cleaning, shopping, spending, working, exercising, and care-taking of others. These behaviors can bring about short-term euphoric feelings for women that replace negative feelings about themselves. Because the euphoria is short-term, the behavior will be repeated.

Anxiety

- Persistent and uncontrollable feelings of anxiety that are accompanied by thoughts of impending harm to self or a loved one, especially one's children.
- Physiological responses that accompany anxiety feelings such as tightness in the chest; inability to breathe normally; chronic muscle tensions; sweat and perspiration more often than not; trembling in the hands, arms, legs, and feet that sometimes appear as spasms; and an inability to relax or sit still.
- Emotional overreaction that is sometimes experienced as anger, irritation, or frustration in response to normal incidences and occurrences in daily life. A pattern of intense reaction or defensiveness in family relationships or in relationships that are more distant, such as with coworkers and friends.

Body Image

- Dissatisfaction with body and appearance is persistently experienced.
- Inability to accept compliments about physical appearance from others.
- Choosing clothing to cover up the body, reduce shame, avoid attention, or reject one's femininity and femaleness.
- Overeating/excessive weight gain is also a means to cover up the body and avoid (male) attention or a way to feel more powerful and "safe" in the present.
- Development of eating disorders that are related to the experience of body shame arising from the sexual abuse include bulimia, anorexia, overeating, yo-yo dieting, and excessive dieting. Eating disorders can occur in combination with one another, or a particular eating disorder may occur at a certain stage of development.
- Behaviors that typify eating disorders seem to also exemplify or involve reenactment behavior of the abuse or behaviors that women engage in to purge the acts, memories, words, and feelings of the abuse from the body.

- Purging behavior may take the form of starvation, vomiting, laxatives, diuretics, or excessive exercise.
- Cosmetic surgery can also be a means of reenactment and may occur with or without an eating disorder.
- These behaviors may or may not be kept secret, but they can be misdiagnosed or misunderstood as problems that are culturally driven rather than as originating from the trauma of childhood sexual abuse.

Chronic Pain
- Frequent pain and discomfort felt in areas of the body where sexual abuse occurred. Pain can also be emotional and physical when the sexual abuse is thought about and reexperienced.
- Frequent or occasional pain and discomfort throughout the body when the experience of sexual abuse has not been integrated into memory.

Depression
- Chronic or periodic depression brought on by persistent feelings of helplessness or stress that feels hopeless to resolve.
- Excessive guilt and self-blame for life's problems that are felt as shame about self.
- Difficulty asserting control over one's life, inability to act for one's own self-interest, or viewing oneself as a victim of other people's desires or expectations.
- Thoughts of suicide, plans to attempt suicide, or acts of suicide that arise from wanting to escape overwhelming feelings, memories, and thoughts of the sexual abuse.

Fearful Thoughts and Behaviors
- Fears, unidentified anxieties, chronic nervousness, and excessive worry.
- Ruminating thoughts and repeated behaviors that seem to be unrelated to any specific cause in the present or that do not seem to make sense in relation to what is identified as causing or maintaining them. Excessive worry about dirt, neatness, cleanliness, and orderliness are common ones that disrupt and control daily life.
- Being overly protective and/or overly cautious when making decisions or choices, which prevents normal risk-taking in order to act independently of others, to change decisions that could affect the direction of one's life, or to make choices for oneself or others, especially children.

Memory
- Avoiding thoughts of the sexual abuse.
- Forgetfulness or difficulty with concentration when thoughts and images of the abuse are present.

- Spacing, blocking, drifting off, or disconnecting from conversations when images of the abuse are intrusive.

Parenting
- Excessive fears and overprotection of children to the point of restricting children in their activities, friendships, and development.
- Overcontrolling of and domineering toward children.
- Being harsh, rejecting, critical, and reactive to children's needs and appropriate required care.
- An inability to speak up when children are being mistreated or when other's interactions with them are inappropriate.
- Unable to show love, affection, warmth, and genuine feelings toward children or with specific children.
- Excessive anger and hostility toward children when they misbehave or behave outside of expectations.
- Expecting children to be "little adults" and expecting them to take care of your needs and wants rather than you taking care of theirs.
- Not trusting one's ability to parent.
- Overindulging children, such as with excessive spending on or overdoing for them, rather than asserting appropriate limits and boundaries based on their age and development.
- Inability to safeguard children by keeping them from a known perpetrator in the family or from other individuals who would harm them.
- Confusion and a lack of information about parenting and mothering, including how to nurture and guide children in their development of a healthy identity.
- A tendency to use the abusive family system as the model for family interactions and one's basis of parenting.
- A displaced anger toward children that finds its basis in the belief that they do not deserve to be happy or loved because you did not receive happiness and love.
- Inconsistency and lack of structure with children. Difficulty in communicating appropriate expectations.
- Inability to touch children in terms of hugging, holding, and comforting.
- Excessive or intrusive physical touch with children.
- Intrusiveness in regard to a child's right to privacy and sense of self separate from yet a member of the family.
- The child is not able to share emotions or experiences or ask questions due to viewing the parent, based on the parent's behavior, as not being safe or stable.

Physical Responses
- Gagging and difficulty swallowing that is persistent, especially when attempting to talk about the sexual abuse.

- Multiple physical health problems such as ulcers, irritable bowel syndrome, chronic urinary tract infections, venereal disease, migraines, or chronic headaches.
- Does not liked to be touched in or near the face.
- Easily startled and aroused by loud noises or when surprised by someone's presence or by loud voices that denote anger. Startled responses can provoke anger, crying, anxiety, or being frozen in place.
- Constantly needing to be busy, overworking, or doing the work of others, leading to chronic fatigue and feelings of being tired and stressed.
- Being inactive, lacking energy, procrastinating, lacking independence as an adult, and not being motivated to accomplish goals or daily activities.
- Engaging in self-harm behaviors that are reminiscent of the sexual abuse or reenacting aspects of the abuse as a way of expressing it or to release overwhelming emotions of rage and shame.

Relationships
- Loss of meaning for relationships and unsure if relationships are desired.
- Inability to form secure attachments in relationships either with partners, children, other family members, or individuals outside of the family.
- Few if any close and meaningful friendships, leading to isolation and loss of relatedness and connection to others.
- Marrying to get out of the home where the abuse is or has occurred; marriage is based on escape of the abuse rather than choice of spouse.
- A view that people are nice because they want or expect something rather than that they are simply nice people, which leads to distrustfulness, lack of closeness, and few long-term relationships.
- Controlling, demanding, manipulating, and bullying in relationships with others.
- A view that men are untrustworthy and not deserving of respect.
- Excessive anger toward men or people in general.

Revictimization of Self or Others
- A consistent pattern of unhealthy and damaging relationships especially with individuals who are similar to the perpetrator or other significant family members who were a part of denying the abuse.
- An inability to protect oneself and to identify risk, whether in relationships, circumstances, or surroundings.
- Being hurtful and/or controlling toward others, especially children. As a child may have been aggressive and a bully.
- Abuse to others, especially children. Abuse may be verbal, emotional, physical, or sexual. Abuse toward children may occur as the sole perpetrator or with a partner.

Self-Image

- Driven by the need to be perfect or to be viewed as perfect and problem-free.
- Views self as incompetent and incapable of accomplishing adult independence.
- A sense of being different and not like others.
- A strong desire to hide the inner self from others, which deters intimacy and closeness.
- A belief of not deserving good things in life or not being worthy of respect or admiration.
- Driven to prove self-worth and value without experiencing the satisfaction of accomplishment or a sense of completion.
- Views self as an extension of other people or as an isolated and lonely individual rather than as an autonomous and separate individual.
- A need to view oneself as an omnipotent and invincible individual who does not need anyone and who was never affected by the abuse.

Sexuality

- Avoiding or disliking sex or viewing sex as unnecessary.
- A loss of sexual desires or feelings.
- A lack of sexual fantasies that are fulfilling and that develop a sense of healthy female sexuality.
- Fear of sexuality that leads to no relationships in which sexuality would be expected or a history of very few relationships in which it was expected as part of the commitment.
- May be sexual early in the relationship but then lose an interest in sex.
- May use sex to gain control in relationship or punish partner. May punish self by performing demeaning sex or engaging in aggressive sex with a partner in which harm is inflicted to herself or the partner.
- An inability to say no to requests or demands for sex.
- Not able to state a preference for or against specific sexual acts.
- Confusion about sexual pleasure when engaged in sexual acts similar to those committed by the perpetrator.
- Views sex as equaling love. Seeks affection, care, and comfort through sexual relationships and from sex.
- Experiences confusion about sexual identity or sexual orientation. This confusion can be delayed and not occur until after adolescence or in adulthood.
- Feeling restricted or being unable to explore sexual preferences and desires. May view certain sexual acts, feelings, or thoughts as abnormal and perverted when connected to the perpetrator's sexual abuse.

Sleep
- Disruptions in sleep patterns in which there is a problem falling asleep or staying asleep, or not being able to sleep for periods of time.
- Nightmares of the sexual abuse that intensify when around the perpetrator or other family members associated with the sexual abuse.

Trust Issues
- Inability to trust one's own judgment, opinions, decisions, and actions.
- Unable to trust other people even when they show they are trustworthy.
- Difficulty differentiating trustworthy people from those who are not trustworthy.
- Unable to trust that happiness and life's goodness can be maintained or sustained for more than a short period of time, which indicates a pessimistic and negative attitude toward self and life that disrupts imagined or actual plans for the future.
- Dependent upon other people's approval, acceptance, and affirmation to the point that either anger occurs when these dependencies are not fulfilled or one experiences overwhelming feelings of rejection that devalue self-worth and lead to self-images of defeat.

Taylor (age seventeen) shares how the sexual abuse to her during the ages of eight to eleven has created problems in her life:

"I view my body as fat and ugly and that I am unattractive. I do not want to show my body because it does not look good. I am ashamed of my body, and I want to hide it. I do not want any attention from boys. I have a hard time trusting people, and I do not believe people when they give me compliments. I think 'they are just saying it to be nice.' I do not want to get close to anyone, and I do not want people to get close to me. I hide behind a wall where I do not have to show my emotions. I feel like I am a weak person when I show my feelings, and I do not want to be weak. I feel I need to be strong, and emotions let people know they can get to me and that feels like a weakness. I do not show the real me, and I am not sure I know the real me. I want my distance from people so I do not get hurt again. I do not want the pain of relationships and people being close. I feel sadness because I am alone. I have such a negative view of men that I cannot trust them and I do not like them. Sex and physical touch feels wrong; it does not feel good, and I do not like it. The reason I told about the sexual abuse is that I was tired of being behind my wall. I was tired of being alone and having to do everything on my own. It was killing me. I could not live life or live it completely. I could only live as much as the abuse would let me. I could not act anymore as if nothing was wrong or that nothing had happened. I could not let him win. His abuse of me was going to ruin my life, and I decided it was not going to ruin my life and he was not going to keep me from being the person

I am supposed to be. I want to be human and be able to feel and be able to express my emotions. I want to hate the person who abused me, but I also want to forgive him; I have these emotions at the same time. I want to come out from behind my wall and be the real Taylor. I do not want to hide anymore. I do not want to be scared and afraid, even though I am still scared and I feel scared about the abuse. I do not want to be hurt again, but I do not want to stay behind my wall of protection."

DISCUSSION OF THE PROBLEMS RELATED TO CHILDHOOD SEXUAL ABUSE

As you read this discussion of problems related to sexual abuse, keep in mind the following:
1. They resulted from childhood sexual abuse and became more problematic over time due to a delay in treatment.
2. Women can experience these problems as patterns that change with time. One day you are depressed, the next you are anxious, or there may be times when you overeat and other times when you do not eat at all.
3. Adaptation to problems can occur as they become established as a part of life.
4. Women do not choose what problems will develop from sexual abuse.
5. Some of these problems will increase or worsen when treatment first begins or periodically throughout treatment.

Depression

Depression is experienced at some time, if not most of the time, in the majority of women who have been sexually abused. It often begins at the time of the abuse in response to a sense of hopelessness and helplessness in regard to the perpetrator's actions. This early depression can begin a pattern of negative thinking that over time becomes more pervasive in a woman's life. As the child grows, the abuse eventually ends while the depression continues. Memories and flashbacks of the abuse cause depression to reoccur in cycles, so that even on good days women have the bad days that follow. This cycle of depression can also cause and reinforce a mind-set of pessimism toward self, relationships, children, work, life, and future. As shared by Tony Bates in *Understanding and Overcoming Depression: A Common Sense Approach,* "Depression generally provokes a withdrawal from others and a turning against oneself. Sufferers are left with the conviction that they have not merely suffered some setback or important loss, but they themselves are losers, and that nothing will ever be resolved in their life."[7]

Teresa (at age forty-one) describes her experience of depression from childhood sexual abuse this way: "For years I have been depressed without really knowing why. It seems I can never remember when I was not depressed or anxious. My father abused me periodically starting at age five. It was hard for me to admit to his abuse. The last time he abused me, I was in my teen years. After it stopped, I still felt I was worthless and that no one would ever love me. I grew up believing that if someone loved you, he would hurt you. What a hopeless way to feel."

Depression involves thoughts, physical symptoms, behaviors, and feelings. Depressive thoughts include extreme self-criticism, a lack of self-confidence, indecisiveness, a lack of hope, a negative view of the world, and an inability to concentrate. Physical symptoms can include lack of energy, tiredness and fatigue, reduced appetite, problems with not sleeping or with sleeping too much, and weight gain or loss. These physical symptoms can coincide with somatic symptoms of sexual abuse such as chronic headaches. Depressive feelings include hopelessness, discouragement, despair, sadness, confusion, fear, guilt, shame, and a sense of inadequacy. Behaviors related to depression include inactivity, sluggishness, slow movements, drifting off mentally, restlessness, withdrawal, and dependency. Depression is like a low-grade fever that peaks and then subsides but never really goes away. Women report that they can function better on some days than others, and some women adapt to this up-and-down aspect of depression in much the same way they learned to live with the abuse.[8] These women seem to be unaware that there is another way to think, feel, and behave.

Medications can help manage depression in the short term and are often a first step in addressing this specific problem. Medication treatment for depression usually consists of controlling the level of neurotransmitters at the synapses in the brain. There are four groups of antidepressant medications, and each has its own particular benefits that target specific symptoms of depression. The pharmaceutical industry has created various types of medication such as Wellbutrin, Prozac, and Zoloft that fall within these four groups of antidepressants. Because of the variety of medications on the market, women need to ask for a clinical assessment to help determine which kind of antidepressant or other medications recommended by physicians is right for them based on the symptoms they are experiencing.[9] The drawback for women sexually abused as children is that while antidepressants help the symptoms, they do not address the cause. Not addressing the cause can contribute to the cyclical aspect of depression in women who have been sexually abused.

A woman who seeks therapeutic treatment may or may not be taking an antidepressant. If she is on medication, her physician has probably been treating her physical symptoms but may not be aware of the cause of her depression (emotional trauma due to childhood sexual abuse) or how long the depression has disrupted her life. In addition, if physicians have focused more on current events that are contributing to and maintaining depression, then women are not going to understand its prevailing cause in childhood. Depression will most likely reoccur once the current stresses subside and/or women stop taking antidepressants. In addition, taking medication, stopping medication, and starting medication again is part of this cycle and can itself contribute to feeling depressed!

When we compare studies on depression and those on childhood sexual abuse, we see a prevalence of each within family histories. It seems likely that depression is an indicator of childhood sexual abuse. By putting this information to use, physicians could inquire into the cause of depression when diagnosed for their patients—children, adolescents, and adults. This inquiry by physicians could improve their ability to identify underlying causes of depression, hopefully increase their referrals to mental health practitioners, and create a coordination of care for women to treat and heal this trauma. In addition, if physicians are better today at making a diagnosis of depression in children, and they ask children about childhood traumas and describe the kinds that can occur such as sexual abuse, they have the potential to intervene on behalf of a child to stop the sexual abuse by exposing it within the family.

As women understand their depression—where it began, how it developed over the years, and how current situations maintain it—they can seek effective treatment for it and heal this prolonged effect of sexual abuse. As women heal, they begin to feel hopeful and no longer view themselves as helpless in effecting change in their lives. They can understand that the label of "chemical imbalance" is more than an imbalance of neutortransmitters or a depletion of serotonin. Rather, it is an imbalance in their lives that was brought about by childhood sexual abuse. The trauma of sexual abuse depletes a woman's energy, zest for life, belief in self, and trust in the world. As women disclose the sexual abuse, they understand the cause of their depression. They find lasting relief from the depression at a mental, physical, emotional, and spiritual level. As women identify their losses, grieve what was taken from them, and allow feelings to be experienced and expressed, they feel alive. As the fog lifts, they find that life is not so gray and there are vibrant colors to behold. As women move through the stages of healing, they move through the depression. From helpless victims and hopeless survivors, they become women who have healed by understanding and treating the cause of their depression.

Suicide Thoughts, Plans, and Attempts

Suicidal thoughts, plans, and attempts are not coincidental with childhood sexual abuse. Rather, their occurrence is often reported as a result of the trauma and can include depression, chronic physical and emotional pain, trying to escape from the memories of the abuse, and at times attempting to draw attention to the problem.[10] As a society, we need to be aware that physical abuse is not the only type of abuse that kills our children. Sexual abuse does too, for it can kill the soul and the spirit of the child and the woman she could become. If the act of abuse does not kill a child, then the woman might end her life through suicide. How many women who have died from suicide were sexually abused and believed their lives were either worthless or hopeless? How many believed they were helpless to heal from the trauma or could not tell what another person had done to them? How many died with the secret and the shame that went unnoticed? How many have been institutionalized or emotionally cauterized through treatments that were supposed to help but instead prevented women from feeling or remembering?

Women sometimes describe depression as a slow suicide that saps the joy, happiness, and meaning from their lives. When this happens on a continuous basis, women can come to believe that life is no longer worth living. As Penny (age forty-two) describes, "I lived daily with thoughts of suicide. I even attempted it a few times only to find myself still alive and in the hospital. The first time, my family was shocked, but by the third time, I think they came to accept it. I could not explain it to them—the reasons—because I did not know myself. Then, when the memories came, I knew. I knew why I wanted to die. I remembered how I wanted to die when my brother was sexually abusing me. I did not think I could survive, but I did. Then I had to survive the memories, and I am doing that, too. I feel hope more often than not and even though I struggle, life is more hopeful at least right now."

Preventing Depression

Even after she has healed, a woman may still be vulnerable to depression at certain times in her life, and she will need to be aware of this at such times as experiencing repeated stresses. If women start to experience early signs of depression, they can take steps to prevent a more severe reoccurrence. Preventing depression is possible if women act on the information they learned through their recovery. As children, they had no choice but to endure the depression along with the abuse; as adults, they have the information they need to take care of themselves. The time of being a depressed person who knows no other way to think, feel, or act has passed. Jami (age thirty-six) is a good example of how a woman can and should take care of herself. "Through my recovery, I learned that I am worth caring about, and that I can take control of my life. After all, it is my life! I know when things are bothering me and, more often than not, I can figure it out. I pay attention to what my body is telling me. This may sound like no big deal to some people, but for me it is a great deal. I live my life today without being abused, and that makes all the difference. If I need to make an appointment to talk things out, I feel good about doing that. I do not have to deal with things on my own ever again. I take care of me because I love myself enough to do so!"

Depression and Current Stresses

A woman will also need to work through other issues in her adult life that may be contributing to or maintaining cycles of depressed feelings. Such issues might include being in an unhappy marriage, not feeling fulfilled in her job, wanting to change direction in her life, or contemplating a move from one location to another. A woman often finds that as the depression from childhood sexual abuse lifts, she is able to start addressing other decisions about her life.

Anxiety

Anxiety can be prevalent among women who have been sexually abused. When we look back to the symptoms of chronic shock, we can understand the relationship between adulthood anxiety and childhood sexual abuse. I am not sure that the anxiety a child experiences at the hands of a perpetrator can be adequately described. The anxiety that women recall experiencing is a repeated one and tends to accumulate with each incidence of sexual abuse and each contact with the perpetrator.[11] Each time the perpetrator violated her body and betrayed her trust, she experienced anxiety; each time she was left alone to deal with the aftershock, she experienced anxiety. When he would walk into a room or her parents would leave the house, she experienced anxiety. The terror of not being able to stop the abuse or defend herself is often as real to women today as they were to the child. The absolute loss of control over one's body is a desperate feeling to live through as a child, and it is not much easier for women.

The anxiety that women experience in their adult lives can become more intense during times of stress, but even normal occasions can be stressful because a basic level of trust for most situations is not felt. One mother describes how her anxiety would escalate with her children: "Each time my children left the house I would sit and think about all the bad things that could happen. I would worry myself sick, literally. I would feel such relief when they finally got home or I would be extremely angry if they were even a few minutes late. I do not think they ever understood until I did. I only knew I was afraid, and what I was afraid of was that they would be hurt. I could not trust them out of my sight for even a second. I knew it was not normal, but I didn't know what to do." This catastrophic thinking—assuming the worst—is common for women who have been sexually abused.

Anxiety can also be maintained by memories of the abuse along with the effort women put into trying to prevent them from being experienced. The blocking of memories and simultaneous anxiety about them can leave her fatigued, irritable, edgy, and keyed up. Sandy (at age thirty-two) describes this pattern in her life: "I would go days doing everything I could to keep busy so I would not think about the abuse. I would get tired and then irritable, and others would ask me, 'Why do you do so much?' It is what I did as a child. I would leave the house and not come home until I had to because I did not want to be where my brother was so I would not have to remember what he did the night before. I did not want to remember."

Anxiety is different from depression although they do share common symptoms such as irritability or loss of appetite. Depression tends to decrease energy and motivation; anxiety feels like every neuron in the body is firing at the same time and creating an excess of energy. This excess energy occurs because of the rapid firing of neurons, which in turn can cause symptoms such as heart palpitations, trembling in the limbs, gasping for air, and increased arousal. Therefore, anxiety uses a lot of energy but does not replenish that energy. Some women have spent a lifetime with anxiety, and somehow they have adapted to the difficulties of this excess and depletion of energy even while their bodies have suffered from it. These women often keep busy by hurrying to get somewhere or to do something.[12] Anxiety contributes to sleep disturbances because women cannot relax enough to fall asleep; when they do sleep, their sleep can be frequently interrupted.[13] Even with medication, there are women who simply cannot go to sleep or stay asleep.

As Sandy describes, "I would wake up out of a sound sleep and not be able to get back to sleep. Other nights I would start out not being able to get to sleep. I would get up and try to read, only to find it was impossible. It was the same pattern as when I was a child. Either I was too anxious to fall asleep, or the nightmares would come and I would be awake. This problem would happen whether I took medication or not." Nightmares of the sexual abuse can cause some women to avoid sleep. This affects their sleep patterns and eventually their relationships with family since many are too tired to participate in even daily activities. When they are finally exhausted, they can fall asleep almost instantly but then they have a difficult time waking up.

A woman's anxiety may be heightened during times of the day when the sexual abuse occurred or when she anticipated the sexual abuse would occur.[14] This is why a woman may find that during the late afternoon and evening hours, as night approaches, she experiences symptoms of anticipatory anxiety. The abuse is what has conditioned this anticipation response in women. Women can experience symptoms of anxiety across the various anxiety disorders diagnosed in the field of mental health. Women can have symptoms of panic disorder, phobia, post-traumatic stress disorder, obsessive-compulsive disorder, and generalized anxiety disorder since there is often a "significant overlap among them, and although each can occur separately, two or more are often found together."[15]

Obsessions and Compulsions

Obsessive thoughts and compulsive behaviors develop as a survival technique for the child and for the woman she becomes. Frequently, they are a means to distract a woman from memories of the abuse and can symbolize a way she gains control over her anxiety. If she obsesses about places, things, or other people, she will not have to think about the abuse. Her anxiety about the abuse can be attached to something else that, although disturbing, is often less frightening to her than thoughts about the sexual abuse and the perpetrator. Her chosen obsession replaces the real object of her fear, and this replacement brings her relief by distracting her from memories of the abuse. These thoughts and behaviors are another way women can convince themselves that the obsession or the compulsion is the problem. Until they make the connection between the sexual abuse and the anxiety it creates, their obsession and/or compulsion will continue as a means to distract them from abusive memories and to control the anxiety they experience. The obsessive thoughts and compulsive behaviors that develop in response to childhood trauma are similar to trauma reenactment behaviors because of the rituals and patterns that accompany them and the use of dissociation to engage in them.[16]

Familiar obsessions reported by women who have been sexually abused are perfectionism, order and control, cleanliness of home or body, physical appearance, body image, school and work accomplishments, money, children, other people's opinion of them, and high expectations for themselves. These obsessions allow a woman to create scenarios in her mind that replace the terror, fears, and worries originating from the abuse. In other words, it is less traumatic to fear that she will not get an A on the test, to keep checking if the door is locked, or to clean her house repeatedly than it is to remember that the abuse happened or that someone might find out her life is not perfect. While these thoughts and behaviors are disturbing for some women, for others they have become adaptive ways to live with the trauma of sexual abuse.

The compulsions that women develop and display because of sexual abuse are reminiscent of the behaviors a child develops to gain a sense of control. In acting out the obsession through compulsive behavior, she feels temporary relief from the images of the abuse. Because the relief is temporary, she must continue the compulsion. Compulsions can change over time and start to take on a life of their own. Often, compulsions begin to control and disrupt a woman's daily life and can affect her relationships with others. Even when she feels that her life is out of control, she is not sure what she can do to stop these thoughts and behaviors from continuing.

Panic Disorder Triggered by Anxieties

Panic disorder, or what some women call panic attacks, is often triggered by situations that a woman associates with the sexual abuse and is unable to cope with at the time they occur. Panic attacks have physical symptoms that can include shortness of breath, heart palpitations, headaches or migraines, muscle tension, chest constriction, breathing difficulties, and shaking and trembling. As with other anxiety disorders, panic disorder includes fearful or catastrophic thoughts that occur before or during the panic attack. Emotional symptoms of panic include feelings of wanting to flee, escape, or get away; edginess or irritability; disassociation; rage; scanning the environment to sense for danger; and an inability to relax physically.[17]

As described earlier, flashbacks of the abuse can trigger panic. Women describe the panic they felt when the abuse occurred and the fear they felt when they believed it was going to occur. Celia (age forty-four) described the relationship between the anxiety and panic she experienced: "To me, the anxiety was the fear of knowing the abuse was going to happen; I just did not always know when. The panic was the terror of the abuse when it was happening, and I would feel a lot of rage when these feelings happened." The pattern of anxiety and panic is repeated throughout the abusive cycle. Panic disorder is familiar to women because it has often reoccurred throughout their adult years.

Eating Disorders, Body Image, and Reenactment

Eating disorders are prevalent among women who were sexually abused as children. They seem to have components of other symptoms such as obsessions, compulsions, avoidance of food, and anxiety, and they primarily include a distorted body image and feelings of body shame. For some women, eating disorders are related to the loss of control over their bodies during the sexual abuse and serve as a means of feeling in control of their bodies now. Eating disorders can also be indicative of the developmental stage and age at which the sexual abuse began.[18] Women with anorexia and bulimia report that they were sexually abused either at the age of puberty or during puberty, when their bodies were beginning to develop and they felt a great deal of body shame from the abuse. By contrast, women with compulsive eating report that the sexual abuse occurred before the age of puberty; they used food for comfort. Further study is needed of the relation between the child's age and stage of development when the sexual abuse occurred and the onset of an eating disorder to determine if there is a differentiation among women based on these factors. If so, then treatment methods for the eating disorder that focus on assisting in the completion of the developmental stage that was disrupted by the sexual abuse may be most beneficial for women. We may also discover that sexual abuse helps to explain the high prevalence rates of eating disorders among women and may lend some insight into why we are starting to see more documentation of eating disorders among boys as we see the reports of sexual abuse for male children increasing. Culture alone cannot explain the phenomena of such high rates of eating disorders.

Eating disorders are complex, but what they all seem to have in common is the ability to distract women from the memories, sensations, and experience of the sexual abuse through starving, bingeing, purging, or exercising. They keep the focus on food, body image, weight, fat, calories, diets, miles, and numerous other factors that women focus on during the course of an eating disorder. These disorders also have the ability to numb a woman from the overwhelming emotions resulting from the sexual abuse—especially loss of control, terror, and shame about her body.

Women often have a combination of eating disorders in their history. Some women are anorexic during one period of their life, bulimic during another, and compulsive eaters at yet another stage. They may have a history of one or more or all of these eating disorders upon entering treatment. An eating disorder may be what women identify that brings them to treatment. Women who were sexually abused as children tend to have a greater prevalence of eating disorders than women who were not, and they are more vulnerable to the cultural pressures about women's bodies and appearance due to existing feelings of shame from what the perpetrator said to them and did to them during the abuse.[19] Sometimes, a parent overemphasized (or still does!) the importance of appearance and body perfection or taught the child to use food as a way to numb emotions and provide comfort.

In a study of childhood abuse and neglect, the age at which these traumas took place preceded and played a role in the severity of self-destructive behavior by women and the form it took. "The earlier the abuse, the more self-directed the aggression." The authors go on to report that "abuse during early childhood and latency was strongly correlated with suicide attempts, self-mutilation, and other self-injurious behavior. In contrast, abuse in adolescence was significantly associated only with anorexia nervosa and increased risk-taking. Histories of sexual abuse, in particular, predicted continued suicide attempts, self-mutilation, and other self-destructive acts." The authors concluded that while "childhood abuse contributes heavily to the initiation of self-destructive behavior," it is the "lack of secure attachments [that] maintains it." Women who, as children, "could not remember feeling special or loved by anyone were least able to utilize interpersonal resources to control their self-destructive behavior during the course of the study." The results of this study are typical of other studies that report the correlation between childhood sexual abuse and eating disorders. The relationship between childhood sexual abuse and the family beliefs that sustain it are also supported in the above study. When parents are not attached to their children, they are not able to protect them nor are they able to intercede for them when problems are occurring.[20]

These particular issues within the family belief system or the parent's behavior that occurs along with or follows childhood sexual abuse contributes to the development and maintenance of an eating disorder. Women who grew up with negative beliefs about body image, used food as comfort, experienced insecure attachments, and who were sexually abused may be at even higher risk of developing an eating disorder. The intergenerational aspect of sexual abuse is also a risk factor, because mothers who were also victims of sexual abuse may be teaching their daughters by modeling the thought patterns and behaviors of an eating disorder.[21]

Compulsive exercising is a characteristic behavior of eating disorders. It is a way for women to purge overwhelming emotions while receiving compliments about their discipline to exercise. Women with eating disorders obsess about how many times a week they need to exercise, and many are compelled to exercise in order to rid (purge) their bodies of "excess fat"— overwhelming feelings (shame) and memories (of abuse). Exercise can also symbolize escaping the abuse or the perpetrator—something she was not able to do as a child. As with other obsessive-compulsive behaviors, the obsession with exercising, eating, not eating, purging, weighing, fat, starch and calorie counts, and thinking about food all serve to distract women from memories, overwhelming fears, and extreme shame related to the sexual abuse. Eating disorders can also be a way for a woman to punish her body if she blames herself for the abuse, or they can develop as an attempt by a woman to protect herself. Eating disorders are viewed as self-injury not only because of the behaviors that accompany them, but also because of the reenactment component and the secondary problems that often result as well—obesity, eruptions of the esophagus, and heart failure. When women increase their body size by gaining weight, they believe this prevents unwanted male attraction and attention.[22]

At the core of an eating disorder are intense feelings of inadequacy, lack of safety, loss of trust with self and others, overwhelming memories of sexual abuse acts, and intense body shame. Women believe that the thoughts and behaviors associated with eating disorders are ways for them to rid themselves of negative feelings and beliefs, but they never really experience either of these outcomes. Instead, women lose weight to the point of dying; attempt to purge the abuse from their bodies through vomiting, diuretics, or laxatives; and respond to overwhelming feelings of helplessness by bingeing or by being "bigger" than the perpetrator.[23] They continue the cycle of starving, bingeing, and purging to control what feels uncontrollable: remembering, reliving, and reexperiencing the sexual abuse and the lack of protection from the perpetrator, only now the perpetrator is food. The eating disorder now has control, which is similar to how the perpetrator controlled her during the abuse, but she has convinced herself that she is in control. Women do find some degree of relief from eating disorders, but as with other obsessions and compulsions the relief is temporary so they must continue the destructive pattern to find continued relief only to realize that relief never really comes.[24]

A woman with a history of eating disorder has a skewed view of how to manage the shame she experiences about her body that accompanies memories of the sexual abuse. Some women have lived for years keeping the eating disorder a secret from others or not allowing anyone to talk about it if they do know. In this age of health and nutrition, women with eating disorders are sometimes admired or envied for their low body weight. Family and friends can even encourage the eating disorder by complimenting them on the weight they have lost. Conversely, women who have developed eating disorders that cause them to gain weight are not so admired; instead, they are often ridiculed and further shamed for their "lack of control." Eating disorders of all types, however, are another example of how the effects of sexual abuse can cause a woman's life to be out of her control. The damage to a woman's body from eating disorders can include loss of hair, eruption of blood vessels in the esophagus, heart failure, multiple and reoccurring injuries to the bones, dizziness and blackouts, loss of menses, infertility, high blood pressure, and other health problems that develop as her body is further assaulted.[25]

As eating disorders become progressively worse, they seem reminiscent of the cycle of abuse where a woman once again experiences what she did as a child—that she will never be able to stop this (sexual abuse/eating disorder) from happening in her life. But, as one woman put it, "Now it is me abusing my body." As discussed earlier, the helpless and hopeless feelings and disruptive prolonged effects that accompany sexual abuse perpetuate depression throughout the after-years of this trauma. This is why depression, more often than not, is also identified as an underlying factor in eating disorders for a certain group of women. Depression can be a source of maintaining a negative view about self, life, and the ability to solve problems.

Eating disorders reflect an extreme form of dieting that deprives the body and mind of the nutrition they need to function. Women who are not eating cannot think clearly; their brains are lacking the basic nutrients to process information. Consequently, women report forgetfulness and struggling to concentrate on tasks such as reading or driving. Women who starve, binge, or purge describe feeling confused, not being clear about what they are doing, not always being able to focus, and having days in which they feel generally befuddled; many lose track of time and have a loss of recent memory. Women who purge describe feeling "like a drunk with a hangover." Women who binge on food or exercise excessively experience a euphoria or "high" similar to what someone using drugs experiences. The imbalances occurring in the body and brain are like a roller coaster ride mentally, emotionally, and physically for many women.[26] The books *Body Wars* by Margo Maine and *Fat Is a Feminist Issue* by Susie Orbach are excellent resources for women who want to learn more about the past and current assaults on women's bodies that often begin with trauma and are maintained by culture and perpetuated by women. These books can help women to change the lack of satisfaction they have about their bodies to satisfying acceptance.

Women with eating disorders benefit from working with a nutritionist, who can give weekly support, educate them about healthy eating habits, and help them to determine their natural body weight. More than likely, a woman with an eating disorder does not know what her natural body weight is or what it would feel like to live in her body at an acceptable weight for her. A nutritional support group can help as well, as long as women are not exchanging information about how to have an eating disorder but rather learning how to change and heal these maladaptive patterns. Women can learn to focus on food in a healthy way and not as the cause of their problems.

Cosmetic surgeries can occur along with an eating disorder, or they can stand alone as another way women attempt to eradicate the sexual abuse by remolding, reshaping, erasing, and at times destroying their bodies. While not as well studied as eating disorders or other self-injurious behavior, cosmetic surgeries are beginning to be questioned and researched. Cosmetic surgery that is "frequent and often unnecessary" is described as one of the ways women harm their bodies in reenacting the experience of childhood trauma.[27] Given our culture's invasive high expectations of women's bodies and the stigmatism and fear of disclosing self-cutting, cosmetic surgery for a group of women who can afford the cost of someone else cutting on their bodies seems a likely outlet for ridding themselves of associated shame from sexual abuse. There are surgeons who perform countless cosmetic surgeries on women without ever questioning or evaluating the necessity of these procedures. There are now television shows where surgeons promote their services to women and advocate making these surgical changes. Women can "recover" from these types of body cuts in a community hospital that views this behavior as acceptable and normal, whereas women who cut on their own bodies are often hospitalized in psychiatric units because this behavior is viewed as unacceptable; these women may be thought of as "crazy" and are often diagnosed as having borderline personality disorder. The women who seek repeated cosmetic surgeries or other treatments such as liposuction or chemical peels can also point to popular culture as their reason for needing to stay thin, young, shapely, and desirable. Rather than admitting to the sexual abuse, it is easier for them to acknowledge these cultural pressures. I have also found it interesting that with surgery a woman is anesthetized, which is exactly what most women seek who self-injure—to stop feeling the cause of their pain. The effects of childhood sexual abuse can at times be as well hidden and covered up as the actual abuse was by the perpetrator, and like family members, surgeons will collude in this coverup while women, traumatized as children, continue to be their victims.

Chronic Pain

Chronic pain—defined as pain that has lasted longer than six months—is estimated to affect the lives of nearly fifty million people in the United States.[28] Women who have been sexually abused report a history of chronic pain that include migraines, pelvic and vaginal pain, chronic urinary tract infections, chronic yeast infections, nonspecific muscle and joint pain, lower- and upper-back pain, and nonspecific physical pain that increases during times of stress. How do we acknowledge what a child's young body went through without medical attention and expect there not to be long-term physical problems resulting in chronic pain? Women frequently report that they have seldom had a physician listen to them, take them seriously, and ask meaningful questions about the pain they have endured most of their lives. Physicians and other health care professionals need to learn about the types of persistent physical pain that can result from childhood sexual abuse in order to better diagnose it in women when it is a symptom of the physical damage from sexual abuse.[29] Chronic pain can exacerbate already existing problems that women experience from sexual abuse. Physicians who work in the field of chronic pain identify secondary problems resulting from the mind's response to pain. Secondary problems such as depression, anxiety, rage, irritability, fatigue, and insomnia may already exist for most women and are intensified with chronic pain. Chronic pain disrupts women's lives by taking away or diminishing the joy of living and decreasing their ability to engage in life's experiences of marriage, family, children, leisure, and work.

Another way women experience physical symptoms from the trauma of sexual abuse is referred to as somatization disorder—emotional trauma transformed into physical problems. Bessel A. van der Kolk, a well-known physician and researcher of trauma, defines somatization as "speechless terror, which in some individuals interferes with the ability to put feelings into words, leaving emotions to be mutely expressed by dysfunction of the body." Van der Kolk goes on to say that "verbalization of traumatic experiences decreases psychosomatic symptoms."[30] In a reserach study reviewed by van der Kolk and his colleagues, "over 90% of 100 women with somatization disorder reported some type of abuse, and 80% reported being sexually abused as either children or adults." They further note from their own research "that somatization rarely occurred in the absence of severe histories of trauma."[31]

Somatic experiences associated to the trauma of childhood sexual abuse for women include vomiting, abdominal pain, pain during urination, difficulty swallowing, throat constrictions, gagging, loss of voice, difficulty walking, or muscle weakness. Other somatic experiences women report are burning sensations in the sexual organs or rectum, sexual indifference, pain or bleeding during intercourse, painful menstruation, irregular menstrual periods, excessive menstrual bleeding, and vomiting throughout pregnancy. It is easy to see the similarities of and confusion between chronic pain resulting from physical damage to a child's body and somatization of the traumatic experience from an inability to express the trauma in words. Their similarities lie in what has caused them—that is, childhood sexual abuse; the confusion occurs from the need to differentiate symptoms in order to provide appropriate treatment.[32] Women who experience chronic pain seem to do so as a result of direct physical damage from the sexual abuse or as transference of the emotional trauma from sexual abuse to a physical experience.

Historically, women with chronic pain resulting from childhood sexual abuse have not always been appropriately diagnosed by physicians, and their medical treatment, when it does occur, may not include therapeutic intervention for sexual abuse. Pelvic pain alone accounts for 10 percent of consultations with gynecologists each year, but this statistic does not mean that a woman walks out of her physician's office with an accurate diagnosis, let alone a treatment that will work to ease her suffering.[33] There are three possible reasons for the lack of systematic diagnosis and treatment of women's experience of pain. One reason is that women's health care in general has not always been taken seriously, and consequently there has not yet been enough research on how specific traumas affect women's health. Women can be told that "it's all in your head" rather than having their pain and physical problems understood as being in their body and related to traumatic experiences. A second reason is that women have not recognized childhood sexual abuse as an underlying cause of their pain or physical problems. This lack of recognition by women can be contributed to either not connecting their present pain with past trauma or to their denial of sexual abuse that results in their avoidance of discussing it. A third reason is health care professionals who were not and are not well trained in diagnosing and treating chronic pain in the general population of patients, so they are not trained to diagnosis it in relation to childhood sexual abuse as a specialized population of patients.[34]

We still have much to learn about how the body stores or remembers traumatic experience and the impact to emotional and physical health that trauma causes to a human being. Chronic pain and chronic physical problems affect the quality of a woman's life, limit what she can do or feels capable of doing, cause her to feel different from those around her, and create persistent self-doubt. Women are helped when extended the understanding that the trauma to their bodies is as real as the pain they experience. In doing so, we will move toward developing more effective diagnosis and treatment methods that help women to heal emotionally as well as physically.

I attended a medical consultation with Sandy when she was twenty-seven years old. She had suffered from chronic severe pelvic pain, intermittent lower-back pain, and urinary tract infections for most of her life. She had been tested and examined on repeated occasions and by various physicians and specialists in the medical field. She acknowledged that the pain she had always experienced was becoming worse and that it was most likely due to being repeatedly raped and physically brutalized from ages three to fifteen by her father and older brother. At the consultation, when we were discussing the sexual abuse to Sandy, I asked her gynecologist if he would be able to identify what the damage to her uterus would look like so many years after these traumas had occurred. His answer was "no." After Sandy's surgery, her physician confirmed the internal damage to her body as a result of the abuse; he had not taken her report of chronic pain seriously because he did not know how to diagnose it in an adult woman's body as a result of childhood sexual abuse. His lack of training and expertise in this area of women's health was not intentional, but it existed nonetheless. Children who are sexually abused today and taken to the hospital are diagnosed and treated for the physical damage to their young bodies by sexual abuse. The physicians and other medical staff can see the damage; they do not question it because it is right there before their eyes. Today, there are child specialists who are trained to examine children for sexual abuse and provide expert medical witness in court. However, women whose bodies were traumatized years ago and are years later examined in a physician's office may not have apparent damage that shows up in a regular vaginal exam or even on the most modern diagnostic tests. Until the effects of childhood sexual abuse to women are accepted, understood, researched, diagnosed, and treated, women are at risk of either being ignored by the health care system or misdiagnosed when it comes to problems resulting from childhood sexual abuse.

The most important information is that women need to trust that they know what the pain felt like during the abuse and what it feels like today. When women honor their bodies, they will believe the truth about the pain they suffer. Women can then move forward in an assertive manner, sit down with their physicians, and disclose the sexual abuse so that the origin of their pain and problems can begin to be understood and appropriate treatment made available for it. I encourage all women not to give up until they receive the medical attention that they deserve and that is long overdue. The book *The Chronic Pain Solution: Your Personal Path to Pain Relief,* by James N. Dillard with Leigh Ann Hirschman, is one resource that can help women in the treatment of chronic pain and may be a good resource for their physicians as well.

Addictions

Women who were sexually abused as children can develop addictions that numb the pain and help them escape the reality of the sexual abuse. They use alcohol and/or drugs to fade memories of the abuse, and sometimes substance use began because the perpetrator gave her drugs or alcohol to control her during the abuse.[35] Addiction to substances in response to childhood sexual abuse can include the use of street drugs or the abuse of prescription medications.

Drugs and alcohol are readily available to women at all stages of their life from childhood to adolescence and into adulthood. A woman can use alcohol to numb her body and mind during reenactment behavior, to deaden emotional pain, and to find relief from the memories of sexual abuse. As one woman said, "I started drinking when I was a teenager because it made me forget about the abuse. I did not have to feel his hands on me anymore. It was so easy to get pot from my friends. The feeling of getting high and going somewhere where the abuse was not happening worked until getting high was all I was doing." Prescription drugs can also be abused by women. I have known women who have seen several physicians and received multiple prescriptions or who take prescription medications from family members. They became dependent on medications to help them avoid memories of the abuse, deaden the emotions that came with memories, or cope while in the presence of the perpetrator.

Sexual compulsion is not readily recognized in our society as addictive behavior, although compulsive sexual behavior can and does create much damage in a person's life. Women who consider themselves compulsively sexual describe the ways this damaging behavior resulted from the sexual abuse. For example, their bodies were objects to the perpetrator or the sexual abuse was how the perpetrator showed he "loved" her, so that is how she came to think of her body as an object or to define love as only sexual. Unmet childhood needs for affection and caring are met through sex, and some women sexualize their relationships as a way to feel powerful instead of powerless or to prevent emotional intimacy by making sex the focus of the relationship. Women have described how they have felt desired through compulsive sex while at the same time viewing it as a way to punish their bodies for the shame of the sexual abuse. These women are used sexually and use other people sexually because they do not feel worthy of respect or love or they do not know how to have or trust a relationship based on these attributes. Some women may use sex as an outlet to convince themselves that they do not have sexual problems because they "like" sex so much.

Women who develop addictions often need a dual approach to their recovery and healing. They may need Alcoholics Anonymous or other 12-step programs to help them through the process of recovery from drugs and alcohol coinciding with a history of sexual abuse. They might also benefit from Al-Anon or Adult Children of Alcoholics if alcohol and drug addiction was a secondary trauma to the sexual abuse. Women can attend these self-help meetings while in therapy to recover from the sexual abuse. Therapy and support groups work well together when they are coordinated as part of a woman's treatment to heal. The book *Women, Sex, and Addiction: A Search for Love and Power,* by Charlotte Kasl, is a good resource to further understand this damaging set of behaviors.

Shame and Reenactment

The sense of shame that a woman experiences from childhood sexual abuse is a deep-rooted feeling that something is wrong with her that she is not able to explain. The shame is not only about her body but also about who she is as a woman and a human being. The shame originates from the secrecy of the sexual abuse, the particular acts of sexual abuse she endured, the disgusting feelings about her body that she experienced during the acts of sexual abuse, and the overwhelming powerlessness she endured at the hands of another. Shame is a deep feeling of not being worthwhile, of never feeling good enough no matter what you accomplish, of feeling revulsion at your own image in the mirror, and of believing that everyone knows just how worthless you are. It started when the sexual abuse began and was buried deeper within the child as each act of sexual abuse was perpetrated against her.

Shame also grows from blaming oneself for what another did and not understanding or accepting that the shame belongs only to the perpetrator. It kills feelings of joy, happiness, and worthiness; it replaces light with a terrible blackness. Shame is often at the core of self-damaging behavior, and it causes isolation and a loss of connectedness to other people. As Susan (age twenty-two) described, "I would scrub my breasts where I was touched by the perpetrator; sometimes I would leave horrible marks and abrasions. I hated my breasts for attracting him or because I did not stop what he was doing." Self-harm can also be a means to feel when she cannot feel anything else. As Penny (age forty-three) stated, "When I cut myself, I could at least feel that. It was better than feeling the numbness. The cutting gave me the release, and the release came only when I cut so I would [cut] again." Many women have had some history of self-abuse, which can include cutting, burning, scratching, punching, hitting, or scouring their bodies to rid themselves of the shame and the feelings of the abuse. Constant self-criticism is also a means of expressing self-hatred or humiliation in reaction to memories of the abuse and disappointment in oneself for not being able to stop the perpetrator.

Women punish themselves for not being able to stop the abuse because today they see themselves as adults who could stop it while forgetting how small or young they were as children or adolescents. Women need to accept that the abuse was never their fault—they did not cause it, and they could not have stopped it. The shame a woman feels is not hers; it belongs to the person who sexually abused her. Holding the perpetrator, not the child, accountable is critical to a woman's recovery and healing. This is equally important when a woman has confused her body's response to the abuse with the experience of pleasure, which is viewed as giving permission and consent. Women need to recognize that any body response during childhood sexual abuse was not their way of consenting or giving permission—it was another way that the perpetrator manipulated them.

Women also experience the shame of their family when they come from a history of sexual abuse. They cover up their embarrassment of the family's behavior by keeping silent and taking to heart the family's need to protect its reputation instead of protecting the child. The family may even promote silence at the expense of a woman's recovery. Other women believe that the family would hate them and never talk to them again if the family knew they had told someone about the abuse. As one woman put it, "My family would rather believe I am crazy than know that my brother sexually abused me." This woman felt anger and shame toward her family's belief that it was better to be crazy than break the silence and tell the truth.

Numbing to the Abuse

Women are often numb to the experience of the abuse, and when they talk about it they may do so without any emotions or feelings. I call this the neck-up effect: they know it in their heads, but they do not feel it in their gut. More often than not, women are not aware that they are without emotional reactions and feelings when disclosing and describing the abuse. Dissociation has a role in this response to trauma. When a woman is numb, she has shut down and separated from what she felt at the time of the abuse. Dusty Miller further explains the relationship between dissociation and a loss of feelings. "Dissociation takes a variety of forms, one of which is analgesia: becoming numb, both physically and emotionally. The woman who dissociates may report feeling nothing or having no clear mental response to significant events or communications."[36] As Jodi (age twenty) said to me, "It has been so long since I felt anything, it does not surprise me [that] I do not feel anything while telling you about the abuse." These women feel dead inside and have long forgotten what they felt around the time of the abuse, let alone how they feel now. Numbing is how they survived the sexual abuse; if they did not feel it, it was not happening to them. Numbing is also about remaining in a state of shock. All too often, women who have been sexually abused do not cry. They simply do not allow themselves to cry because, as some put it, "It wouldn't change anything." Women might believe that crying makes them vulnerable or gives the perpetrator additional power: "Then he would know he hurt me, and I never want him to know he hurt me!" They have convinced themselves that this inability to feel or show feelings is strength or a test of endurance. The muted battle cry of "no more tears" is part of the resounding silence of feelings lost over the years.

Numbing is also the experience of never being allowed or able to grieve their losses and pain for what was supposed to be but never was a childhood once the abuse began. Women feel they were old while they were young. Women do not know how to give in to their grief, or they feel unjustified in their grieving. To grieve is to be human, and to be human is to be alive with the pain. The emotional state of being numb allows a woman to get through the day. What women slowly realize is that as dissociation ends, they begin to feel, and while the feeling is painful, it is a release from the trauma. The numbing of emotions from childhood sexual abuse also interferes with a woman's ability to connect emotionally in her present relationships and to events within her environment. This loss of emotional connectedness has a role in the dissociative response during reenactment behavior of the trauma. Women who self-harm will speak of "not feeling" while they cut, burn, or purge their bodies. Numbing is the means by which women disconnect from their feelings. This aspect of sexual abuse also has a role in women's revictimization. When a woman is not able to feel what is occurring to her or around her, she is not able to act on feelings of self-preservation that signal harm and danger. Finally, without emotional connectedness her relationships feel empty and her response to others can be misconstrued as cold and distant. Children in particular suffer from this effect of their mother's childhood sexual abuse. What children need—warmth, nurturance, and caring both emotionally and physically—is not given when their mother is not able to feel and express herself in this most human of ways.

Inappropriate humor is another way women disconnect from painful emotions. Debbie (age fifty-one) explains it best: "I learned to laugh about the abuse with my older sisters. We would actually joke about how the men in our family were all 'perverts.' We seem to find strength in our humor. We make fun of men and their apparent weaknesses. In time, I began to laugh at anything that was painful to me. If I did not laugh, I knew I would cry and then I would be in trouble. I would be found out; they would know I was not strong and that I did not just get over it." The ability to laugh at life's absurdities is a gift, but to laugh at childhood sexual abuse is absurd and diminishes what this trauma does to a child and later to the woman she grows to be. In recovery, women learn that it is appropriate to cry, to feel sad, to express anger and fear, to feel vulnerable, to give and receive emotional support from each other, and to experience and share all the emotions that help to heal from this trauma.

Eventually women do learn to laugh again. They laugh with each other and at each other's humor. True laughter comes from the joy of the moment. They experience this true laughter with other women who have regained their joy of life. For those of us who have been so serious, knowing that we can laugh again and be humorous—but not at the expense of our pain or as a way to numb our traumatic experiences—is healing. Women come together to express their feelings about the unfairness of childhood sexual abuse. Women recover and give each other strength and support along the journey of healing. When they reconnect with themselves, they can connect with other people as well.

Anger and Rage

Women who have been sexually abused in childhood have accumulated anger that can develop into rage. Each act of abuse fueled her justified anger. A woman's anger is about violation, betrayal, and not being protected by family members. Underlying rage are emotions related to loss of control, terror, anxiety, and experiencing a violation of personal boundaries. Triggers that can release anger or rage include someone trying to control a woman or touch her in a certain way, hearing certain words or phrases, or a sense of threatened safety. Anger and rage can be expressed either outwardly toward others or inwardly toward oneself. Rage is dangerous; it is dangerous to the woman because it is experienced as a loss of control, and it is dangerous to others when they are the target.

Children in particular are vulnerable to this rage. A thirteen-year-old child who was often the target of her mother's rage described her experience: "My mother would get mad over just about anything I did. If I talked on the phone too long, if I did not clean my room, if I wore makeup or I did not come home right after school. It never took much, but the explosion was always out of proportion to what was occurring. The worst was when she would come at me with what I called her 'demon eyes.' I knew I was in for it then. I carried the bruises to school, and when a teacher reported her, I was scared. I knew she would blame me and not herself." Rage that is displaced onto others can cause a woman to become physically, emotionally, and/or verbally violent and harm other people.[37]

Anger is a healthy emotion. It speaks to us and tells us when others are hurting us, violating us, or not treating us well. It can let us know when we need to speak up and say, "No, you cannot do that to me." The child felt her anger just this way, but she had no way to express it safely so it continued to accumulate and build over the years. She suppressed it just as she suppressed her other emotions during the abuse. Learning to direct her anger toward the perpetrator, and eventually toward the other adults in the family who did not protect her, is where a woman needs to begin. This releases her rage about the sexual abuse so that she can live with healthy anger that she is free to understand and express safely. There are steps women can take to identify, understand, and express the rage that accumulated with the sexual abuse. Their goal is to direct it at the perpetrator and family members who did not protect her, not at herself or others. Women need to express their feelings of rage and intense anger in a controlled and assertive manner, not as a perpetrator. Anger can be expressed safely if a woman is willing to learn to do so constructively.

Rage can also cause feelings of jealousy and possessiveness toward others, which are more covert feelings of expressing rage. Women relate how they become jealous if the man they are with is perceived as looking at or if he talks to other women. Envy is another emotion heightened by rage and can be created by both the loss of what was taken from a woman and feeling that others do not deserve what she did not have as a child. Envy and a sense of entitlement—a feeling that the world owes her—are emotional effects of sexual abuse that are not always recognized. They reinforce the distorted belief that "If I did not have it, you do not deserve it either." The "it" is the happiness, security, warmth, love, trust, and sense of belonging that she never knew as a child. Susan (age twenty-two) said, "I have finally learned that not only do other people deserve good things, but so do I, and that while we are not necessarily entitled, it is our right to have a happy life. I do not have to envy others their good fortune, for I have found good fortune of my own. And while my childhood was not fair and I did not deserve the abuse, I do deserve to have the life I choose for myself today." In learning this, Susan stopped antagonizing other people and became more successful in her work and in nurturing friendships.

Sexuality

The effects of childhood sexual abuse on a woman's sexuality are multiple. A woman who was sexually abused as a child had the most basic of emotional needs, that of trust, violated. Without trust, she can never feel safe with another. She is unable to differentiate between who is trustworthy and who is not. She is unsure whether she can trust or that trust is safe. Without trust, she cannot explore relationships, and if she is unable to explore relationships, the development of healthy female sexuality will not occur.[38]

A woman's sense of control over her body is also affected. Women report either having no sense of control over their bodies or being afraid of losing control, which does not allow them to share intimately with another person and enjoy the freedom of sexual exploration. Control affects the pleasure of sexual experience between two consensual adults. Women who have never experienced control over their bodies have felt obligated to be sexual and do not often know what they enjoy or do not enjoy sexually.

A woman who experiences sex as an obligation rather than as a consensual or initiating partner is a woman whose body experiences relate to forced sex. Consensual sex is relaxing, enjoyable, and gratifying. Forced sex is tense, one-sided, and not enjoyable. Forced sex causes a woman to dissociate and emotionally travel somewhere else while she endures the act of sex. She is not present, and she does not actively or fully participate with her partner. Forced sex triggers the experience of the sexual abuse, since she once again feels violated without being able to tell her partner.

A partner is more often than not aware that a woman has seldom found enjoyment in their sexual relationship. While confused by this absence of pleasure, the partner has also consented to it. Partners have to learn that a woman's body is hers—not theirs—and that if she does not give verbal consent or initiate making love they should stop and ask her what is occurring. As one partner stated, "It took me a while to understand that my wife could not tell me that she did not want to be sexual. I had to accept that she was going along to appease me. I always sensed this but did not know how to talk about it. This was before I knew about the sexual abuse by her father. I had to learn to let her initiate our making love and to be affectionate with her before she could feel safe enough to be with me and know that I was not with her for sex." Partners who are supportive understand that it will take time for the woman they are with to be able to say "no" and then "yes." If a partner continues to expect sex on demand, he will only delay the woman's sexual healing. Often a first step for these women is to ask for nonsexual touch from people they trust; in this way, they start to experience what safe touch is to their bodies and to participate in mutual consent.

Often, women who have been sexually abused believe that they do not deserve happiness in their lives in general, and this extends to their sexual life as well. This is related directly to the shame and to not knowing what their own preferences are. Think about it: if a woman does not know the daily things she needs to bring her joy and have her needs met, how would she believe she deserves sexual pleasure? How can she ask for what she needs sexually when she cannot even ask for a day off from work? Feeling that they deserve good things in life is foreign to most women who have been sexually abused. The child learned that "other people deserve good things, but not me." This does not make a woman a martyr. She does not purposely ask others to "use me and abuse me," just as she did not ask that as a child. She is simply acting on the beliefs she developed from childhood sexual abuse. Learning that she does deserve good things, that she has a right to personal enjoyment, that others do care about her needs, and that she is not a victim moves her past the underlying belief that has maintained her self-sacrificing.

A woman who has been sexually abused as a child is often sexually inexperienced. Most women find this difficult to believe; even though they have experienced these thoughts and feelings throughout their adult lives, they wonder how they can be inexperienced when sexual acts were done to them or they were made to do horrible things. They are experienced in that they know about sexual abuse, but they are inexperienced because their sexuality did not develop fully and they did not have natural sexual experiences. There are always areas of female sexuality that women do not know and need to learn about because the sexual abuse prevented them from learning about their sexuality. Sexual abuse is an unnatural act perpetrated by an abnormal person. As a child, the woman was made to be sexual, had sexual acts forced upon her; her young body was manipulated and used by another. She never consented to the sexual abuse and did not find it naturally pleasurable. She was made to believe that sex is something someone does to her, not an expression of love for another. She was never free to explore her sexuality as a natural process of her adolescence and young adult years. What she did not experience was the first kiss that she chose to give or perhaps the excitement of the first boyfriend who held hands with her, cuddled, made out, or explored her body without her feeling shame and with the option to say "no" or "yes" with the confidence that these were her true feelings and would be respected.

Women who were sexually abused as children miss these developmental steps that girls normally go through as they grow up and are involved in relationships with people that they trust, choose to be with, and grow to care about. Women sense they are still "virginal" in terms of the emotional aspects of being a sexual woman. Experiencing sexual abuse is not experiencing natural sexuality. Childhood sexual abuse skews and distorts a woman's sexuality and prevents her from exploring sensual feelings and mutually inclusive sexual behavior with a partner she chooses.

Avoiding sex altogether is a prevalent effect of childhood sexual abuse. Avoidance is not the same as choosing celibacy. Women in recovery from childhood sexual abuse will at times consciously choose to be celibate in order to facilitate their sexual healing. This can be a very healthy experience for a woman. Women who avoid sex frequently do so by numbing and shutting down before or during the sexual experience. As Sandy (age thirty) described, "Whenever my husband wanted to be sexual, I would simply 'freeze.' I felt like a deer caught in the headlights of a car. I could not move. It was always painful because I was so tense and nervous. Sometimes I would bleed afterwards, and my husband would never know. He did not know what was wrong." Women who avoid sex are not able to relax and allow themselves a gentle and slow exploration of their sexuality with a partner. Often during sex they are having flashbacks of the abuse. A woman cannot be in the present while having a flashback; she is in the past, and the feelings she had then are the feelings she is having now. Learning how to control flashbacks is possible for a woman when experiencing a partner who provides gentle touches, gives understanding, does not rush her or force her, and can teach her to trust him in a nonsexual way. Women can learn to have a healthy, enjoyable, sexually satisfying relationship if they are willing to heal and are with a partner who is willing to be the kind of person she can trust. *The Sexual Healing Journey: A Guide for Survivors of Sexual Abuse,* by Wendy Maltz, is a good resource for women to use in identifying where sexual healing has occurred or still needs to occur and in exploring ways they can approach sexual healing that is comfortable for them.

Parenting

How childhood sexual abuse affects parenting is often not apparent to women or is not something they readily want to acknowledge and discuss. A woman who has been sexually abused is at risk of not protecting her child from the perpetrator because she may need to believe he would never hurt her child the way he hurt her; this is especially true when the perpetrator is a family member. Too often, women who are now mothers allow their child to be around the perpetrator. This leads to the tragic perpetuation of sexual abuse, which the mother hopefully acknowledges once her child tells. The secret of the sexual abuse by the perpetrator and the silence of the family members who know reinforce the silence of the woman. Until the silence is broken and children are protected from the perpetrator, all children are at risk of the trauma of sexual abuse.

If a mother has managed to keep her child away from the perpetrator but not broken the silence, she has still raised her child with the effects of sexual abuse. Children who are raised by a mother who was sexually abused but has not healed are children being affected by the abuse in other ways. Children can be raised with a mother full of anger and rage or crippled with anxiety and depression. Mothers who were sexually abused may not have their own sense of identity and self-worth or may not be comfortable establishing their own boundaries and beliefs. A mother who is in chronic pain or who has addictions and eating disorders is not always available to her children in a consistent way.

Mothers who have not healed from childhood sexual abuse can neglect children. Children often know that something is wrong even if they do not know what that something is. They know it because they see it, hear it, and feel it, just as their mother did. Rather than actual abuse, they experience its repercussions, and this is traumatic to children because it denies them of their right to a healthy mother who is able to function in the present and be available. Mothers usually do not affect their children on purpose, but as one woman said, "I was fooling myself for years, wanting to believe my children were not being affected by my problems. I was affected by my mother's problems, and mine affected my children. I just did not want to believe it. I wanted to believe I was different." Women come to realize that what Jodi (at age thirty) said is true: "We are not sexually abusing our children, but they are being affected by the sexual abuse."

Promoting a child's sense of individuality and independence in relation to the family and the world is a priority in healthy parenting. Women who have been sexually abused as children are often observed as being either at one extreme or the other when it comes to meeting their child's needs in this area of development. They may not allow their child to be independent or have friends out of fear of what might happen. At the other extreme, they allow their child to do anything because of not knowing what is or isn't appropriate for a child at a given age. They may expect too much from their children at one age and too little at another because they had no role model for healthy parenting. As Tammie (age thirty-six) shared, "I would often expect my four-year-old to take care of the two-year-old. After all, this is what my mother expected of me. In therapy, I came to realize that neither child could take care of the other. I was the adult, and they needed me to take care of them." Another mother said, "I had such difficulty trusting my own judgment as a mother. I knew I was making mistakes with my children, but I did not know what to do. My indecisiveness and inconsistencies confused my children."

At the other extreme is the mother who enables a child to become completely dependent on her when the child needs to separate and start the process of independence to gain a sense of competency in the world. Sharon (at age fifty-three) explains how she learned to parent her daughter who is now a young adult. "It was difficult for me to be able to let my daughter do things on her own. I used to dress her for school and then yell at her later that she was lazy. Who made her that way? I did. It was so unfair to her and to me. I had to learn what was appropriate for her to do for herself and what was appropriate for me to do with her, or for her, all the while considering her needs at the age she was. It took a lot of work on my part, but it has been worth it, for her and for me." Mothers need support in parenting so that they can have good information and find the sense of balance they need to raise children who are competent and healthy adults.

Reparenting oneself in conjunction with learning about parenting and child development is an important aspect of healing that helps mothers who were sexually abused as children trust their true abilities as parents. Doing the opposite of what our parents did is seldom the answer; doing what our parents did is no answer. Reading books, sharing with other mothers, going outside the family for advice and guidance, and identifying the needs of children are good steps. Learning to trust one's ability to parent appropriately, believing that healthy parenting is possible, and asking for help enable women to become competent mothers who can meet the needs of their children. Women need to have the courage to examine their parenting so that as mothers they can develop skills and keep their children from being affected by childhood sexual abuse.

SUPPORTING YOUR HEALING

1. As you read the list of prolonged problems, identify the ones prevalent in your life today.
2. To help lift depression and anxiety, act to reduce current stress, challenge your negative and fearful thinking, take care of yourself physically, understand and respect what makes you vulnerable, set boundaries with other people, increase the time you spend on you, try new ways of relating to others, and seek appropriate support.
3. Have you talked to your therapist, physician, partner, adult family members, parents, or friends about how childhood sexual abuse has continued to affect your life today? If not, why not?
4. What effects were the most problematic for you in the past? How have they changed?
5. Discuss current effects of sexual abuse with your therapist and with your doctor if you are being followed medically. Start healing your life one effect at a time. Start with the most problematic and see what else begins to heal.

Ending the Pretense

Now you understand
Just why my head's not bowed
—Maya Angelou, "Phenomenal Woman"

The above quote by the poet Maya Angelou reflects the increase in self-esteem that women experience after they have stopped pretending either with, or about, the person who sexually abused them. For most women, giving up this long-standing pretense is another step toward reconciling that the abuse and its harm are real. Women who have continued contact or a relationship with the perpetrator share how they have mirrored his behavior by interacting with each other as though the abuse never happened. When the family connection has continued, both he and the woman he abused interact in a manner that is reflective of his denial system and more than likely the expectations of the family belief system. He does not express remorse or state that what he did was wrong and harmful, and she is afraid to speak to him about the truth and remains worried that he will blame her rather than be accountable for what he did. The continued pretense and lack of accountability by the perpetrator is a source of anger for women. A woman's own continued pretense is a source of reoccurring shame that in turn maintains her silence about the perpetrator. Whether the contact was yesterday, a week before, last year, or ten years ago, a woman can experience long-lasting shame, anger, and regret about not speaking up to the person who harmed her. As women stop pretending, they raise their heads and use their voices. They are no longer the silent child who cannot speak, the helpless victim who cannot escape, or the fearful survivor who must continue his denial. It is at this point in recovery that a woman begins to consider whether it is time for her to speak to the person who sexually abused her and to tell this person that she remembers what was done to her. Women come to believe what they have always known but have never acknowledged, "that before perpetrators can be forgiven, there first needs to be an honest accounting and restoration of honor and dignity to victims; the facts need to be fully acknowledged in order to heal the wounds of the past."[1] As stated by Bessel van der Kolk, clinician and researcher, "We believe that the spirit of squarely facing the facts as a prelude to healing should guide both our clinical and our research work with victims of trauma and violence."[2] Women who have faced the facts of sexual abuse are often ready to face the perpetrators who harmed them.

Speaking with the perpetrator is a decision that requires thoughtful consideration. For example, a woman needs to determine how talking with the person who sexually abused her will aid her healing. If it will not help her to heal, then there is no reason to have this discussion with the perpetrator; if it will, then thinking through what her expectations are about this disclosure would be her next step. For many women, their decision to go forward with confronting the perpetrator is based on a need to relieve themselves of the burden of his secret or to request financial compensation for damages and payment of therapy and medical bills. However, for many their reason is based on the growing need to act on the courage they feel through healing and the accountability they seek from the perpetrator.[3]

Women use the following terms interchangeably when referencing this decision: "talking with," "confronting," "disclosing to," and "meeting with" the perpetrator. However, what they are all considering is stating in their own personal way what was done to them to the person who did it. They are not considering something harmful or damaging to themselves or the perpetrator, and they are not acting out of a sense of rage and vengeance. At this time in recovery, women have passed through these emotions and moved on to wanting to resolve the abuse at this level of healing. This is not a decision that all women need to make or want to make, but it is a decision that women do consider.

Women are aware of the risk they are taking when making this decision, since it is most likely a family member they are considering speaking to and confronting. Because of this family relationship, a woman will need to identify her thoughts and feelings about how this disclosure will affect her relationships within the family and realistically assess what emotional repercussions she may face. Often, the family belief system that was there when she was a child is still in place. This belief system still has at its core the rule of silence. Her decision to disclose to the perpetrator and confront him about the abuse will break the rule of silence and be in direct conflict with what the family believes or expects of her. The rule of family silence can also be one of the reasons a perpetrator does not initiate his own acknowledgment about the abuse or why he may retaliate against the woman who confronts him.

At the same time, women who are making this decision have already acknowledged that maintaining the family's maladaptive beliefs are not healthy. As women heal from the betrayal of sexual abuse, they often choose to withdraw their silence, either publicly or privately, about this trauma.[4] While not all women will choose to talk about the abuse openly, women who are in recovery certainly no longer deceive themselves about what they know to be true. Women acknowledge and talk about the abuse because they are motivated by a desire for honesty in their lives, not because they are motivated by a need for retaliation or revenge. Exposing sexual abuse or the perpetrator is not done to hurt the family. In fact, what women often desire is that with disclosure the family can start to heal. However, whether disclosure will bring about healing within the family is not something a woman can determine or control, and she needs to be very clear about the possibility that this desire will not be met.

Disclosure can be healing for women because it is a means of holding a perpetrator accountable; therefore, when it does take place, the sense of shame women have felt decreases dramatically. When a woman expresses her feelings about the sexual abuse assertively and directly, she experiences a newfound sense of self-esteem because she has redefined her belief about the trauma or her view of the perpetrator. The feeling of being free from the hold he has had over her life is another reason a woman is motivated to disclose. Women give responsibility for the abuse back to the perpetrator by not carrying it for him any longer.

Deciding to speak to a perpetrator is a highly personal decision. Whether the perpetrator is alive or deceased, women can confront this person and achieve the same outcome in her healing; the only difference is the process. If the perpetrator is alive and women are considering a direct confrontation, their safety is the most important consideration. Women should never directly confront a perpetrator who is known to be violent and aggressive. The risk of repeated abuse is too great. He is not, nor will he ever be, a safe person for her. As a therapist, I will not participate in disclosure to a violent perpetrator. This decision is made for her safety and mine as well. If the perpetrator is alive and not violent, then women can consider what options they have for disclosure. As a woman considers disclosing to or confronting the perpetrator, she should understand that this decision makes sense when she is clear about his responsibility for the abuse; whether he admits to it or not, her healing will be facilitated.

THE PROCESS OF DISCLOSURE

The following options are presented for women as they consider disclosure with a perpetrator:

1. Confronting him in a session with her therapist, and one other person, who is there for support.

2. Planning a symbolic confrontation.
3. Writing a letter to the perpetrator with the decision to mail it to him.
4. Meeting in a public place with someone she trusts nearby.

The type of disclosure a woman decides upon is based on her personal recovery needs. In addition to her safety, an important consideration is whether a woman is ready. The disclosure needs to be thought out so that women have control over the disclosure, are prepared as to what they will say, anticipate what they expect to happen, are clear on their expectations as to the outcome for themselves, and plan what they will do after the disclosure.

Questions about Readiness

The following questions can help women to assess if they are ready for this decision. Women can discuss these questions and their responses with their therapist or someone else they trust.

1. How do I know I am ready? What are my current strengths? What are my expectations? What are my fears or worries? What people are my support system through this decision? Who, besides my therapist, have I told about the abuse that I can trust and can talk through this decision with me?
2. Is the perpetrator safe or not safe? Is he available or not available for the disclosure? How will I feel about the type of disclosure I choose?
3. Who would I ask to be there for support? Why would I ask this person? What would be her or his role?
4. If the disclosure is to take place at a therapy session, then consider the following: How will the perpetrator be contacted for an appointment, and how will the appointment be scheduled and confirmed? What will my therapist say to the perpetrator if he calls or comes to her office before the appointment? What do I say or do if he calls me before the appointment? Will he and I be in the waiting room together? Will I arrive first? How long will he be there? How much time will I need afterward to talk to my therapist about the disclosure?
5. What do I want to share about my memories of the abuse? What do I want to share about how the abuse has affected my life?
6. What do I expect from the perpetrator today? What are my boundaries with him? What kind of relationship do I have with him now? How will the relationship change?
7. What will I say if he denies the abuse? What will I say if he admits to it? How will I feel if he apologizes? How will I feel if he does not apologize? Do I accept his apology? Am I ready to accept an apology from him? How will I respond if he minimizes what he did or denies the harm done to me? What will I say if he tries to blame me for the abuse?

8. Will I choose to answer his questions? Are there questions I want to ask him?
9. How will I feel if I choose not to disclose to the perpetrator? What are my reasons for not wanting to have a disclosure with the perpetrator?
10. What do I anticipate will be my family's response? Who do I expect to be supportive of me? Who has been supportive? Who in my family will be angry with me?
11. What do I feel about forgiveness? Am I ready to forgive him? How will I feel if I do not forgive him? What do I believe about forgiveness? How do I respond if he asks me to forgive me?
12. What else do I need to consider?

Disclosure in a Therapy Session

Disclosing to a perpetrator in a therapy session gives women structure, support, and control. After all, a therapist's office has been her safe place. A therapist can help women to gain confidence about their reasons for wanting a disclosure as well as help with planning it, identifying expectations, and determining the possible outcomes. This process is how women gain a sense of control over the disclosure and feel prepared. Women are reminded that this is not about revenge or behaving in an abusive manner toward the perpetrator. Disclosure is not about yelling, screaming, or being violent. One act of violence never justifies another. Acting out a revenge fantasy is not constructive to healing and brings women closer to a perpetrator's behavior rather than the behavior of a woman who is healing. If a woman is feeling and thinking more about revenge than honest disclosure, she may have more outrage and grief work to do before she is ready for a healing disclosure with a perpetrator. Remember, adults can express their thoughts and feelings without being abusive.

Therapeutically, I have shared in this process with women. I have found it interesting that a perpetrator who is determined to be safe (not actively violent) for contact chooses to attend the session. First, I send a letter requesting the appointment. I state in the letter that "Lucy Smith has been in treatment for childhood sexual abuse and would like to meet with you." I do not state that he is the perpetrator. I give the time and date of an available appointment. I ask that he call me, not Lucy Smith, to confirm his decision to attend the session. Usually, when he calls he wants to know the reason for the meeting. I state, "She is requesting the appointment to discuss the reason." I then ask whether he is willing to attend. I do not tell him what will be discussed at the appointment since that would be a breach of confidentiality. I do ask him to plan on fifteen to twenty minutes of his time and not a full hour. I have concluded thus far through my own experiences that perpetrators seem to attend these appointments for two reasons: They want to know (1) what a woman remembers about the sexual abuse and (2) with whom she has discussed his behavior.

I have found that when perpetrators admit to the sexual abuse, most of them have taken some responsibility for it even as they made excuses for it. They do not necessarily show remorse for what they did or the harm they caused to her; rather, they show remorse for being exposed and may give some indication of the harm, but not on an emotional level. They do not seem capable of emotional vulnerability within this context of their behavior. Some of the men do apologize and ask to be forgiven; others do not apologize or ask to be forgiven. When an apology is made, these men do not seem to grasp the level of harm they have inflicted upon the child or understand at a meaningful human level the damage they caused to the child or the woman she became.

In planning this disclosure with women, I make sure the boundaries for the meeting are very clear. The client and I have reviewed the disclosure procedure, and she has answered questions pertinent to disclosure. We go over these a few times as she continues to clarify her reasons and expectations for the meeting. She has written a letter to the perpetrator that determines what she wants to say to him. This letter is written and refined prior to the meeting. She has also determined what questions she might ask, what questions she will answer if they are posed to her by the perpetrator, and what her thoughts and feelings are about forgiveness. My role in the meeting is to ensure that her boundaries are respected by pointing out to the perpetrator when he violates her stated boundaries. I meet with her and the support person prior to the scheduled appointment. This meeting is to answer questions regarding the support person's role, clarify what she might ask of this person during the meeting, and review what questions the support person might have as well. I have the client, along with her support person, arrive a few minutes early and wait in a confidential office until the perpetrator arrives. I do not structure the meeting with her waiting in the reception area with the perpetrator. When he arrives, I introduce myself and ask him to join us.

As the session begins, I tell the perpetrator that the reason for his presence is that the client requested the appointment, she has been in treatment for recovery from sexual abuse, and she has a letter to read to him. I ask that he listen to the letter all the way through and not interrupt her. I ask him to wait and ask questions after she finishes reading the letter. The woman acknowledges his presence and reads her letter. She reads the letter slowly and with deliberation. If she needs to pause, she is encouraged to do so and to continue when she is ready. The perpetrator is asked to respect her pauses and not speak out. If he does try to interrupt, I ask again that he please wait until she is finished.

After she reads her letter, it is her decision to ask questions, respond to questions, listen to what he has to say, and accept or reject an apology if given by him based on her readiness to do so. These are her decisions to make throughout the time that he is there. I am present to give support and guidance through this process and to keep the boundaries in place with the perpetrator. I also find that this is an excellent time for her to practice how she might interact with the perpetrator in the future: by stating what she knows to be true, staying focused, and keeping her boundaries. If he asks intrusive questions or questions that are uncomfortable for her, I remind her that she does not have to answer questions. This is an opportunity to point out to the perpetrator when he is behaving disrespectfully, acting inappropriately, or violating her boundaries. Usually after fifteen to twenty minutes, the session with the perpetrator ends, but there are times that this process takes longer. I ask him whether he understands what has occurred here today and if he is clear on what she is stating she wants or needs from him. I take a few minutes and reiterate what he heard in the letter, thank him for coming to the appointment, and then I confirm that he may go.

After he leaves, the client decides whether to meet with me alone or with her support person. We process the disclosure in terms of how it felt to her, what she is feeling now, and how she plans to spend the rest of the day. There needs to be a plan in place for after the session. I reiterate the importance of what she has accomplished in her recovery, and I ask her to be aware of her feelings and thoughts over the next few days and to keep her boundaries with the perpetrator. I ask that she call the office within a couple of days and let me know how she is doing. She is encouraged to spend the next couple of days taking care of herself and to participate in activities that affirm her recovery. For some women, the accomplishment of disclosing to the perpetrator is a time of celebration and jubilation.

Women report a sense of relief and personal empowerment following disclosure with a perpetrator. The anxiety of having the perpetrator sitting in a room with her diminishes as feelings of self-respect take over. These feelings of self-respect come from telling him directly what he did to her and how it affected her. Women often report that letting the perpetrator know her boundaries as an adult is the greatest sense of control they have ever had with him. Other women share that having spoken clearly and in their own voice to the perpetrator confirmed their healing in a profoundly meaningful way. The disclosure is an affirmation of the empowerment women experience as an outcome of their healing and a release from the perpetrator's hold on them.

Symbolic Disclosure

A symbolic disclosure usually occurs when a perpetrator is deceased or unsafe to confront directly or when a woman decides that this kind of confrontation is best for her. The purpose of affirming her recovery, releasing any remaining sense of shame, and breaking the silence of the abuse is still met through symbolic disclosure; it is just accomplished by different means. Women choose a symbolic way, personal to them, that transfers the shame and accountability to the perpetrator, even though he is not directly there to receive them as his responsibility.

In preparing for a symbolic disclosure, a woman has planned a ritual that is significant to her. Women choose a place for this disclosure to occur, a place that has emotional significance to them. I have accompanied women to the house where the sexual abuse occurred or to their homes where they have felt safe and free of the abuse. We have met in my office where women have felt trust and understanding about the trauma of sexual abuse. We have also gone to grave sites where women have burned or buried letters to a perpetrator. Some women have burned an effigy or a picture of the perpetrator. Others may want to cut him out of pictures or destroy a significant gift he gave her. Sometimes they want to include something that is symbolic of a specific memory of the abuse. One woman chopped up the toy chest her grandfather gave her and burned it in her backyard while she told him what he had done to her as a child. She stated, "I never knew that I could feel so good getting rid of that toy chest. As I burned it, I cried, and it was for both of us. I felt clean afterwards and exhausted. It was a good feeling, an incredible feeling." Symbolic disclosure happens at a location that each woman decides is important for her emotional healing; the disclosure often has a spiritual meaning to women and can include a prayer of gratitude for their healing. Emotionally, women who symbolically disclose experience the same kind of relief and empowerment as women who confront a perpetrator directly. As with the direct confrontation, we plan what she will do afterward and we process her experience on the day of the disclosure. I have her call and check in with me a few days later to see how she is doing.

Sending a Letter

Sending a letter to the perpetrator is also an option for women. I may send a brief cover letter to accompany it if a woman asks me to do so. In my letter, I simply state, "Enclosed you will find a letter from Lucy Smith who has been in treatment for childhood sexual abuse. I am forwarding this letter to you at her request." If she gives me permission, I also state that she desires no contact from him at this time other than to receive and read the letter. Just as in a direct or symbolic confrontation, the woman has decided what she will state in the letter and has identified her boundaries with the perpetrator. She brings the letter to a session to read, think through, and refine before mailing it; she may choose to send it registered mail so that she receives a receipt upon its delivery. We discuss her feelings and the process she has been through in writing and sending the letter. She decides how she will respond if he chooses to contact her after receiving the letter. Writing a letter to the perpetrator sometimes leads to a meeting at my office. It can also occur in conjunction with a symbolic confrontation or meeting with him in a public place. The decision is up to each woman and is based on her needs.

Meeting with the Perpetrator in a Public Place

A woman may choose to contact the perpetrator herself and request a meeting with him outside of her therapy. She does so with the recommendation and intent of meeting him in a public place with at least one support person present. Women have chosen to meet in restaurants, churches, museums, and libraries. These places have a sense of openness. They are not isolated, and a woman can leave at any time; other people are there, which adds a sense of comfort, safety, control, and security. As with the other disclosures, a woman has written a letter and has identified her boundaries. We schedule an appointment after the disclosure for her to process and relate what occurred. She is encouraged to have a support person present, either nearby or inside the public meeting place. Again, it is important for her to know what her plans will be after the meeting and to check in a few days following the disclosure. Like the letter-writing option, this type of disclosure can occur in conjunction with a symbolic confrontation.

Similarities of the Confrontations

The four types of confrontations discussed here have the following similarities. First, a woman has chosen to have the disclosure and thus comes to that decision from a position of strength. Second, she has written a letter stating what she plans to say to the perpetrator about the sexual abuse, its effects on her, and what her boundaries are with him today. Third, she chooses who will accompany her to the disclosure for support and what people she will tell within her support system. By having someone she knows attend the meeting or be nearby, she has also identified to this person what kind of support she needs at the time of the meeting with the perpetrator and afterward. Fourth, she meets with the perpetrator and completes the disclosure. After the disclosure, she attends a therapy session to process her thoughts and feelings and to share what occurred during the disclosure and what her plans are for the next few days. Fifth, she shares the disclosure with her recovery group. The women in her recovery group are one of her main support networks, and they are encouraging during her decision to have the disclosure. The women in her group, who have already completed this process, can share their experiences. Sixth, she writes a letter to herself stating what the disclosure means to her healing and her life today. It is a letter about strength, empowerment, courage, knowledge, closure, and truth.

After the Confrontation

What to expect after the confrontation will depend upon what a woman has decided she needs from the perpetrator and how much contact she plans to have with him. She does not have to have any expectations of him, nor does she have to have any contact with him. Whether or not to have ongoing contact is not about what he needs or expects or what the family needs or expects of her; it is about the choices she has the right to make in her life today as an adult woman who is healing. One of those choices may be that she does not want a relationship or any contact with the perpetrator. She chooses whom she will tell about the disclosure, and she is encouraged to tell people she knows she can trust—people who believe her about the sexual abuse, have been supportive of her recovery, and will respect her boundaries.

She will consider what decisions she may need to make about family gatherings if the perpetrator is still a part of the family. Whether or not she attends these gatherings is her choice; if she does attend, she needs to plan how to interact (or not interact) with the perpetrator if he is there. Now that he knows she remembers, has exposed him, and will no longer keep his secret, he may not want to attend family gatherings. Some women decide to attend family gatherings even if only for a set amount of time predetermined by them. Others decide to have their own family gatherings without the perpetrator present. These are examples of the decisions a woman makes in the coming weeks, months, and years after her disclosure with the perpetrator.

Whether to see or be around a perpetrator if he is still present in a woman's life is always an immediate question. The fundamental choice of having any contact with him is her decision; however, her first concern should be about keeping herself safe and free of deception. She no longer has to live by the family's rule of silence or believe that she has to continue to protect the perpetrator by denying the truth about what he did. If she has children, their safety is also of primary concern. To keep children safe, women must acknowledge that children need to be kept away from known perpetrators.

What a woman learns from her own experience of disclosure with the perpetrator is that he no longer has the same power he once had over her. She learns that his power stemmed not only from the abuse but also from the secret that she carried for him. As Teresa (at age forty-two) stated after her disclosure, "I no longer fear being around him. I do not like to be where he is, but I do not have to stay and endure his presence. It is not the same as it was before I confronted him; he just does not have that kind of power over me anymore. It is an incredible feeling." A woman learns that she has nothing to prove by being around the perpetrator. Other women have shared similar sentiments after disclosing to the perpetrator: "I feel toward him as I would a stranger or a casual acquaintance." "He is more to be pitied than hated." "I do not like him, and just as I would not choose to be around other people I do not like or have anything in common with, I do not choose to be around him." "I can be around him, but I do not feel the need to associate with him."

For a woman in recovery, learning how she feels about the perpetrator today will help guide her decisions. The closer the perpetrator was to her as a child in terms of love and trust, the more feelings a woman may have to sort through in determining her boundaries and her relationship with him today. Women often need to continue working through their feelings about the perpetrator. One of the truths women learn is that while they may love the person who abused them, they may not be able to be near that person and recover. In consideration of their decision, women can ask themselves, "What are the reasons I expect myself to continue to have a relationship with someone who sexually abused me?" Women answer this question in order to affirm that the choice is theirs, not his or the family's.[5]

Women may find that a distant relationship defined on their own terms with their boundaries very clearly stated works best for them in the immediate present if the perpetrator is still a member of the family. Most important is that women know how to keep themselves and their children safe because they now know not to trust the perpetrator; they trust that they can determine what is healthy for them today, and this includes no more secrets, deceptions, or distortions about the truth. A woman will need to break through the long-held family belief that it is safe to be around the perpetrator, since she may continue to feel pressure from family members to accept the perpetrator in her life. Letting go of the family belief system that allowed sexual abuse to continue will enable women to make these kinds of decisions clearly. Women also face the belief held by many people in our culture and society that they need to forgive the perpetrator in order to heal. The person she needs to forgive is herself. If and when she does forgive the perpetrator, it should be her own choice, not because she is forced into believing it is necessary for her healing. Women also need to understand that forgiveness is not about forgetting, nor is it about believing that they must be around the perpetrator and have a relationship with him. Women do not have to prove their forgiveness. Forgiveness is what women feel when they have healed. It is personal and something that no one else defines or decides for them. It exists in a place within each woman where she finds solace and peace. Appendix I offers support to women on the process of forgiveness.

WOMEN WHO HAVE DISCLOSED

The following are letters written by women who have disclosed to perpetrators within the family. The first letter is from Sharon, who expresses what confronting the person who sexually abused her has meant to her life. These letters describe the essence of what women feel and experience when they have acknowledged that childhood sexual abuse has occurred to them or in their family, and in doing so they have held the perpetrator accountable. Sharon's letter captures the positive feelings that women experience years after they have confronted the person who sexually abused them.

Marsha's letter speaks of the betrayal and pretense within the family when sexual abuse has occurred and the family chooses to be silent. Marie's letter is as a sibling to her brother and is an example of how a family member can confront the perpetrator and give support to the children who were his victims. It exposes the family code of silence about sexual abuse and holds out the hope of forgiveness while being honest about what will need to happen if the family is to heal.

Carolyn's letter speaks of the pain that a daughter feels toward a father who betrayed her. Her letter is a statement of rebuilding her life after the abuse once she is able to speak the truth of what her father was: a perpetrator of sexual abuse. Jami's letter is one of hope that a woman does forgive, and in that forgiveness she finds the love she has for herself and for those around her. Her letter describes how women go through a process of reclaiming their lives and their voice when they heal from childhood sexual abuse.

I hope other women will gain confidence from the experience and words these women have to share. Their letters are examples of the healing power women have when they use their voice, trust their memories, find their words, and affirm their life.

A LETTER OF SELF-ESTEEM

Dear Karen:

I want to let you know how grateful I am that with your support I was able to confront the family member who sexually abused me. On the day that the three of us met, even though I was nervous, I felt ready. I had waited for over forty years to confront this person and tell him how much I hated what he did to me, how the acts he committed had affected and influenced my life, and the way I felt about myself. I was encouraged to say what I needed to say and even though I will probably always have more to say, what I said that day was enough because it freed me. I felt a tremendous weight was lifted from me when he admitted what he did to me; a weight I had carried for many years. With your encouragement and support, I was finally taking another step in my healing. I no longer felt the rage and bitterness I had felt for so many years.

Even though it has been several years, I still feel the powerful effects of that meeting. I have moved on with my life. I seldom think about the abuse anymore, and for the first time, I feel in control of my destiny. While not everything is easy, I feel I deserve good things in my life and for that, I am forever grateful.

Thank you,
Sharon

LETTERS TO PERPETRATORS

Marsha's Letter

Larry,

I have tried to think about what I would say to you. I keep trying to figure out why you picked me, but then I remember it was not just me you sexually abused, but other cousins as well. Every time I think about what you did to me, I get so full of rage. I want to tell everyone in the family about what you did. I told some of the family, but the rage was still there. My life and the life of my children have been affected by what you did to me. When I should have been there for my girls, I was trying to deal with what had happened to me. Over the years because of the way the sexual abuse affected me I could not give them the guidance they needed.

Every time I hear what a pillar of the community you are, I want to throw up. When my family has a problem, and believe me we have had more than our share, I want to scream out that everything that has happened to us goes back to the problems in our dysfunctional family. You and our grandfather both molested children who are in the family; our grandfather molested my brother. No one in the family would ever talk about what you two did, and we have all suffered because of it. I was secure as a child until you abused me. You took that safe and secure feeling away from me. I have had nightmares about what you did. I have never had a healthy relationship with a man. Sexually I can hardly stand to have a man touch me because of the flashbacks that occur.

I hope you will own what you did and be accountable for your actions. Our grandfather is no longer alive, but his death makes him no less responsible for the damage he has done. I have nothing else to say to you except that what you did was wrong and it can never be taken back.

Marsha

Marie's Letter

Matthew,

I am writing to you because I need to tell you how I feel. I am not comfortable being around you or having you in my home. I am not comfortable being with you because you sexually abused our sisters and brother and you have never taken ownership or responsibility for the abuse. You have never even made an effort to explain yourself. That is your whole history. You have done some things that are not right and the family protects you by never confronting your behavior. I cannot look at myself in the mirror after I am around you because I feel like a hypocrite. I feel by being around you I am saying it is okay what you did and it was not okay. I cannot and will not do it any more. I hold you accountable for your behavior. This is something I do not think you have ever heard from anybody especially a person in our family. That is where I am. I am not comfortable being around you until you can sit down and talk with your family about the sexual abuse. I believe there can be healing in our family but not if we continue to maintain the denial about the long-standing problems in our family.

Marie

Carolyn's Letter

To My Father,
The last letter I wrote to you was full of anger and pain. This letter still has pain, but it also has a lot of sadness and loss. The sadness of a little girl who never got what she needed from her father. She loved her dad with all her heart. She tried so hard to please you, but you made her feel that she was never good enough. All she ever wanted was for her dad to love her as much as she loved him. She wanted him to be proud of her. She wanted him to claim her as his daughter and to protect her.

As an adult woman, I realize that I protected the child I was and the person who hurt her from the rest of the world ever knowing or understanding the reason for her pain. I feel sadness that as my father you will never know how loving and caring your daughter is and how much loss you have caused in her life. Sadness that as a father who died you will never be able to understand the harm you caused when you abused me and then left me with strangers, never to return.

There is also pity for you in this letter because the child lost a lot of her life, but you lost the best part of your life when you hurt her. You lost something you can never regain—a daughter.

The child and the woman can rebuild and go on to a better way of life, but you died a perpetrator. That is something you cannot take back or undo. The only anger left is that I could not say these things to you while you were still alive. I love you.

Carolyn

Jami's Letter

To all of those who have harmed me,
Please pay close attention to what I have to say because what you have done has been so damaging and destructive that I deserve your undivided attention. You robbed me of my innocence and you had no right to impose yourselves or your will onto me. I have suffered greatly.

You took something that did not belong to you and I am here to reclaim it. The pain and deadening numbness I have endured have been burdens I have carried for my entire existence. The loss of self, feeling empty and completely unworthy, not knowing how to trust or love, being made to feel ashamed and guilty, told to lie and deny, feeling totally disconnected and unattached to myself and this world and completely cut off from my own life force. These are just some of the effects that your abuse caused. I wish I could convey to you through this pen just how much you damaged and altered my life. It is my life not yours. To those of you who have taken it upon yourselves to make sure that my life would be dark like yours I have some news for you. It is a headliner, a real page-turner. It did not work!

It definitely started out that way, I will give you that, but it just did not work. I have taken back my power and control. I have made a brand new start. I have managed to find myself even in all the blackness. It turns out that all I had to do was turn the light on. There I was waiting to be discovered. I must say, I like what I found. I admit to being surprised at first, but now it is as natural as how I came into the world. It is a hard and long road, and I have gotten lost along the way, but with help, I found my way back.

I know I can proudly walk away knowing that I am a very strong—and I mean that in every possible way—and a worthy human being who fought her way back, because I am who I am. I always will be, and that is just fine. Yes, it turns out that I am okay after all. I was never to blame for what happened. I was just a child, an innocent, loving child of God. I can say that because of my healing. I have learned many lessons and gained quite a bit of life experience in the few years I have been alive. I am moving on now. I am finally letting go of you. It is time to forgive and to free myself. The world has much glory to offer me and I want to have room for it in my life. I deserve it.

I forgive those souls who have harmed me. I am turning my back and walking forward. It is the present that I live in and not the past. I release you to your proper time. I carried you with me and to be honest, you are weighing me down. I have forgiven you. I do so for myself and my loyalty is with me. As a human being who tries to understand this world and for the most part does not do all that bad, I pray for your souls. I pray for what you have to endure. We all have lessons to learn, and I definitely do not envy your path. I am grateful for my life and for what I have learned. Somehow, you have been a part of that learning. I believe we all choose our lives ahead of time, before we enter into the physical; and believing that puts a different perspective on things. If I chose this life then that is that, and I must accept and learn what I came here to learn.

A few minutes from now your doorbell will ring. There will be a package addressed to you with no return address. Go ahead and open it. It belongs to you. I am returning it. I have held onto it much too long. It belongs with its rightful owners. I do not wish its contents on anyone. I pray and hope for the sake of this world that you get the help you need. You see, you are going to need it. What is inside of that package is lethal and must end. I have done my part. It is time to do yours. God be with you!

Jami

SUPPORTING YOUR HEALING

1. Review the questions about readiness regarding disclosure with a perpetrator; always consider your safety first.
2. Imagine the meeting with the perpetrator and let this help guide your decision.
3. Who are your support people right now? How will it help you to talk with these people about your decision?
4. What are your feelings for the perpetrator today? What kind of a relationship have you had with him? How will you redefine your relationship with him?
5. What are your thoughts about forgiveness? What do you think forgiveness is? What were you taught about forgiveness? Appendix I can help women identify what forgiveness can mean to them.
6. How strong is your family's denial about the perpetrator's behavior and character? Who considers the perpetrator a safe person for children? Who in the family tolerates his inappropriate behavior? Who does not?
7. If you are married or in a committed relationship, what support do you have from your partner? What has his relationship been with the perpetrator? Do you trust your partner?

Moral, Legal, and Family Issues Related to Exposing a Perpetrator

> At last I can reveal my sufferings, for the strength I once felt in silence has lost all its power.
>
> —Deidra Sarault, from *Each Day a New Beginning: Daily Meditations for Women*

Our society has come to believe that one of the most effective means of safeguarding children and preventing them from becoming victims of childhood sexual abuse is to identify and expose perpetrators. This belief has become established through legislation that was passed in response to the repeated victimization of children by perpetrators released from the criminal justice system after serving time for committing the crime of child sexual abuse. In 1994, the U.S. Congress passed the Jacob Wetterling Act, which required all states to establish registries of sexual offenders who victimized children.[1] Consequently, law enforcement agencies throughout the nation set up databases to identify and track individuals convicted of sexual offenses primarily against children. In 1996, Congress amended the Jacob Wetterling Act and passed Megan's Law.[2] This law allows state and local law enforcement agencies to make available to the public information such as names, offense committed, and the location of convicted sex offenders. These laws increase the exposure of known sexual perpetrators residing in a community and assist parents in protecting their children.

These laws are named after Jacob Wetterling, who was abducted and has never been found, and Megan Kanka, who was raped and murdered by a sexual perpetrator.[3] The man who raped and murdered Megan Kanka had been convicted of two previous sexual assault crimes and had served time in prison. After his release, he lived across the street from Megan without her parents ever knowing about his prior criminal behavior. Even though local law enforcement had information about his criminal past (from the state registration of sexual offenders under the Jacob Wetterling Act), they were prevented from releasing it to the community because at the time the Wetterling Act did not provide for public access and notification about known sexual offenders. What makes the abduction of these children so reprehensible is that if both laws had been in place prior to their abduction, perhaps the assault of these children would not have occurred and the tragic loss endured by their parents and family could have been prevented.

With this in mind, it is difficult to believe that Megan's Law was recently challenged in the U.S. Supreme Court.[4] The opponents of Megan's Law argued whether public access to offender information was constitutional. Opponents of public notification and access to sex offender information purported that"some states unconstitutionally punish convicted sex offenders twice, first with jail time or probation, then by putting their pictures on the Internet." There was also a second challenge that put forth the question of whether states should give offenders a chance to prove they are no longer dangerous. If offenders could prove they no longer present a danger to children, this would prevent public access to their criminal history and disallow their photos and addresses being placed on the Internet.[5] The basic argument of opponents to Megan's Law hinged on whether community notification and public access to information infringes upon the convicted offender's right to privacy versus the public's access to information—information regarded by proponents as the public's right, and especially the right of children, to be safe. The Supreme Court upheld Megan's Law and granted states the right to provide community notification on the Internet.[6]

The primary reasons for the passage of this legislation and the Supreme Court upholding it—the protection of children and a child's right to live in a safe community where parents can have knowledge of known offenders— are the same reasons women will consider talking to family members about the perpetrator who sexually abused them. The only difference is that women who can identify known perpetrators are focused first on the safety of children in their families and when possible children who are outside the family but come in contact with the perpetrator. Therefore, women believe that they should contact parents and let them know that a perpetrator with access to children exists within their family. Just as individuals in a community may not be aware of when a perpetrator is nearby, women are seldom sure who in the family knows about the perpetrator's behavior. While women feel a personal responsibility to alert parents in their families, they question if parents will be receptive to hearing what they have to say due to the secrecy and denial that surrounds this family trauma; they also wonder if parents will act on the information once it is received. Therefore, notifying family members about a perpetrator becomes a *moral decision* for women— keeping silent while children are at risk of sexual abuse does not feel like the right decision to make, and their silence often weighs heavily on their consciences. Just imagine how the police in Megan Kanka's community felt. They knew this sexual perpetrator with prior convictions was living there but were not allowed to notify residents, especially the parents of children, and then the known perpetrator abducts, rapes, and murders a child who perhaps could have been protected with notification and warning to her parents. At the same time, women face additional concerns when considering exposing a perpetrator because they are aware that telling this family secret, which has sometimes been hidden for many years, may cause unintentional hurt to other family members. For example, the perpetrator's immediate family members may face rejection and ridicule within the family. They might experience unwarranted shame about the perpetrator's behavior even though they are not the one who abused a child, or they might feel guilty about the abuse even if they did not have prior knowledge of his behavior.

Women also realize they are at risk of being ostracized for talking about this problem, which some family members would just as soon keep hidden. Given the belief system in families where sexual abuse occurs, women are justifiably concerned about being labeled troublemakers, told they are mentally ill, or even accused of lying. One woman, who chose to remain anonymous, shared that "I wrote my nieces that their father had sexually abused at least five children known to me in our family, and that I was concerned about the safety of their children. I received a letter back from one of my nieces telling me 'I was not a forgiving person nor was I a Christian since I wanted to bring up the past.' In the next sentence I was told by my niece that 'yes, their father had sexually abused her and her sister, as well as their children, but he had went before their church and asked for forgiveness and if God could forgive him then I should too.' I felt such anger at the denial and ignorance of my sister, her daughters and even the church members. I also felt tremendous sadness for the children he had harmed."

Women are not naive; they know there will be people, inside and outside the family, who will not believe them or who will want them to remain silent about the abuse. They recognize there will be people who refuse to accept the truth about the perpetrator and what he has done. Any therapist who works directly with families has experienced how members can react with intense anger, defensiveness, and rejection toward the person who has exposed a perpetrator's history of sexually abusing children.[7] Anne (age thirty-five) is a mother who learned that her husband's father sexually abused their six-year-old daughter, Lucy. Anne and her husband were supportive of their daughter telling about the sexual abuse. They even got through the emotional conflict of the grandfather lying about them to the detective who investigated the case and trying to lay the blame on them. What caused more hurt was when they had to deal with the grandmother's rumors about them and Lucy to other family members. Each time they thought the grandmother was through making her accusations, they would hear another one from a sister or a brother. This behavior by the grandmother continued for months. Lucy was at first confused and then sad about her grandmother's behavior. As a six-year-old child, Lucy had an uncanny insight into her grandparents' behavior. She would consistently tell me, "I am sure they are lying because they are scared to tell the truth because they do not want to go to jail." During one therapy session, Lucy even offered to speak with her grandparents to assure them she still loved them and that she did not want them to "get in trouble." Lucy would tell me, "I just want them to tell the truth." I was in awe of this child's compassion for her grandparents in light of the fact that there was no compassion or empathy from the grandparents for what Lucy or her parents were going through. The grandmother remained angry and accusatory throughout the legal process. She did not choose to seek professional assistance that could have helped her learn about family sexual abuse, offered her guidance, and taught her how to support her family during this difficult time. The grandmother could have been a person who became a source of strength for her family; instead, her behavior and her husband's split the family further apart, caused a permanent rift with their granddaughter, and hurt their son in particular. This grandmother's behavior seems to typify the intense denial that occurs by some family members. These case stories exemplify what women need to be prepared for when they choose to expose a perpetrator within their family.

Women are aware of their right to talk about the sexual abuse that was committed against them. With each conversation that women have about the trauma of sexual abuse, the effects of it, the perpetrator, and their healing, they become more confident, self-assured, and clear on what they need to do to live their lives according to their own set of values and morals. Understandably, women feel they have a responsibility to help keep children safe. Women who were sexually abused as children feel this responsibility perhaps more deeply than people who have not been sexually abused because they have lived through the trauma and its long-term effects. Therefore, talking to people within the family whom they believe will benefit from knowing about the perpetrator and would take a stand in keeping children safe becomes worthy of their consideration.

When a woman speaks with other family members, she may learn that the perpetrator who abused her also abused other children or that there is more than one perpetrator in the family. In addition, some family members confide that there are perpetrators in the family who have committed acts of physical or emotional abuse. This mutual disclosure can create a bond with family members who have also experienced the trauma of abuse. It can also create an opportunity to talk about recovery and healing. When Susan (age thirty-two) disclosed to her two younger sisters that their father had sexually abused her, they disclosed that he had sexually abused them as well. Susan was able to help her sisters talk with their mother and tell her about the abuse by their father. Statutes of limitation—laws that set guidelines about the length of time a person has to report sexual abuse to the legal system based on when the abuse occurred and when the report is made—prevented Susan from reporting her father; however, her sisters were young enough that the abuse to them had occurred within the specified legal limits, and they chose to report their father. Their mother was supportive of her daughters even though she was still married to their father; she went with her daughters to meet with the prosecutor and find out what needed to happen to protect them. Their father was arrested, prosecuted, and sentenced for the sexual abuse of his daughters. Eventually, Susan, her sisters, and their mother came to therapy together, which helped them to heal and rebuild their family. As part of his sentencing, their father entered a treatment program for perpetrators. He continues to participate in a weekly program for the sexual abuse of his daughters, and he goes to treatment for his history of alcoholism. Susan's mother attends therapy for herself and with her spouse. Susan and her sisters have not yet made a decision about having therapy with their father or reestablishing contact with him.

Two questions for women to consider as they decide to speak with family members are "Why do I want other people to know about the perpetrator?" and "What do I want to share about the perpetrator's behavior?" Identifying who they view as trustworthy in terms of breaking the silence and secrecy about this problem in the family is a matter of self-protection for women.[8] At the same time, women also need to recognize that they cannot control what others in the family will do once they learn about a perpetrator and his behavior. While most women hope that the people they tell who are parents will warn their children and keep them away from the perpetrator, this outcome is not always the case. By talking to her family members, a woman has given them the opportunity to have information about the perpetrator. However, the people she shares with will decide for themselves, individually, what actions they will or will not take. Women will need to accept these decisions by others whether they agree with them or not. Women also need to consider the possible legal ramifications, since there are perpetrators who bring lawsuits as a means to protect themselves from exposure and accountability regardless of their ability to win their case within the legal system.[9]

Paula (age forty-three) chose to tell her brother's girlfriend about his sexual abuse of her as a child and teenager. While she feels she made the right decision to expose her brother as a perpetrator, his girlfriend continues to allow him around her two young children. Paula has accepted that there is nothing more she can do to protect these children from her brother. Paula has also not received the support she wanted from her older sister in exposing their brother. Her sister either denies the abuse altogether or minimizes it. Her sister will invite the brother to her house while excluding Paula from most family activities. Her sister's behavior has been painful for Paula to experience, but she is accepting that "It is not up to me to decide for my sister what decisions she will make about my brother." It is sad, frustrating, and at times dejecting when women experience these negative and confusing responses from family members. These less-than-positive attitudes are in some ways a reflection of residual beliefs in our society that women either should not talk about their past, should not confront what has been painful in their lives, or should keep secrets about family members who have harmed them. Women simply need to be prepared that they will experience individuals who are, as well as individuals who are not, supportive of their decision to expose a perpetrator and talk about the sexual abuse. Women need to follow their own beliefs and trust that what they believe is right for them will lead them through the decision they are making.

Since the time of Betty Freidan's *Feminine Mystique,* published in 1962, women have become more open about this and other traumas that they have endured throughout their history. In talking about the female experience, women share their collective knowledge and wisdom, and in doing so they discover that they can help other women who have had similar experiences. They identify that helping others also helps them to find their own voice—a voice that most feel was silenced long ago. While the trauma of sexual abuse is particularly difficult for women to talk about, this pain has not prevented them from sharing their experiences. The ability of women to share has built a bridge between their past and their present. As Gloria Steinem reveals in *Revolution from Within: A Book of Self-Esteem,* "Given the pain of so many childhoods, there are three riddles: why many people pass the pain on to their children, why many do not, and what makes the difference."[10] Women who heal from the trauma of sexual abuse find that they can make a difference when they use their voice to expose sexual abuse and the perpetrator. Steinem also provides a plausible explanation as to why some people may find it difficult to accept women choosing to expose a perpetrator and the abuse he committed: "Because many adults are proud of surviving, and therefore believe the damage wasn't serious, or even that it toughened and helped them."[11] Perhaps this belief explains why some people believe that others should be tough and strong and should keep silent about what they suffered and endured. Our culture seems to have a consistent expectation that women should suffer in silence or follows the old adage that what occurs in a family stays in a family. Of course, enduring in silence is what women find they need to change if they are to restore their lives—an inner strength is shown with breaking this silence rather than keeping it.

Carol Gilligan, researcher and author of *In a Different Voice: Psychological Theory and Women's Development,* offers another perspective as to the reason women are at times ridiculed, disbelieved, or belittled for their desire to speak out against sexual abuse and why women persevere through these negative reactions to achieve a moral decision even when they are somewhat "reluctant to speak publicly in their own voice." Gilligan shares that the "moral judgments of women differ from those of men in the greater extent to which women's judgments are tied to feelings of empathy and compassion and are concerned with the resolution of real as opposed to hypothetical dilemmas." She explains the double standard that exists in our culture for women who do speak publicly. "However, while society may affirm publicly the woman's right to choose for herself, the exercise of such choice brings her privately into conflict with the conventions of femininity, particularly the moral equation of goodness with self-sacrifice. Although independent assertion in judgment and action is considered to be the hallmark of adulthood, it is rather in their care and concern for others that women have both judged themselves and been judged." As discussed previously, when a woman's sharing comes from her desire to prevent the trauma of childhood sexual abuse, she does so within the context of a very real dilemma for herself, the family, and the children she wants to protect from a perpetrator. A woman's intention is not to harm; rather, it is to prevent harm. As Gilligan asserts, "The conflict between self and other thus constitutes the central moral problem for women" and is what women struggle to resolve in their "effort to reclaim the self and to solve the moral problem in such a way that no one is hurt."[12]

Women find that they can turn to each other for this support, and when they do healing occurs. Perhaps women find that from their sharing, a profound change is experienced. The immense and satisfying change that can come from mutually supportive sharing with other people is something that Steinem talks about as building and enhancing self-esteem. "What made the difference for those who were able to break the [harmful] patterns in which they were raised was the support of family and friends and an ability to be open and angry about their own past abuse. Sometimes, a whole group begins to change, and because we share that group identity, paths for our own change are opened up, too."[13] Openness, sharing, acknowledging anger, and support from others are suggested by Steinem as paths to change. These attributes are like the steps of recovery—openness (honestly acknowledging the abuse), sharing (disclosure and talking about the trauma), acknowledging anger (expressing feelings about how the abuse has affected your life), and support from others (encouragement to seek help)—and like recovery they will restore a woman's life.

With the change that comes from restoring her life, a woman experiences a profound desire to prevent the trauma of sexual abuse from occurring to her children and to other children as well. Women want to use both their collective and individual voices to expose the core of this trauma: a perpetrator who hides his behavior from the family and then expects refuge within the family belief system when the people he has harmed expose him. When perpetrators are exposed, they can be stopped. Women of this generation deserve much of the credit for the changes that have occurred within our society in accepting that this trauma happens to children. They have helped to educate the legal system, which, in turn, has improved its ability to prosecute this crime. As the forgotten victims of the crime of child sexual abuse, women have had to accept that they are prevented from seeking justice in the courts because statutes of limitation prevent prosecution. They are not allowed the legal privilege to seek prosecution of the person who profoundly harmed them as are children of today. While women realize they could seek a civil lawsuit, some may find they are not supported to do so while others do not trust the legal system to stand by them. Women can experience criticism within their families or skepticism within their communities, and their actions may be reported on in a negative manner by the media.[14] Many women feel that for crimes committed against them, they have to prove their own innocence rather than the person who committed the crime proving his innocence. Perhaps the next changes that occur will be that our legal system will not place on trial the people harmed by the behavior of others and that the media will become better educated and informed in regard to reporting about these crimes and legal actions.

The limitations of legal justice combined with the personal desire to protect children also influence the reason a woman may want to expose the person responsible for the sexual abuse committed against her. As Sharon (age fifty-two) explains, "Each time I saw my cousin, I could not help but feel that I was continuing to allow his sexual abuse of me to silence me within my family. When he was with the family and me, he behaved as such a hypocrite. He acted as though he had never committed this crime against me. He would speak in a manner that denied and contradicted what he had done to me as a child. The family admired him because of his job, the house he had, and the money he made, while my life had been devastated for so many years. I was often looked down upon by my family as the one 'with all the problems and always screwing up.' When I would see him playing with the children, my skin would crawl. When I finally confronted him and talked to my family members, I felt that justice, not vengeance, had somehow been served. I also hoped that he would not be allowed to do to other children what he had done to me. I felt better about myself because I had not kept quiet like I had for so many years, pretending as though nothing was wrong with him. That kind of pretending is what I did when the abuse was happening."

The laws that are in effect today to protect children and prosecute this crime are a vast improvement compared to thirty or forty years ago. The legal system's knowledge and expertise about this crime, and how to prosecute it more successfully, has greatly improved. Daylon Welliver, deputy prosecuting attorney for Johnson County in Indiana, explains: "The statutes of limitations have changed, and the legislature has recognized that there is a delay in the reporting of sexual abuse. The laws today have extended the statutes of limitation accordingly, allowing more time for the victim to report the sexual abuse. While this is good for children today, it may not help women who were sexually abused twenty to forty years ago. Some of the statutes that were in effect at that time and applied when women were children have expired." Welliver gave an example of a woman who came to him because she had seen the individual who had sexually abused her at a recent family function, and she was concerned for the children in her family. "She thought the statutes were in her favor, but it turned out they had lapsed and we were not able to prosecute. I was in support of pursuing the case, but my hands were tied by the laws that govern when I can prosecute."[15]

The passing of laws that extend statutes of limitation and make possible the prosecution of perpetrators has come about because women and men fought to have their voices heard within the legal system on behalf of children. When I make a report of child sexual abuse today, the first question I ask is whether the statutes have passed or if they are in effect based on the amount of time that has passed since the abuse occurred. Fifteen to twenty years ago, I dreaded telling a child, a woman, or their family that even though this crime occurred and the prosecutor was willing to pursue the case, prosecution was not possible because the statute of limitation had expired. How could it ever feel good to a child (in the past or the present) to know that while she had been sexually abused and so much had happened to her, nothing was going to happen to the perpetrator? I am grateful that the laws have changed and that progress has been made within the legal system to better understand some of the specifics of this particular crime, such as that it may take several years before it is reported. However, it is both frustrating and frightening to know that identified perpetrators will not be held legally accountable for their crimes against children because the same legal system that makes it possible to hold them accountable also prevents this accountability from occurring due to statutes of limitation. Laws need to be passed that allow for longer reporting periods if we are to stop perpetrators of child sexual abuse who operate within families.

We have a child protective system in place that works within the current laws to remove a perpetrator from the home where sexual abuse is substantiated and eventually prosecuted. At the same time, this system will not, cannot, and perhaps does not know how to act to investigate sexual abuse that occurred when statutes have expired. How frightening is that for parents and children? Every April, we recognize National Child Abuse Prevention Month. During this month, there are conferences scheduled around the country to promote the exchange of information about how to prevent child abuse, communitywide rallies to remember the children who have been the victims of perpetrators, and marches organized by coalitions to promote awareness of child abuse. Yet, how often do presenters at these conferences or individuals at the rallies or marches speak about the perpetrator who is in the family today and is not exposed even when he is identified by a victim he abused? Television shows produce and air programs about the topic of family violence and child abuse, billboards display slogans, and public service announcements give a hotline number to call if we suspect a child is being abused. However, how to expose the perpetrator that the legal system will not or cannot investigate or prosecute remains a question that needs to be answered. While continued awareness is needed about this crime against children, the steps taken to increase awareness limit the effectiveness of programs as long as they omit steps to protect children within their own families and skip over the important fact that most perpetrators of sexual abuse are family members or someone the family knows.

Because of the laws passed in the last ten years, action to protect children against individuals whom the legal system has identified as sexual offenders can occur. This is possible because our lawmakers have said that citizens have a right to know if a sexual perpetrator is living next door to them, in their neighborhood, or around their schools. Parents are outraged, and rightfully so, when they learn that a known perpetrator of child sexual abuse is living near their children. They do not want these men or women in their neighborhoods, because they believe that perpetrators are not to be trusted near their children. Parents have heard news report of repeat offenders released from prison sexually abusing other children. Yet, these same parents may not have enough information to realize that the real danger to their children is often right within their own family.

While there are parents who will assert their right to have information about sexual perpetrators, speak out against this crime, protest if a sexual perpetrator is living in their community, and demand that the safety of their children take priority, there are also parents who will keep the secret of a perpetrator whom they know is in their family. These parents remain silent even when they know that it is not the stranger on the street they have to fear but the family member who just walked through their door. Other parents have no idea there is a perpetrator in the family and feel betrayed when they find out he has sexually abused their child while other family members knew his history and said or did nothing to prevent the sexual abuse. How do parents who are not aware of a sexual perpetrator in their family protect their children? What motivates a parent who knows there is a sexual perpetrator in the family to remain silent and allow this person access to children or deny the trauma altogether? While some of the questions about protecting children from sexual abuse have been answered, other questions remain that still need to be answered. These questions may not be easy and may make some people uncomfortable, but the ones thirty years ago were not easy to answer and made people uncomfortable as well; however, thirty years ago we began to understand that if we did not find the answers to and about sexual abuse, children were going to be the victims of our unwillingness to try.

Perhaps what we need is a family awareness program to identify known perpetrators, expose them within the family, and hold them accountable for the harm they cause to children—children who had a right to trust and to believe that they were safe within their own family. Such a program would teach families how to stop the perpetrator by exposing him to the children he would harm. The outcome of such a program could be that families are empowered and assisted in safeguarding their children. While this idea may seem idealistic, unrealistic, or even radical to some people, consider that for each individual who is on a sexual offender registry, more than likely the first child sexually abused by this person is a child in that perpetrator's family. A perpetrator gets close to a child and starts the cycle of sexual abuse by either being a member of the child's family or by getting close to the family. Whether the family is his or not, the family is the means by which he gains access to the child. This is a known part of child sexual abuse that all parents need to understand so that they can help keep their children safe.

Just consider that for each one thousand women who recover and heal from childhood sexual abuse, there are one thousand women who can identify a sexual perpetrator—a perpetrator who is in a family or living in a neighborhood and whom the parent or the child knows nothing about because he has not been exposed. How can a parent act to keep a child safe if the parent is misinformed or steadfastly believes that the only perpetrators to fear are the ones prosecuted and sentenced? How informed are parents if they do not have a resource to utilize that helps them to learn how to identify individuals within their family who sexually abuse children? As stated by Ainscough and Toon in their book *Surviving Childhood Sexual Abuse,* "For each child or adult Survivor who can talk about her abuse, there is an abuser who can be prevented from harming other children. For each abuser who is prevented from having access to children, there may be dozens of children protected from abuse and saved from years of suffering. Adults who disclose can receive help for themselves, overcome their feelings of powerlessness and learn how to protect their own children from abuse and act to prevent their abuser (or abusers) from harming other children."[16] The same process is occurring within the Catholic Church. As known perpetrators are exposed and no longer protected by a system of secrecy, there are children who are being protected from future sexual abuse.[17] The courage of adults today who were victims as children is making this protection possible.

We continue to face the moral and legal dilemmas of how to protect our children and prevent childhood sexual abuse because our legal system cannot always expose or investigate perpetrators due to statutes of limitation or does not always prosecute due to a lack of expertise. This is not a criticism of the legal system; rather, it sheds light about a naivete in the identification of known perpetrators that strikes against the safety of children. Despite these complex and multiple dilemmas, most women hope that at some time in the near future, there will be a way for them to address exposing perpetrators who are in their families with some level of support from their family members, the legal system, and society. The only reliable way to prevent children from being sexually abused is to put our efforts into making sure they are not available to perpetrators, and we can only do so when the perpetrators are known to us and exposed for the harm they cause.

FAMILY DISCLOSURE: WHAT TO EXPECT

As women recover, they talk about the trauma of sexual abuse in a way that is comfortable and forthright yet also maintains their privacy about details of the abuse. The more comfortable women become within the healing process, the more confident they become about what aspect of the abuse they choose to share with others. Considering whom she will talk with is usually based on the closeness of her relationship with a particular family member or on whether a woman believes a particular person will benefit from what she has to say. Women realize that they may receive various responses from family members when they do expose the perpetrator and discuss the sexual abuse they experienced as children.

Often, conversations with family members take place over time since sharing about childhood sexual abuse seems to occur in two steps. The first step is the initial disclosure in which an immediate discussion about the sexual abuse and the perpetrator occurs. The second step consists of follow-up conversations that occur when the family member has had time to absorb what he or she has learned and may have other questions or want to talk more about the perpetrator. Rhonda (age forty-seven) is a mother of two daughters who, when they were young adults, disclosed about the sexual abuse to them as children. She shares that when she told her parents of the sexual abuse, "We talked about it initially and they asked a few questions. Then we seemed to talk about it at different times over the next several months. It seemed each time we did, they asked more questions. They continued to express different emotions as they learned their granddaughters had been sexually abused. I feel we all have gotten to a point of where we accept it happened and that our relationships are better for having this secret in the open. We seem to communicate better than we ever did before."

Because family members will ask questions, women need to decide which questions they will answer. Sometimes family members ask questions that make a woman uncomfortable, and she needs to acknowledge this to the person asking the questions. As a general guideline, a woman can keep her privacy by setting boundaries about what she feels comfortable telling family members and being confident in stating what questions she does not want to answer. During this second conversation period is when family members may also ask how they can be supportive and perhaps what may need to happen within the family. When other parents are told, they may express concerns about their children's exposure to a perpetrator and have concerns about the contact their children have had with the perpetrator.

Women also need to anticipate their own reactions. As with any disclosure, women need to be prepared for this step and take their time in deciding how they want to go about each disclosure within the family. This thoughtful consideration of their emotions will assist women through this experience. As women have these discussions with family members, they can reexperience feelings or thoughts about the sexual abuse that they had previously resolved. This is a normal part of the process of family disclosure. Women simply need to review what they already know about what they are experiencing and reaffirm their recovery in whatever way helps them. When Jodi (at age twenty-seven) disclosed to her husband about the sexual abuse from her childhood and adolescence, she was not surprised to find that while she felt confident about what she had to share, she did experience some past feelings and memories. "I felt okay about these feelings, and the memories did not bother me as they had before."

Women also need to be prepared for the possibility that not all family members will believe them about the perpetrator. Sometimes women experience anger toward family members who do not believe them, while other women experience sadness. Whatever a woman feels when a family member acts from disbelief about the perpetrator and the sexual abuse, it is important for her to stay focused on what she knows to be the truth. Women need to remember that their recovery is not going to change other people, nor is it necessarily going to change the beliefs that people have when they refuse to accept the truth.

While women heal, they become comfortable setting boundaries as they gain experience identifying what they need from their relationships to be healthy. Boundaries promote safety and trust in a woman's life. Trust is an integral part of a relationship, and since recovery is about a woman learning to live her life with people who are trustworthy, she needs to identify the people she can trust. Family members who are respectful of boundaries will be people who are safe for a woman to include in her life. Without trust, safety is unpredictable; when safety is unpredictable or inconsistent, a relationship is unstable. Instability in a relationship creates chaos and crisis. These two attributes are ones from the past that women want to prevent from occurring in their lives today.

Sandy (at age thirty-six) shared the frustration she felt with her mother over a lack of respect for her boundaries. "I have not told my mother that my brother sexually abused me. She knows something happened because I no longer talk to him. She will insist on bringing up his name and tell me about him even though each time she does I remind her that I do not want to hear about him. It makes me angry that she does not respect my request about this. It also makes it difficult for me to tell her about the sexual abuse because I do not trust she will respect my boundaries about what I want to share or I do not want to share about what he did to me."

Honesty, along with being more open with others, is an outcome of recovery. Honesty is a gift that we both give and receive from our relationships. To be honest about the past is how women honor the struggle they have been through, the strength they have shown, and the journey they have traveled to heal. Ultimately, it is through honesty that a woman decides how she will live her life today by the choices that she alone has the right to make as she goes about creating her future without the trauma of the past preventing her from doing so. Boundaries determine the parameters of treatment by others that women find acceptable and play an important part in the relationships they establish today. Boundaries define what relationships will be like as women determine how they want to be treated by others. Women often find that some of their first boundaries are the outcomes of challenging, and changing, the unhealthy patterns that existed in some, or most, of their relationships prior to healing. Boundaries form a triangle with our values and beliefs. Together, the three sides of the triangle guide our lives, give meaning to the decisions we make as women, and keep us centered as we face the future we all hope to live.

Appendix G reviews boundaries that women in this recovery program have established. These boundaries have helped other women to gain confidence in determining their own destination and to develop self-assurance that their relationships in the present will be healthier than perhaps they had been in the past.

CHANGING THE FAMILY LEGACY

Women are changing their futures as they move away from the past and their family history of abuse. This positive outcome brings about positive changes in the family a woman has established today. While a woman's recovery has the potential to bring about positive change in the family she grew up in as well, it is up to her family members to make that choice for themselves.

Preventing child sexual abuse is possible in families today. I hope that we will continue to make progress in decreasing or outright eliminating the potential of this trauma to children now and in the future. We have public service announcements about sexual abuse, child awareness and parent education programs, and a legal system to report abuse. There are laws for prosecuting perpetrators, shelters for women and children who are victims of abuse and family violence, education and information programs, books and articles about abuse and how to heal, and movies that center on the themes of family violence. While all the above steps are a positive means by which to expose family sexual abuse, I believe it will be, and is, the courageous healing each individual woman and man experiences that will have the greatest long-term impact on preventing family sexual abuse and its effects on children and families. Each woman who heals unburdens herself of this trauma. As her life changes, she puts in place her own individual prevention program that she establishes within her life and the family she has today. One woman at a time can, and does, stop family sexual abuse from occurring to the next generation of children.

While it is always my hope that a woman's family of origin will join her journey of healing, this is not always the case. The belief system of some family members is often so entrenched in the historical denial of sexual abuse that they refuse to believe what they already know to be true: that sexual abuse has existed within the family, sometimes for years or for several generations, and has never been exposed. Due to this entrenched denial, some women may find it necessary to distance themselves from their family. Women will know whether they need to make this decision as they spend time with their family and notice how they feel and whether they are affected in a negative way. Women do not have to sacrifice their own recovery or place themselves in harm's way because of the family's damaging and entrenched belief system. Women no longer have to feel bound by the misguided loyalty in their family that allows for the abuse of children to take place—either past or present—and hides the behavior of a perpetrator by continuing the silence that allowed him to exist in the first place.

Families can and do come together to heal from the trauma of sexual abuse. I have worked with mothers, fathers, daughters, granddaughters, stepparents, sisters, brothers, cousins, and grandparents from families where sexual abuse has been exposed, discussed, confronted, or prosecuted. Often, these family members share that they have been waiting for someone to tell about the abuse and guide them through healing the pain they have felt for so long. There are family members who share that they did not know about the abuse, and they are loving and supportive during the process of healing. Hope can be restored and families can reunite, but not while the secrecy of sexual abuse is intact and children are vulnerable to the harm caused by a perpetrator. There are families who have made the decision to stop protecting the perpetrator and to start protecting themselves—especially their children. When the trauma of family sexual abuse is exposed, the entire family has an opportunity to heal. Self-esteem as a family becomes possible as each family member commits to restoring hope, trust, and safety. Each woman has to make her own decision about sharing and telling her family members about the perpetrator's abuse to her. It is my belief that each woman will make her decisions from the strength of her recovery and the wisdom she gains from healing. Women do learn to trust that they alone know what decisions are right for them to follow. When women learn to have confidence about what they know, this self-knowledge and self-confidence guides them as they gradually make these decisions with thought and consideration based on their own beliefs and values.

Jami (age twenty-eight) wrote a letter to her family during her recovery from childhood sexual abuse. She wrote about coming to believe that she deserved to receive their love and support. As she worked through her recovery, she realized that she struggled to feel worthy of love. The deep shame she had always felt about the sexual abuse caused her to believe that she did not warrant either love or support from those around her. Fortunately, she has a family who believes differently. They supported her in exposing the sexual abuse by perpetrators who had been hidden for many years because of fear, silence, and secrecy existing within the family. Her family was there for her through each step of her healing. Jami's expression of gratitude typifies what most women feel and need when they have the love and support of people who care about them. Here is what this young woman wrote to express the gratitude she felt toward her family:

> Dear Family,
> This letter is to express my eternal gratitude for your very special and selfless acts of generosity to me. I witness the true meaning of love in each of you. You show me that in the mere act of giving, there is dignity, grace and an expression of one's true self. Your love for me is pure beauty. I have come to understand that there is honor in receiving love. I can now accept that I am worthy and deserving of your gift of love by simply allowing the exchange. The acceptance of your gift is felt on a deeper level than what I am capable of expressing. For me, when I felt I did not deserve your love it created an emotional block that prevented me from accepting your support. I know the pain this emotional block creates because it made me feel numb. I thought since I felt so numb that I would not feel pain either. However, I did feel the pain. The pain I felt was an ache in my soul, and no matter how hard I tried, I could not ignore it. It was always there, always felt.
> Each of you had a major role in helping me to heal that pain, and emptiness, and the void it created. My growth as a human being is important to me. I understand my personal growth is a major part of whom I find myself becoming as I heal. Whenever I view my life with eyes wide open, a heart ready to embrace, and a soul ready to experience, I truly feel alive and connected. Each of you, through your simple

acts of kindness, and gestures of love, helped me to grow and learn about myself. You have helped me evolve into the person who now believes she deserves all the love the world has to offer.

Through your support, you helped me to find myself again. You showed me the path I needed to take to find my way back to my true self. I am grateful for what comes so natural to each of you. In your love, I am shown how to admire and respect myself. Your love proves that by simply giving to someone it is possible to change a person's life. That is what you have done for me. You showed me that I deserve love and all the goodness the world has to offer. You will forever have my deepest gratitude for the gifts you bestow upon me.

All My Love
Jami

SUPPORTING YOUR HEALING

1. Write down the name of each family member whose relationship you value and list the reasons you value these relationships.
2. Make a list of the people you trust in your life today and identify the reasons that you trust them. Now, make a list of the people you do not trust and identify the reasons you do not find these people trustworthy.
3. If the people you do not trust are in your life today, write down the reason they are and decide if these reasons are valid for your life today.
4. Who do you identify as important to talk to about the perpetrator? List at least one reason for each person you identify. What responses do you anticipate from the people you have identified? Is there anyone that you anticipate will be difficult for you to talk to about the perpetrator? What are the reasons that talking to this person will be difficult for you?
5. Write a letter to your partner telling him about the perpetrator. Once you write this letter, set it aside and review it in a few days. Do you want to give the letter to your partner? Do you want to wait a while longer to talk to your partner? Do you choose not to talk to your partner about the perpetrator? Have you talked to your partner about your recovery? Identify a reason for each response to the questions listed above.
6. How well do you trust your own judgment about who to trust at this time in your life? Identify decisions you have made in the last three months that have helped you to gain confidence in your judgment on who to trust.
7. Write down what you will say to each family member you have identified that you want to talk to about the abuse or the perpetrator. Be

specific about what you will tell a parent in the family about the perpetrator. How will you feel if these parents continue to allow their children to be around the perpetrator? How will you feel if they do not allow their children to be around the perpetrator?

8. Identify the expectations you have for yourself if you decide to talk to your partner and family members. Now, identify the expectations you have for yourself if you decide not to talk to your family members.

9. What do you need to consider about the impact that disclosing or not disclosing will have on your recovery and healing?

10. Who are you grateful for having in your life today? Whom do you want to thank for being there for you? Is there someone in the past you remember with gratitude? If so, why?

The Therapeutic Relationship

Being whole is a journey. It involves growing in different directions, developing potentials, and becoming fully human.
—Lesley Irene Shore, *Healing the Feminine: Reclaiming Woman's Voice*

The recovery process can seem long and arduous at times, causing women to question if the effort is worth the time, expense, and most of all the emotional pain. As Taylor (age seventeen) said to me, "Maybe there should be a caution sign on your door." Other women have shared a similar sentiment, but they always seem to follow with something like "but I would still come through the door!" The above attitude exemplifies one of the most important personal qualities that women bring to their recovery—the attitude that they want to heal. This attitude is conveyed when a woman can accept and then acknowledge that the distress from childhood sexual abuse has interfered with her life. It is also conveyed when she admits that she cannot, on her own, resolve the problems that she is experiencing and needs help to do so.[1] This accepting attitude provides the basis for women to make a commitment to heal. Women also identify consideration for those they love, especially their children, as an aspect of their commitment. I think this part of a woman's attitude is a reflection of the integral role relationships have in the lives of women. Since sexual abuse can affect a woman's capacity to interact, relate, and connect at an intimate level, she views treatment as a way to heal the harm that has resulted within her most significant relationships.[2]

Women may find that maintaining a consistent attitude and willingness for healing throughout the recovery process is difficult. One reason for this inconsistency is that healing from the trauma of childhood sexual abuse is painful and at times disturbing, so they may reengage in avoidance. Outside influences such as problems in a marriage or a child's illness can cause a woman's commitment to wane. At other times, she may experience people who discourage her from therapy. When a woman faces these kinds of barriers, it is a good idea for her to talk with someone she trusts. A woman may need to explore how current disappointments are felt in relation to the feelings she experienced at the time of the abuse. In addition, as women go through various stages of their healing, they may experience some avoidance to returning to an aspect of the sexual abuse that is particularly difficult for them or they might prefer not to face how the sexual abuse has influenced their life in a particular way. For example, a mother who learns that she has not protected her own child from sexual abuse may find the victimization of her child difficult to reconcile because as a child she was not protected either. Feelings of shame about the sexual abuse and the embarrassment of the acts committed by the perpetrator can also deter women from seeking help. The label of "victim" can be a deterrent to women because of the feelings of blame and helplessness connected with this label, while some women simply do not like having this word applied to them. A backlash of the feminist movement is a cultural belief that as women gained independence, they escaped the problems of the past. This belief (and myth) has a double edge to it for women—if you ask for help, you are not independent and self-reliant; if you are independent and self-reliant, then you do not ask for help![3] Other women have expressed that they do not identify with the term "survivor" either since it can imply a sense of existing rather than living and thriving. When women enter treatment, they do not necessarily come as "helpless victims who survived." Many are there as women who have made a conscious choice to heal. They experience this choice as empowering and within their control to make as the adults they have become rather than the children they were.

How women are viewed by the mental health system in terms of the understanding they receive about childhood sexual abuse as a trauma and how their problems are related to this trauma and understood can cause them not to choose therapeutic intervention or can affect their commitment to continue once they are in therapy. When clinicians fail to pay attention or do not understand the significance of past traumas in relation to current problems, or when they fail to accept the fundamental reality of a past trauma in order to understand what a woman has experienced, then clinicians will be limited in the approaches they are able to take to treat child sexual abuse effectively. Since "interpersonal traumas are likely to have more profound effects than impersonal ones," the knowledge and understanding the clinician gives to a woman who seeks help for the trauma of child sexual abuse is essential to effective treatment.[4] Another issue women have voiced is their concern at being labeled "borderline personality disorder," "mentally ill," or "abnormal" if they seek help for what they are experiencing and have lived with for many years. These psychiatric labels often stigmatize women, as well as other individuals, who seek help for trauma.[5] Treating symptoms only or in isolation from the trauma will not help a woman to come to terms with the trauma or reengage in a life that is fulfilling and rewarding for her. While post-traumatic stress disorder (PTSD) is one category that provides a general reference for therapists and doctors to understand symptoms of trauma,[6] it is not necessarily adequate for women sexually abused as children. When the social context, historical cause, memory disruptions, and gender-specific effects of the trauma are overlooked by the mental health system, this can affect the type of therapeutic understanding and treatment that women will receive.[7] Since most women seek treatment for how the trauma of sexual abuse has affected them over the course of their lives, the female experience of prolonged problems associated with this trauma needs to be considered and understood within a proposed diagnostic and treatment approach. Examples of associated problems that need to be understood within a diagnostic and treatment approach for childhood sexual abuse are a pattern of revictimization, disrupted development, loss of a self-sustaining identity, an inability to nurture and bond with one's own children, somatization, repeated hospitalizations, suicide attempts, self-harm, and eating disorders. These may be more predominant for women and are not included in the diagnostic category of PTSD, but they are often the primary reason some women seek treatment. Associated problems such as these need to be understood within the historical cause and context of their existence if women are to receive and participate in effective therapy. In general, a woman needs a therapist who understands that treatment of trauma should be considered along "three domains." Effective treatment first helps to stabilize stress responses (chronic shock and dissociation) that can be expressed in such ways as panic attacks or sleep disturbances. Once stabilization is apparent, then the focus turns to helping the woman to process and come to terms with the trauma. This aspect of treatment may take longer than stabilization and goes beyond the treatment of symptoms or simply reporting the trauma experience. It addresses at an individual level the somatic, emotional, physical, and mental dimension of the trauma. The final focus of treatment helps the woman to fully engage in her life. This would include reestablishing a sense of fulfillment and connectedness to others.[8]

Women should be aware of the kind of barriers they may need to overcome as they follow a course of treatment to heal from the trauma of childhood sexual abuse. Even the most motivated and positive woman can experience periods of needing to step back and evaluate where she is in her commitment to heal. When women need to pause to take some brief time away from therapy, this temporary rest can rejuvenate them to return and continue their recovery. Healing from childhood sexual abuse is not about how easy or how soon the problems that developed from the abuse are "fixed." Rather, it is about a permanent healing that sustains and endures throughout life. To that end, women can and do persevere to overcome these barriers and find their way through a recovery process that works for them.

FINDING AND CHOOSING A THERAPIST

Finding a therapist a woman is comfortable working with is one of the first challenges she may face in her choice of healing. When I first meet with a woman to discuss what a therapeutic program will involve in healing from childhood sexual abuse, we cover the attitude and commitment she is prepared to bring to her therapy. For example, women are asked to share what brought them to recovery at this stage of their life and to share if something has occurred recently to influence their decision to seek help at this time. We also go over how they came to choose a therapist, what they have shared or not shared with their physician if they are receiving medical treatment, how long they can expect to be in treatment, and how they view their willingness to make changes. In addition, we discuss how much time they plan to give to recovery and what questions they might have about therapy.

This type of information, along with the opportunity to ask questions, is helpful for women in the beginning of the process so that they can make a decision about their choice of a therapist and the treatment approach taken. Women should think about what this commitment will mean to their lives and, if need be, continue to think through their decision. In other words, they do not have to schedule an appointment right then; they can wait and give their decision more thought.

Qualities of the Therapist

Women need to think about the qualities, experience, education, and training they are seeking in a potential therapist before they call to inquire about an appointment, because it is within the therapeutic relationship that women will establish a healing process. This process will be based on mutual trust, safety, and cohesiveness in order for recovery to occur, making it one of the most important relationships that a woman will have during her lifetime. The significance of the therapeutic relationship is what makes the choice of a therapist worth the thought that women need to give it. Turner, McFarlane, and van der Kolk, in their essay "The Therapeutic Environment and New Explorations in the Treatment of Posttraumatic Stress Disorder," point out the importance of this relationship, which "depends on both a sensitive understanding of the unique issues that make every individual different from all the others, and clinical knowledge about the accurate timing of appropriate interventions. What occurs between a patient and a therapist is a function not only of the particular diagnosis of the patient, but also of the unique and personal relationship between patient and therapist."[9] Because of the unique level of trust required within this relationship and the intrinsic vulnerability that women can present arising from childhood sexual abuse, the ethics that guide a therapist are critical.

Women are at risk of revictimization by unethical therapists as well as by poorly trained or inexperienced therapists who can misguide them even unintentionally.

To that end, women need to do some research, practice good consumerism, ask questions, and identify their preferences when contacting therapists. If this sounds like too much work, then think of the outcome of a therapeutic choice based on inadequate information that lacks the knowledge a woman needs to ensure that she is not contributing to a historical pattern of setting herself up to be revictimized by not asserting a mature level of control over her choices. Knowledge is empowering, and the more knowledge women have about childhood sexual abuse, the approaches that are found to be effective in its healing, the experience and training of a therapist, and the commitment they bring to recovery, the less likely women are to find themselves with a therapist who cannot help them.

The Female Preference

Most women express a preference of working with a female therapist for this particular trauma because they relate better to another woman and have more confidence that a female therapist will better understand the effects of childhood sexual abuse to a female child than a male therapist will. Perhaps this is a stereotype or a female bias; nonetheless, it does exist and when considered makes sense to most women. Women also explain that they feel less challenged to trust a female therapist with their treatment because of the belief that women encourage each other. This aspect of the female preference goes against the stereotype that women are too competitive with each other to be supportive. Interesting enough, even women who were sexually abused by female perpetrators relate these same preferences, which may be due in part to multiple abuses that included a male perpetrator and the embarrassment of speaking about sexual abuse to a man. Pat (age forty-six) found that trusting men was difficult for her because it was a male physician who sexually abused her as a child. She had intense anxiety whenever she faced exams by her female physicians; a male therapist would not have been possible for her to trust with the details of the abuse by her family physician.

Some women share that their inability to trust a male therapist impeded their willingness to disclose details of the trauma they believed were important for the therapist to know and that their reluctance to share impeded their recovery. Sometimes women report that they did not have a positive experience with a male therapist due to his lack of knowledge about childhood sexual abuse, or they perceived a bias from a male therapist in not believing them or of being skeptical of their disclosures. Given the continuing psychological and legal debate over "false memories," some women are going to come across therapists, both male and female, who are skeptical of disclosures by women (as well as by men and children) of childhood sexual abuse, or women might experience therapists who may not be knowledgeable about past and current research on traumatic memory. Even with the substantial body of research that does exist on childhood sexual abuse or other types of violence to women, such as rape and physical assault by partners, skepticism and an inability to believe women does still exist in the mental health field.[10] In addition, while some educational training programs might include the diagnosis of childhood sexual abuse, there does exist a lack of experience among some professionals when it comes to the treatment of this trauma. Among the six universities I surveyed in my geographic area, I found only one that offered in its catalog a college course on the diagnosis and treatment of childhood sexual abuse and none that offered courses for diagnosis and treatment of adult women for this trauma. This absence of course work and formal education in colleges and universities is difficult to understand when the prevalence rate for this trauma is so high throughout our nation, especially for females.

Preference for a female therapist who is educated and well trained is not uncommon or unusual for women who have been sexually abused as children, nor is it uncommon or unusual for a woman to encounter the types of experiences and beliefs identified above. Therefore, it is healthy and assertive of women to realize that the criterion in choosing a therapist does need to include their comfort level with the therapist, their willingness to establish a level of trust within the therapeutic relationship, and the experience, education, training, and therapeutic effectiveness of the therapist. When women come to treatment having confidence in their therapeutic choice, this confidence becomes a strength that they can build on throughout their healing.

At times, women express a preference for working with a therapist who has recovered from childhood sexual abuse, because they feel that someone who has healed will understand firsthand both the experience and the effects of this specific trauma and that she can be an excellent source of support and a role model for their own recovery. While being able to relate to this trauma firsthand can create a specific kind of empathy and understanding, equally important would be the healing that has occurred for the therapist as well. The desire to work with someone who has been through this trauma and has healed is understandable. Individuals often seek help from those who have had similar experiences and who seem to have come through life experiences to a place of being restored. In a similar manner, human beings often look to role models to help them identify how they too can overcome difficult times and achieve a life of well-being. However, the childhood experience of sexual abuse does not necessarily translate into a qualification to work as a therapist in the field of trauma recovery.

Conversely, a specific educational degree may not translate into experience or therapeutic effectiveness in working with this trauma, either.

One Woman's Experience

Celia Ferrand (age forty-four) shares her experience in the search for a qualified therapist to support her recovery from childhood sexual abuse. She shares her therapeutic encounters with two male therapists and two female therapists, each with different backgrounds, training, and levels of experience. She tells her story with humor, grace, and resolution. Celia relates well the importance of not giving up the search until a qualified therapist is found. She realistically illustrates what women might face in their search for a therapist. Celia also affirms the right women have to choose a therapist they feel connected to who has the qualities to help them heal from childhood sexual abuse.

Celia's Letter

My journey on the long road to wellness began in a "stress center" fifteen years ago. I packed a bag, called my sister to take care of my two children, and checked myself into the hospital. At the time, to say I was having a breakdown would have been an understatement; I was having a meltdown where I felt my inner core was exposed.

The resident therapist was an extremely book-smart fellow. He had a clinical answer for everything. He pointed out that the sexual abuse I had suffered throughout most of my childhood was having an impact on my life now. Intellectually, it all made sense to me, but my gut kept telling me something was off and not quite right. Eventually I made the connection as to what was causing me not to fully trust the therapy I was receiving. This clinical therapist reminded me of my husband—"keep your chin up, do your work, and all will be fine." Well, it did not turn out that way. I followed his advice, took my medications, but I was simply doing what I was told. So why was I not feeling any better after ten days in the hospital and numerous sessions with him after my release?

I mentioned to him at some point in the therapy that I did not feel we were finding the underlying cause of my "problem." He promptly handed me over to another male therapist. As a minister, this therapist too had good intentions. This man was kind, patient, and very wise, but again, something was off. While I believe that prayer will answer many things in my life, I also believe that God needs us to do the work. After several sessions, he suggested I bring the perpetrator along with me. It seemed liked a good idea at the time. I had visions of my therapist shaming this man into oblivion; I wanted my therapist to make him feel as badly as I had felt most of my life. I could not wait—I was ready for battle! As we sat down, it was quite clear from the beginning that this session was not going to be about what the perpetrator had done to me; it was going to be about finding out what had been done to him! I was stunned when my therapist began by saying to my abuser how sorry he was for him. He asked him what horrible thing had happened in his life to cause him to behave this way rather than asking him to acknowl-edge the horrible things he had done to me that had caused my life to be the way it was and had been for some years. Needless to say, that ended my sessions since I felt he really did not understand my pain at the hands of this individual.

The next therapist was a very young and inexperienced female social worker. She was fresh out of college with no experience in the field of sexual abuse. Our first session began with my telling her about my concerns. I began by letting her know that even after my hospital stay and working with two other therapists that I was not feeling as if I was making progress. I had received intensive group therapy at the hospital, and I thought it had hit on a few things. I wanted to get back to those "feelings" the staff was able to help me recognize. I knew these feelings had to be meaningful or my gut would not keep telling me to go back to them. She was clueless. She did not know where to begin, and she was the professional! She promptly dismissed me and sug-gested yet another therapist. I was beginning to feel as if I was a woman no one had ever dealt with, and neither was sexual abuse. Truthfully, I do not think anyone wanted to deal with it or me.

Therapist number four. I had absolutely no expectations for this one whatsoever, which, as it turns out, was a good thing. Very soon into our first session, she seemed distracted and I asked her what was wrong. (Now keep in mind, I am the one who supposedly needs a therapist!) She shared with me the fact that her six-year-old daughter was recently diagnosed with a malignant brain tumor. We ended up having a very lengthy conversation on the horror of this news for her and her family. I told her very honestly that I did not feel she should be counseling any-body at this point in her life. I needed undivided attention from my therapist, and she was not able to give that to me. Quite understand-ably, I suggested she take some time off to deal with this crisis. I am not sure whatever happened to her or her daughter. I hope all is well. I con-tinued my search.

The fifth and final therapist is the lasting one. I distinctly remember the atmosphere in her waiting room. It smelled of wildflowers and felt warm and peaceful. I thought to myself that this room did not seem at all clinical, but rather cozy. Yet, I brought with me all the months of searching and frustration and held my expectations at a minimum. She

came to greet me in the waiting room. She shook my hand and made me feel welcome. I was given a four-page questionnaire to complete. I thought to myself, "Huh? This is a new twist. I have not been asked to do this before." I completed all four pages and waited for her return. Now, by this time in my life I was resigned to the fact that I would have to muddle through this "chaos" in my head by myself. Why would this therapist be any different from the others? I had no desire to explain once again what had brought me to this point. I fully prepared myself for a quick discussion, and I would be gone.

I cannot remember at what point the infamous "connection" was made, but it was; I felt it. I felt it in my heart and in my gut. I was not sure how this woman was going to "cure" me, but I knew she would lead me in the right direction. As we talked, two things were clear to me. She had experienced similar issues, and she was female. It was a REVELA-TION! We had the same things in common. What more could you ask for? I quickly discovered I was not alone. Here was a woman sitting in front of me who was able to help other women heal. She was a godsend.

I continued to see her for several months. Each time it was as if a little more of the "poison" was being extracted from my soul. She kept pulling it out of me a little at a time. She could relate to what I was feeling and had experienced. As time went on, I began talking with my sisters about my therapy because they began to notice something about me that was different. The rage and anger were subsiding, and an understanding of my self was taking their place. You see, my sisters were also victims of this abuse. They all had their ways of dealing with it and being affected by it. Sexual abuse will manifest itself in one way or another. We all had the symptoms, but at that time, I was the only one seeking help for a cure that would come later for all of them. At the right time, I stopped seeing my therapist on a professional level. She had done all she could; the rest was up to me.

The search for the right therapist can be exhausting but necessary. I am a firm believer in "gut feelings." I trust them implicitly. You can intellectualize each issue of sexual abuse, twist it, and turn it to suit your needs, but it just will not go away. I harbor no ill feelings for the therapists who were not able to help me. I came to realize that they simply were not trained to deal with the issues of sexual abuse. They did not have the experience to know where to begin. Perhaps they did not know that the beginning for each woman is simply to listen and encourage. When you find the right therapist, you will know it because what she says to you will make sense. She will be someone who can guide you through this process of healing. Just do not give up!

If I could give but one piece of advice to women who are seeking help, it would be this. First, find someone who has been trained in this field.

Ask about the therapist's background. Do your homework. It is unfair to say that those who have not experienced abuse cannot counsel survivors, and asking them outright might be a bit too personal. At least start with a female. It has been my experience that men can feel uncomfortable discussing this issue. Sometimes they look at you as if you brought this on yourself. They simply do not know how to respond. Second, if you were sexually abused and still believe it has no influence on how you live your life today, think again. The abuse is the sickness, and your out-of-control lifestyle is the symptom. The abuse is at the core of everything. It is why you do the things you do. Having another woman sit across the room and understand that very complicated fact is invaluable.

I have talked with "K" a few times over the years. She was there when I finally decided to leave my husband. She knew it was coming; it was just a matter of time. Again, she was not surprised, only supportive. She has also been there when my oldest daughter was in a crisis. All I needed to hear was her calm reassuring voice on the other end of the phone to put things back into perspective. She has become for me a touchstone. Something I reach out for from time to time, not because I cannot figure it out on my own, but because sometimes things are still confusing. Our relationship has been as dear to me as other female relationships in my life. She has helped me discover the peace I had searched for and found I could have within my life. While this may be unusual to find in a therapist, it does exist. I have spoken before about the importance of my female friends, and I count her among them. While I was searching for a big strong man to rescue me, along came a soft-spoken woman who became my hero.

Celia Ferrand

Celia's letter describes well the commitment it takes to find a therapist who has the personal and professional qualities that a woman needs. As Celia stated, women should trust their instincts and listen to that voice within that will lead them to where they need to be. Finding a therapist who will meet both the personal and professional qualities that a woman seeks is possible. How well a woman relates to the therapist she chooses and her willingness to discuss her feelings regarding the therapist's approach or proposed recommendations are essential. Since assertiveness does not always come easy for women who have been sexually abused, taking a direct approach in discussing something will cause discomfort and will be a personal challenge. However, assertiveness within a therapeutic relationship should be one of the safest relationships in which women can practice discussing their feelings openly and honestly. If the discomfort is resolved, then continue; if it is not, then choose to contact another therapist. Just be sure that a pattern of withdrawal is not occurring, and if you suspect it is, then pause and ask, "What is creating this pattern of not choosing a therapist I can maintain a therapeutic relationship with for a period of time?" or "What is causing my repeated discomfort within a therapeutic relationship?"

The Choices Available

Today, there is an array of mental health services offered to the public. While the profession is growing, it is challenged in its effort to try to be all things to all people. Given the broad field of psychology and related areas such as social work and mental health in general, it is not unusual for clinicians, psychologists, counselors, therapists, and social workers to specialize in particular areas and to work in private individual practice, in a group practice with other therapists, with physicians, or at hospitals. Physicians such as psychiatrists offer specialized services just as gynecologists, internists, or surgeons do. When mental health professionals specialize, it is typically in an area where their interests are and where they focus their postgraduate training. Individual states offer licensing to qualified individuals, and insurance companies will reimburse for specific mental health services offered by certain types of licensed professionals. The educational degrees, licensing requirements, and insurance reimbursement can vary from state to state and from one insurance policy to the next. It is always a good idea to contact your insurance company to determine the amount of reimbursement for mental health services. At that time, women can ask their insurance representative if the mental health professional they have chosen is covered by their policy. If the therapist is covered, then women can ask what percentage of the cost for therapy will be covered by insurance. When a woman is part of a preferred provider network, she may still be able to see a therapist outside her network, but she needs to ask what level of reimbursement she will receive. Sometimes the reimbursement can be a lower amount than if she stays within the network. However, this network condition can be challenged when insurance providers do not offer specialized services in the treatment of this trauma. The variety of insurance coverage that is occurring today can be confusing for consumers; this is another reason for women to contact their insurance providers, take their time, and do their homework as they go through the steps of choosing a therapist and understanding their insurance coverage.

The Therapeutic Approach

Asking about the approach a therapist takes is helpful because the approach determines the appropriateness of applied treatment and therefore the outcome. As covered in Chapter 5, women are encouraged to inquire about the beginning process. For example, ask if an assessment process is involved in determining treatment recommendations and if clients receive a copy of their assessment results and treatment plan to review and discuss. The assessment process and stages of healing presented in Chapter 5 can help guide women in the kind of questions they may want to ask of mental health professionals they are contacting.

Women are encouraged to ask about individual therapy versus group therapy and how they might occur within a treatment program. For example, the women I work with usually complete at least a year of individual therapy before they begin a recovery group with other women. This individual time in therapy helps them to build trust and establish a level of healing that they bring to their recovery group. The feedback I receive from women has encouraged me to continue this approach. Women also find it helpful when they are given an idea of what topics are presented in a recovery group and what boundaries are in place for the group. These questions are reviewed before a woman is admitted to the group.

Asking questions before making a commitment to a therapist helps to gain some idea of what will be involved in working with a particular therapist and to build confidence in the therapeutic relationship. Writing questions down before that first telephone call is useful. Women need to ask about fees, insurance reimbursement, available appointment times, crisis support, and anything else they might consider important in making a decision about their healing. Most therapists I know welcome questions and want to provide information to potential clients.

Coordinating Care with Physicians

Physicians are in a better position to follow a medical course of treatment that supports a patient's healing when they have information regarding the underlying cause of symptoms their female patients are experiencing. Women who receive coordinated care are more likely to have the effects of the trauma specifically understood by health care providers and have a team of professionals who are working together on their behalf. Physicians and mental health professionals can be a valuable resource to each other, especially when it comes to healing this trauma with women. Unlike several years ago, when women first began to seek treatment for this trauma, today physicians and therapists are more knowledgeable about childhood sexual abuse and the treatment of associated problems such as depression, anxiety, and chronic pain.

The decision for women to talk with their physicians about this trauma can be important to their recovery in the short-term and the long-term. For example, an exchange of information can help identify the most effective medication for depression or anxiety by sharing test results that specify

symptoms matching a particular medication's therapeutic attributes. Exchange of information can assist with monitoring the side effects of medication as well. When women have physical effects of abuse such as chronic pain or migraines, a physician and therapist working together can recommend a course of treatment that might be most appropriate. For example, women may not benefit from more medication for these symptoms during certain stages of recovery; rather, they may be helped by relaxation techniques such as yoga, physical activity such as walking, or perhaps biofeedback to manage and alleviate their discomfort and decrease symptoms of pain.

When a therapist and physician establish a rapport with each other and communicate about treatment, women are the ones who benefit. Their health care does not have to be fragmented even when the physician, therapist, or other health care providers are not in the same physical location. All it takes is time and effort, two areas of practice all health care providers need to make sure they have enough of before accepting an individual as a client or a patient. Women need to consider the benefits to them and any reluctance they may have before they agree to a release of information on their behalf. Remember, women have the right to decide whom they want to share with and what they want to share, and this decision includes sharing with their physician. When women have a reason for not feeling comfortable with their physician or other health care provider, then they are encouraged to consider changing their provider and finding someone they are comfortable being open with.

The Amount of Time in Recovery

Most women ask about the amount of time they will be in therapy. Each woman is unique, and so different factors determine how long recovery may take for an individual woman. As stated previously, foremost will be her commitment to recover and her willingness to make changes in her life. Age can be a factor. The age when the abuse began and ended (if it has ended) and the age at which she begins to heal are considerations. A woman's age at the time of the abuse determines in what ways and for how long the abuse affected her development. How long the abuse occurred (days, months, weeks, or years) and what resources the child had available to her will also influence time in treatment.

Who the perpetrator was determines the closeness of the relationship, the level of trust, the sense of betrayal, and the amount of secrecy about the abuse. For example, a father, stepfather, grandfather, or brother is closer to a child's inner circle of trust than a cousin or uncle; however, what remains important is how the child felt about the perpetrator prior to the cycle of abuse beginning. There are individual differences as to how sexual abuse affects a child and later the woman she becomes. While this may seem vague, and although there are common issues related to childhood sexual abuse for all women, the reality is that the specific expression of the effects of sexual abuse are individualized by a woman's experience of abuse, internal and external resources, personality, age, and relationship to the perpetrator as well as the amount of time the abuse occurred, the specific acts of abuse, and the family belief system of secrecy and denial. The nature of this trauma has a specific and direct impact upon each child it occurs to, and while the impact is similar among children, it is unique to each child.

Another factor is whether there was more than one perpetrator sexually abusing the child. In most families where sexual abuse happens, it is common for more than one perpetrator to exist. Criminal justice reports indicate that perpetrators abuse several children over many years, not just one child.[11] Women who were sexually abused by more than one perpetrator will need to work through the healing process either for each perpetrator or for the specific effects caused by each perpetrator. Also, if there were other traumas that the child experienced while the abuse was occurring, such as frequently changing schools, chronic illness or death of a parent, divorce(s), and alcoholism, these traumas will also impact the time in recovery.

Summary of Therapeutic Choices

The importance of a woman's commitment to heal from childhood sexual abuse and her willingness to make changes in her adult life are significant factors in the effectiveness she will experience in healing this trauma. While a woman never takes responsibility for the abuse, she will need to take responsibility for her recovery. What this means is that women have to be willing to go to therapy, admit that they were sexually abused as children, acknowledge and accept that it is a trauma that has affected them at some level and in specific ways throughout their lives, and talk about the abuse and its effects with their therapists. A woman may face decisions about the family she grew up in and whether she is going to remain a part of her family dynamics or if she will need to stay separate from those who are a part of the painful past.

Therefore, when women come upon difficult times in their healing, and they will have difficult times, they will be able to persevere because they have commitment, willingness, and an internal resolve to heal. Remember: healing from childhood sexual abuse is a commitment a woman makes to herself. She heals because she is worth it. She can do it with the support of others and with the grace of her inner strengths and personal character. Women have to be able to listen to the voice within that was silenced long ago, the voice that tells them it is time for their healing to begin.

Steps to Support Recovery

The following steps are offered to give women an idea of what they can do and will need to do as they recover. These recommendations build on a day-to-day process. The changes they bring occurs over time, not overnight!

1. Listen to therapy tapes and write in a journal the ideas, themes, insights, and content of your sessions.
2. Write down negative beliefs and then write healthy, life-affirming beliefs.
3. Read a daily affirmation book and think about how you might be able to use the affirmations in your life.
4. Read recovery books on topics such as sexuality, depression, and family relationships that are specific to your healing. Identify what you relate to and share this information with your therapist and one other person you trust.
5. Let your therapist know at the beginning of the session that there is something that you need to talk about.
6. Identify and write down your boundaries with other people and review them daily or weekly. Allow your boundaries to guide your decisions.
7. Set one or two daily goals that define how you will live your life that day. Start small and build.
8. Attend support meetings. These can be meetings of spiritual faith, meditation groups, or 12-step programs such as Alcoholics Anonymous or Al-Anon.
9. Plan your day.
10. Get up at the same time every day.
11. Eat healthy and avoid fad diets.
12. Exercise at least fifteen minutes each day. Make it fun!
13. Try a new activity such as yoga, dance, walking, archery, bowling—something you have not tried in your adult life.
14. Identify one leisure activity that gives you joy. Then do it!
15. Write down your memories in a memory journal. Each time you write a memory, close the journal until your next therapy session. Share your memories with your therapist at the beginning of your session. Tear out the page and ask your therapist to keep it.
16. Become aware of the behaviors you want to change and develop a plan to change. For ideas and to stimulate creative thought, ask other people how they made changes in their lives.
17. Write down at least three compliments to yourself a day. Say "thank you" when other people compliment you.
18. Pay attention to your language. How do you speak about yourself or to yourself? How do you speak to or about other people? Do you use sarcasm and criticism more often than not?
19. Identify your fears. List three fears and what caused you to develop them.
20. Practice deep breathing for ten minutes at least three times a day. Driving is a good time to practice breathing.
21. Take time to be proud of yourself. Write notes of encouragement to yourself and read them whenever you feel discouraged.

22. Celebrate life and the joy of healing!
23. Cry and feel your sadness. Do not allow the sadness to be frozen inside of you.
24. Write a thank-you note to at least three people who have supported your recovery.
25. Start with one goal from this list and work with it for thirty days.
26. Reinforce the commitment to your journey of healing by observing consistency.
27. Love the woman you are and the woman you have yet to become; she is right there within you.

Recovery Tools

Recovery tools support the journey to heal rather than diminish it. They can remind women that healing is possible when they follow through.

Recovery Tool	NOT a Recovery Tool
Attending therapy	Not keeping therapy appointments
Taping your sessions	Not listening to your tapes
Keeping a journal	Not sharing your journal in therapy
Sharing honestly with others	Lying or distorting the truth
Leisure time and hobbies	Keeping busy and overworking
Quiet time and meditation	Drinking alcohol or taking drugs to relax
Discovering a spiritual practice	Blaming God for the abuse
Talking to people you trust	Isolation and loneliness
Setting boundaries	Remaining nonassertive
Supportive relationships	Damaging relationships
Honesty with yourself	Denial of the abuse or other problems
Slowing down your life	Rushing around in a state of stress
Making choices about your time	Over-committing yourself
Using short-term coping skills	Survival skills as patterns of responding
Using your voice	Keeping silent

As you discover your own recovery tools, share them with other women you know.

Making Decisions

Recovery is a time when women make decisions that enable them to create and live the life they want today. Women are reminded to be thoughtful about their decisions and not rush them. Women learn to slow down their thinking so that they can have confidence in the decisions they make today. Learning to listen to their feelings and to act with love toward themselves will become more consistent with the life they want to lead. View some of the decisions that were made before beginning recovery as behavior that reflected a maladaptive pattern brought on by the sexual abuse, especially if regret is felt about these past decisions. Women can reframe the decisions they are facing today in terms of how their recovery enables them to make informed decisions that does not follow a destructive pattern from the past.

Some women will face decisions about their marriage, children, family, and/or job. Some women question whether they made the right decision in marrying their spouse. Other women need to learn to remake decisions about their children in terms of the kind of parent they have been. Still others are faced with learning to detach from an abusive family in order to attain the freedom to walk their own path. Some may also want to rethink their job, since some jobs intensify the experience of work compulsions to avoid feelings of pain or to create false self-esteem. A friendship may also need to be reevaluated in terms of whether it is mutual—you receive as well as give—or one-sided friendship in which you are the sole receiver or giver. Women should be prepared if some of their friendships change or they drift away from former friends. Remember: women are creating room in their lives for new experiences. The important thing is to consider what decisions will create the life a woman wants that is fulfilling.

After Treatment

I always like to remind women that treatment ends and recovery goes on. Recovery becomes how a woman lives her life free of the abuse and its effects. Women do not need to continue in therapy for the rest of their lives, but they do need to live their lives mindful of their recovery and healing. A perspective to share with women about the time they have invested in healing is, "From the time the sexual abuse happened you went (fill in the number) years with the effects of childhood sexual abuse creating problems and impacting your life. If you invest one year, or three years, in recovering your life, how valuable has that time been? What has this time been worth to you?" As one woman said, "I will take five years of healing over forty years of pain anytime!"

I also remind women to remember what they know about recovery and how it works. To monitor their emotional health, I encourage them to have a yearly therapy checkup so they can review how their life is going. I also affirm that they can call anytime. They do not have to wait for a crisis to occur, since waiting for a crisis is not really living their recovery. I also help women develop a relapse list that they can review at any time to determine whether former patterns of thinking or behaving are reoccurring in their life. Once they recognize a relapse issue, they develop a plan that takes them back to their recovery. Remember: If you wait for a crisis, it will find you!

SUPPORTING YOUR HEALING

1. What beliefs do you have about recovery and healing?
2. What is your greatest fear about healing?
3. Have you contacted or seen a therapist before? What was your experience? How did you benefit or not benefit?
4. Do you accept that healing takes time?
5. Can you define your commitment to heal?
6. What do you view as your personal strengths? What could be potential barriers?
7. How might others resist your recovery?
8. How might others be supportive?
9. What decisions are you facing in your life right now?
10. Will these decisions have a positive or negative effect upon your decision to heal?

10

The Voices of Women

Know this child will be gifted
With love, with patience, and with faith
She'll make her way, she'll make her way
—Natalie Merchant, "Wonder"

The writing of this book has been a lifetime goal that has finally been fulfilled. When I began my practice as a therapist, I did not know that I would end up where I am—working with women and children to heal the trauma of sexual abuse. I am not quite sure how I chose this area of clinical practice. At times I think it chose me! Either way, it has brought me both personal and professional satisfaction and afforded me the opportunity to continue my quest for knowledge.

As a young graduate student, fresh out of a master's program, I, like most of us, thought I knew more than I really did. I found out that while I knew the basics I still had a great deal to learn, and over the years among my teachers have been the women and children who call me their therapist and sometimes their friend. Each woman and child has taught me something about this trauma and how it affects the child at the time it happens or the person she became as she endured through the aftermath of what I have come to appreciate as a profound and direct change in the lives of each of them. With each interview, assessment, social history, and treatment plan, I learned that not only does this trauma reverberate throughout a child's life, but the spirit of that child somehow is retained. As each one of them allowed me to touch their lives, they touched mine as well.

At times I have been shocked and then angered at the laxness of the criminal justice system and the people who make criminal justice their profession. I have had the opportunity to work with dedicated judges and prosecutors who strive to bring justice to a child who has been sexually abused and who manage to show compassion even after so many years in their profession. I have experienced child protection caseworkers who do not return calls, respond to letters, or seem to care about reported child sexual abuse. I have also witnessed some very dedicated ones who are not given the recognition and financial support they deserve for the job they do. At times I have had calls from detectives who seem to know the right questions to ask about this crime, and at other times I have never had my calls returned from police officers who are supposed to be investigating this crime committed to a child.

In court, I have testified before judges and juries. Some of these judges are educated about this crime and are able to bring that knowledge to a case and assist jurors in understanding this particular type of crime and the people—children—who are affected by it. At the same time, I have often wondered why we do not have seminars and workshops for jurors to receive information about child sexual abuse that would assist them in understanding testimony of both the victim and the accused and deciding the justice that will occur. It concerns me when I see jurors make decisions based on ignorance and misinformation rather than knowledge and when I see attorneys who are as manipulative and contriving as the people they represent.

Families play a particular role in the exposure of child sexual abuse. I keep waiting for the day when all parents support their children in healing from this trauma. As a therapist, I came to a decision that I could only work with children whose parents were supportive of a child telling about this crime and reporting it to the authorities and who would bring their children to therapy. Otherwise, I experienced emotions too reminiscent of my own childhood and frustrations that interfered with my clinical judgments and ability to work with these parents even when I knew I was helping their children. While I look for these qualities in partners, parents, and family members of the women I work with, they, like me, are at times disappointed. Even as adults, they can continue to lack the support, care, compassion, and understanding that they deserve.

The legal system can let down as many children and women as it helps. This crime seems to be like no other that this system investigates and prosecutes. Even now, in the early twenty-first century, the criminal justice system still has not come to terms with cases of child sexual abuse where there are seldom any witnesses to this crime other than the child and the perpetrator, where physical evidence is not always available for them to make for a "good case," and where perpetrators are able to go free due to the limits of the law's ability to prosecute them. While sometimes I believe the ability to bring justice to children will eventually come, I doubt this more days than I believe it. But it is the only system available, so we have to keep working within it to bring about necessary changes so that children are eventually kept safe.

When Megan's Law was challenged, I was truly taken aback. While a firm believer in civil liberties and individual rights, I also believe that when an adult harms a child and is found guilty in our courts of having done so, that adult has abdicated his or her rights to seek protection under the same set of laws. Frankly, I think a vital measure toward keeping children safe is for identified perpetrators to be kept on sex offender registries for life. As stated by William E. Prendergast, considered an authority in the treatment of sex offenders,

> In the aftercare treatment I have conducted with paroled and maxed-out sex offenders for nearly thirty years, there has never been a single individual who has not admitted to me at some time in his aftercare treatment that he had lied during inpatient therapy, either directly or by omission. This occurs most often when the return of a deviant fantasy has occurred, especially if he was somewhere in the release process. The most commonly used justification is that he will handle it when he is released and that if he admitted it at the time it occurred he would be punished by being removed from the release process and delayed another year or more. It is only when the problem begins recurring in the community where real victims, not fantasy ones, are available that he panics and decides to admit it in an aftercare session.[1]

Dr. Prendergast makes the point of never believing what a sex offender tells you. Even during and after prosecution, sentencing, time in prison, and the opportunity to return to society, the offender continues to lie and mislead others about his abnormal behavior. These are the facts we need to know, accept, and act on if we as a society are to protect our children from these individuals who would continue to perpetrate the crime of child sexual abuse.

I hope all women, men, and children who have been sexually abused have the opportunity to travel the path of recovery and restore their lives through healing. Each one deserves to be heard, understood, and believed. I also believe that each individual deserves her or his day in court whereby the perpetrator is brought to justice and not protected by statutes of limitation. Each perpetrator who is held accountable and not excused for his crime due to the number of years since it was committed and hidden is another perpetrator who hears the message that this crime will no longer be tolerated.

Finally, I am starting a research study on the relationship of child sexual abuse to eating disorders and cosmetic surgery. Readers interested in being a part of this study may contact me at my website at www.Healing4Women.com.

Pass the word—healing is possible. May we all walk the path of healing and find our way back to the lives we so richly deserve.

LETTERS FROM WOMEN

As this book was being written, some of the women I have worked with over the years were asked to write letters about what their recovery has meant to them. I hope the reader finds inspiration from what these women share.

Kathy is the sister in a family where sexual abuse occurred to her siblings. I had the privilege of meeting Kathy when one of her sisters asked for a family session and invited Kathy and her other sisters to attend. These sisters shared openly that day and in doing so broke through the remnants of denial and secrecy that had remained within their family for many years. The other letters are written by Penny, Sharon, Pat, Mickey, Celia, and Sandy. They are women sexually abused as children who chose to heal this trauma. I have worked with each of them at some time over the years. I admire their courage, perseverance, and tenacity. To paraphrase Pat, they are all works of art.

Dear Friend in Recovery,

The life that I know and enjoy today would not be possible without recovery. Before recovery, I was merely surviving the days instead of living them. To me, living means that I am no longer a victim of circumstances. Regardless of what happened in the past, I now make the decisions that steer the course of my life. I do not give my power away to anyone and do not apologize for my thoughts, feelings, words, actions and choices. I own all of my life, good and bad.

Recovery began the day that I understood that my life was a lie. As I learned to be honest with others, and myself, I was free to be me (flaws and all). The love I felt for myself would not allow me to lie anymore. Honesty did not make me popular with friends and family who were part of the lie and liked things just the way were. I had to determine who to keep in my life and to whom I would say goodbye. The people who have encouraged me and enriched my life are my angels on this earth. We share an unshakeable bond built on truth.

Self-preservation is the key to my continued recovery and healing. I often remind myself that recovery is a life-long journey and in order to stay healthy, I cannot give to others until I give to myself. There are only 24 hours in a day and I have a limited amount of energy that I can expend so I carefully choose what and to whom I give this precious resource. I thank Karen for shining the light so I could find my way on the path to recovery and healing. She validated my feelings and choices, helping me stand tall until I was strong enough to stand on my own. She and you are my sisters on this journey. I know that I am blessed.

With Love, Kathy

Dear Friend in Recovery,

Healing is a tough journey and I hope you are met with love and support in your disclosure of childhood sexual abuse.

If you have told, I pray that those with whom you have shared will help you, support you and love you. If not put those keys in the car and drive to where you are cared about and understood. Use your voice to talk about the trauma because opening up to one person starts the healing process. Perhaps one day abuse will no longer exist, but until then we need to expose it.

I love Alice Walker's movie and book *The Color Purple*. Ms. Walker believes that God finds great happiness in a field of purple flowers. It is an awe-inspiring picture. I believe that God also finds great happiness when he sees a gathering of persons who start to face what has happened to them from the past and who are now finally discovering what person God truly meant for them to be in this lifetime.

I disclosed to several friends. Three of my friends have been phenomenal. While they all live in different areas of the country, I call them whenever I need to be in contact and feel their support. How much support you need is up to you. If one person is enough and you honor each other, then that is great. If you need more then do your research and find the support you need to heal.

I wish you success. The best of all possible worlds can happen. It will be slow but as women, men and children heal, we act as the spokespersons to expose this trauma and stop the abuse in our lifetime.

With love, Penny

Dear Friend in Recovery,

I am writing to express my gratitude for the healing that I have had in my life. With the help of therapy, I came to realize the secret of the sexual abuse that I had kept for almost forty years was not my secret to keep any longer.

Through my years of growing up and forming relationships, I shut out my mind to the shame and the lack of self-respect I felt. Over the years these suppressed feelings built to a horrible rage. Through sharing and talking about my experience, I began to release myself from the bond of the abuse.

Until my recovery, I had felt that I was not good enough and I let men use me and abuse me. It took my therapy and a wonderful, understanding, compassionate counselor to open my mind and free me so that I could be at peace with myself and realize I deserved to be treated with respect and love and that no one had the right to control me anymore.

I feel sincere gratitude for what therapy and healing brought to my life,

Sharon

Dear Friend in Recovery,

Recovery to me represents truth. The truth about the abusers, the truth about who I am and the truth about how I feel. Recovery means courage to face the darkness within, to face it, embrace it and to accept that sexual abuse really was a part of life and was too long denied.

Recovery means coming into the light of reality instead of living in perpetual denial and hiding. I am now able to accept more of myself and take responsibility for how I feel instead of focusing on how someone else feels. Recovery means freedom, choices, and the knowledge that I have a choice. Recovery has meant understanding my past for the first time in my life and knowing that the sexual abuse was not my fault, which is one of the biggest gifts of all.

Recovery is a constant work of art with moments of great clarity. It is also moments of struggle and doubt. In essence, I see it as a part of life's journey as I heal from abuse and from any other situation that may arise in the future.

Pat

Dear Friend in Recovery,

Recovery is not something I thought I would ever be able to do. I thought the feelings and memories I had were so deeply buried that I would never have to face them again. I did not realize that I had to face them in order to heal myself and be able to live my life to the fullest.

I have gone through the entire spectrum of feelings during this process. Sometimes I do this on a daily basis—sometimes in a matter of minutes. It is confusing and hard to sort out, but I am learning that this too is necessary and a part of the process. I am learning to feel again and that may be the hardest part for me.

I am beginning to listen to my inner voice. I did not seem to have a problem listening to this voice where others were concerned, but it has been a long time since I have listened to the messages I was sending myself. I could not seem to put value in my thoughts or feelings. After the trauma, I felt that I had no worth. My value was so diminished and I felt that no one else listened to me so why should I listen to myself. I am trying to take the time to find out exactly what it is that I want and map out a plan to get there.

I am beginning to feel stronger and more confident in my day to day interactions with people. Some of them are not easy but I am trying not to avoid confrontations that I know will be uncomfortable. At times, I hear something come out of my mouth and I think where did that come from? I feel like I am gaining a better understanding of some of the feelings I have concerning the abuse. I cannot say I am comfortable with them, but I am trying to understand the impact they have had on my life. By trusting my inner voice, I have been able to verbalize the anger and hurt that I feel toward my parents. I may never be able to express these feelings to them, but being able to share the feelings is helpful.

Overall, I think I am experiencing many changes within myself. I am grasping the full impact of all that I am feeling. I am trying not to get discouraged when something does not go as I think it should or feel the way I think I should feel. My comfort level with feelings has inched upward. I still feel there is a long way to go. So much of what I feel is still unclear, unsettled, confusing, complicated and uncomfortable. I know I need to be patient and let it all unfold; it is just so difficult at times.

I think of my recovery like this: I am learning to ride a bicycle for the first time. My therapist is holding the bike and a little at a time she will let go. I know that I may fall, but at least for now I take comfort in the fact that she will be there to pick me up. Someday I will be able to ride that yellow Schwinn with the banana seat alone.

Your friend, Mickey

Dear Friend in Recovery,

To me recovery means that I have finally started to live the life that should have been mine to begin with before the sexual abuse happened. It means to live with no more secrets and that I no longer cover up what I am feeling. Recovery is not only understanding your feelings, but also knowing they are true and real to you. Simply put, recovery is living!

Sandy

Dear Friend in Recovery,

For me, recovery is peace—peace of mind, body, spirit and soul. Sounds like a lot to ask I know, but I had to believe it was out there, and I would not stop until I found it even though I was not at all sure how or where it would come. After years of self-medication, destructive behavior and the "swirl" of madness that surrounds this type of abuse, the layers were peeled away and behold the peace came from within. Yes, it is there.

For so many years, I thought something was wrong with me, when in fact it was not me at all. I was simply a product of my environment that included a perpetrator. Someone and something else created who I was rather than who I wanted to be. This is where women like us make the fatal mistake of blaming ourselves for "letting" this happen. I carried enormous guilt because I did not say "No" or somehow get away from the perpetrator. I was thirty years old when my therapist told me that in talking with the perpetrator she had found out that I was only three years old when the sexual abuse began. This confession of how young I was when he began the abuse came from my abuser. I distinctly remember the feeling that came over me when I learned how young I was at the time it began. I did not know whether to laugh, to cry or to throw up. That was the beginning of my healing. While my abuser admitted to what he had done, he showed little if any remorse. This also ended my fantasy of his falling to his knees and begging my forgiveness. He did however become less and less frightening to me. Today he has shriveled away to a small shadow in the recesses of my mind. The rage and anger are gone and have been replaced with pity for this man. What goes around comes around, and it did for him, for I have healed and he has not.

My life now is as it should be. It is not about finding the perfect man, job, car, etc. it is simply about discovery of one's self. That is truly the journey of a woman. Yes, it may take some of us until we are in our forties to begin, but we must find that beginning nonetheless. As women, we make a choice. We either choose to remain the product of the abuse or begin to rebuild the woman that we all had the right to become. For me it took a divorce after twenty years of marriage, reaching out to other women, building friendships and finding the incredible gift that women can give to each other. In the years since my divorce I have been fortunate to be blessed with the most wonderful female friends. While I was married, I was never allowed friends. Through these friendships, I have come to discover that the women in my life love me for who I am, with all my faults and fears. We support one another through single parenthood, raising teenagers and the realization that we are no longer in our twenties. We have become women who are wise and whole.

I look forward to the journey continuing and I am prepared to face the crossroads and negotiate them the best way I know how. Several years ago, *The Bridges of Madison County* was in the movies. Francesca, a passionate woman, was lost in the reality of everyday life. Determined that her children would know her for all that she was, she writes, "What a tragedy to never have been truly known." Know yourself as a woman so that others, who choose to, will know you as well.

Celia Ferrand

SUPPORTING YOUR HEALING

1. Take out your journal and write about what you visualize recovery from childhood sexual abuse will mean to you.
2. What positive changes do you see taking place in your life?
3. What changes will take place that will indicate you are healed?
4. What beliefs will change? How will your attitude about your self and your life change? How will you feel physically? Mentally? Emotionally? How will your behavior be different? How will your language be different?
5. What boundaries will you have that you do not have today? What will you understand about yourself?

APPENDIX A

Trauma and Memory

OVERVIEW OF MEMORY

Before we can begin to understand how trauma affects memory, we must first understand how ordinary memory occurs. The human brain functions as a center to integrate human experience into memory. Current research indicates that some structures of the brain are more involved with the formation, storage, and retrieval of memory than others. These structures are considered to be affected by trauma.

Memory is formed along the neurotransmissions that occur in the brain in response to sensory experience. The thalamus receives experience via the five senses: sight, sound, smell, touch, and taste. The hippocampus allows us to receive new information and assimilate it into existing memory, while the amygdala registers the emotional aspects of memory. The hypothalamus, along with the brain stem, regulates homeostasis, or the body's internal balance, as experience is transmitted and memory is formed. The interactions of these brain structures and the processes they complete contribute to the formation of normal memory.

The prefrontal cortex of the brain is also involved in memory since it integrates the social, emotional, physical, and narrative aspects of human experience. The right hemisphere of the brain processes the nonverbal aspect of experience such as tone of voice, gestures, facial expression, and the perception of emotion. In addition, the retrieval of personal biographical experiences appears to be mediated by the right hemisphere. In contrast, the left hemisphere processes experience in terms of looking for cause-and-effect relationships that will explain the rightness and wrongness of what is being experienced. In the formation of memory, the left and right hemispheres have a role in forming both a verbal narrative and an emotional context that enables an individual to understand and integrate her experience. How these various structures of the brain process, form, integrate, store, and recall ordinary memory allows a basis for understanding the effect that trauma has on memory.

TRAUMATIC MEMORY AND EMOTIONAL RESPONSE

Although not yet fully understood, the above structures and processes of the brain are thought to be directly affected when a traumatic experience occurs. For example, emotions of terror or fear are often experienced with a traumatic event. These emotions are highly charged neurologically, and this increased level of arousal disrupts the functional process among the structures of the brain. Formation of the traumatic experience into consolidated memory, assimilation of it within existing memory, and storage of it for later recall are interrupted. This is one explanation of how traumatic memory becomes fragmented and isolated from previous memory. The experience of a flashback is often an isolated and fragmented memory where details of the trauma are recalled in a disjointed manner. This highly charged arousal response might explain why the recall of traumatic memory is often emotionally intense and difficult to put into words. This occurrence of emotionally intense discharge could also explain the reoccurrence of chronic shock symptoms such as panic, hyperarousal, anxiety, and sleep disturbances. Therefore, trauma appears to disrupt the normal processes of the brain that would otherwise occur naturally to form memory.

For some individuals, the sensations that accompany traumatic events, whether sensations of touch, sight, smell, sound, or taste, are thought to remain in the mind, separate from other memory, and the passage of time alone does not diminish them. If this is true, then internal and external cues associated with the trauma trigger the reexperience of trauma sensations. Another aspect of the emotional intensity of traumatic memory is how prominent the perceptual recall is for the individual. For example, are the emotions of the trauma experienced in terms of sight, sound, and body sensations or sound and sight only? How often and for how long a particular image of the trauma continues to be experienced is also relevant to understanding the intensity of traumatic memory. Furthermore, while people are not always able to verbalize the traumatic experience, the emotional experience of the trauma still seems to exist. Just because a person is at a loss for words does not mean that the expression of the trauma is not occurring. This aspect of traumatic memory can explain why people engage in reenactment behavior as a nonverbal means to express their traumatic experience; if a person cannot express in words what happened to her, perhaps she is attempting to show through her behavior what went on during the traumatic event. This may also be why some women find drawing and painting or other mediums of art, such as clay, useful in expressing and processing traumatic experience.

LOSS OF MEMORY FOR TRAUMATIC EVENTS

The inability to recall or recollect in sequence memories of traumatic experiences is well documented by reported victim experience, observation in therapy, and findings from research. When loss of memory occurs or sequencing of the traumatic events is disrupted, dissociation is thought to have a role. Finally, general population studies cited by researchers show that childhood sexual abuse seems to result in the highest degree of total amnesia prior to the recall of memories.

These consistent observations and the research on traumatic memory have given rise to the theory that traumatic memories are processed differently from memories for ordinary events and that it is the degree of the trauma along with the individual's experience of it that contribute to this difference. Obviously, as research continues we will better understand the process of ordinary memory and in doing so will understand how the structures of the brain are affected when trauma occurs. From the findings of this research, we can look forward to applying what is learned to the successful treatment of trauma in general and childhood sexual abuse in particular.

TRAUMATIC MEMORIES AND STRESS

The intense emotional, physical, and mental aspects of traumatic memories stored within the brain may be the source of flashbacks, nightmares, and somatic responses experienced by women. Stresses that women experience in the present may also serve as a source of retriggering traumatic memories that are then expressed in intensified emotional responses, vivid mental images, and body sensations reminiscent, if not exact sensations, of the original trauma. Traumatic memories and the responses associated with them may be the underlying reason that traumatized individuals do not respond to stress in the same way that nontraumatized individuals do.

When stresses occur that retrigger emotional responses or mental images of the trauma, these responses overstimulate the individual and intensify her response to current stress. Thus, stress seems to promote retrieval of traumatic memories, and traumatic memories seem to increase the stress response. Perhaps the current stress taps into the emotionally charged aspect of the past trauma. This relationship between stress and trauma would explain why it is often a stress-related occurrence that brings women to treatment years after the sexual abuse. It also supports an understanding of how somatic sensations and flashbacks are often experienced without a direct ability to verbalize them or connect them to the time and place when they originally occurred.

SUMMARY

The structures of the brain responsible for the consolidation of experience into ordinary memory are likely affected by trauma, as indicated by current research, clinical observations, and the narrative recall of victims. As the impact of trauma upon memory is understood, the application of what is learned to the treatment of childhood sexual abuse will be forthcoming.

Source: Adapted from *Healing Trauma: Attachment, Mind, Body, and Brain,* ed. Marion F. Solomon and Daniel J. Siegel (New York: W. W. Norton and Company, 2003), pp. 10–32 and 168–186; Bessel A. van der Kolk, Alexander C. McFarlane, and Lars Weisaeth, eds., *Traumatic Stress: The Effects of Overwhelming Experience on Mind, Body, and Society* (New York: The Guilford Press, 1996), pp. 217–241 and 279–297; and Charles L. Whitfield, *Memory and Abuse: Remembering and Healing the Effects of Trauma* (Deerfield Beach, Fla.: Health Communications, 1995), pp. 39–50 and 91–113.

APPENDIX B

Distorted Thought Patterns

Distorted thought patterns can form during childhood sexual abuse and from the family culture where it occurs. These patterns of thinking can continue to affect a woman's self-concept and identity, influence the choices she makes in her life, and perhaps contribute to a pattern of revictimization. The underlying beliefs that support these thought patterns are in italics. The thought patterns and underlying beliefs were identified from women within this treatment approach. While they are not meant to be all-inclusive, they are meant to stimulate a woman's evaluation of her own thought patterns related to sexual abuse and the underlying beliefs that helped form them or maintain them from the time of the abuse until today.

1. I focus more on what I do wrong or what I fail at than what I do right or well. Consequently, I berate myself when I have failed at something I tried or belittle what I do well. *If I had done more things right, I would not have been sexually abused.*

2. If I am not perfect in what I do, how I look, or who I am, then I am less than and not as good as other people. *If I had been perfect, looked a different way, or acted a different way, then the sexual abuse would not have happened.*

3. I do not deserve the love or respect of other people. *I need to do more, be more, and give more in order for people to love and respect me.*

4. I am not liked by other people because I am not good enough for them to be my friend. *If I had been a better person, the abuse would not have happened. If people knew the real me, they would not like me.*

5. I can never trust that anything good in my life will last because it either ends or goes away and then I am left to pick up the pieces. *People are not trustworthy and neither is life; both will disappoint you and let you down. It's better not to want anything than to be disappointed.*

6. I have no control over my life or what happens to me; therefore, I just have to accept what occurs and try to make the best of it. *What I said or did never stopped the perpetrator from abusing me. Nothing I say or do makes a difference, so why bother?*

7. I am helpless to effect changes in my life. *I was a victim in my childhood and will always be a victim.*

8. When I am giving to other people and helping them is when I feel good about me. *The only value I have is what I can do for others.*

9. I am always right and other people just do not want to admit this truth. *I was wrong to trust that the perpetrator would not harm me. I will never allow myself to be wrong again about whom I trust, so I only trust me.*

10. I do not like it when people break the rules; it is not fair and they should be punished. *If I had followed the rules in my family, I would not have been abused.*

11. I must be the irrational one because other people seem to make more sense in what they say about how I should live my life. *I do not trust my own thoughts or perceptions because I can remember how I was told I was stupid, dumb, or wrong.*

12. Once I am rejected by someone, I should just give up trying and accept that I will never get their approval. If I do not receive approval from other people, I must have done something wrong. *I was never given acceptance and approval in my family, so why would I think I would receive it from anyone else?*

13. I am to blame for the pain I feel. *If I had not done things to cause me to be punished then* _____ *would not have punished me. (Fill in with a name or names.)*

14. I cannot be assertive because then other people will not like me. *If you speak up about what you need, then other people will think you are selfish and rude.*

15. If you do not win the argument, then you were wrong to begin with. *I am not smart enough to state my opinion in a manner so that other people will accept my opinion, support me, or understand me.*

16. Fighting only leads to more fighting, so it is better not to say anything. *Problems cannot get resolved in relationships because all anyone is interested in is being right and getting what they want regardless of whether someone else is hurt or upset.*

17. If other people would only follow what I say, then I could get along with them. *If other people disagree with you or are different from you, then they need to be brought back into your way of thinking and behaving or they deserve to be rejected.*

18. If people do _____ (fill in the blank with a rigid rule of behavior; a rigid rule is one that is meant to control someone), then they are only asking for trouble. *If you do not follow the rules, then bad*

things will happen and you deserve the bad things to happen to you for not following the rules.

19. I should never tell someone how I feel especially if I feel hurt, disappointed, or angry, because then that person will feel hurt, disappointed, or angry, and then I will feel bad for how I made that person feel. *I am responsible for other people's feelings. It is dangerous to tell other people what you feel because then they could use it against you.*

20. I do not like it when people want to do things for me. *You should never let anyone do you a favor or accept someone being nice to you because you end up owing that person or you become obligated to the person. I do not trust that people really want to be nice to you for no apparent reason; they usually want something in return.*

21. You should never talk about what goes on in your family because you are being disloyal. *Secrets are to be kept and never talked about, even with family members.*

22. Never question _____(fill in a name) because he/she will become angry. *Only certain people have the right to question someone in authority.*

23. I do not really like consistency and structure in my life. I like to be spur-of-the-moment and impulsive. *If you do not make plans, then you do not have to keep your commitments. If you say you will do something, then you do it no matter what.*

24. Chaos and crisis are just a normal part of life that you have to come to accept and adjust to. *There is no such thing as having a day free of problems.*

25. My family is like any other family; we have our problems, and we accept that they will always be there. *I can never talk about the problem of sexual abuse even when I know it has not stopped.*

APPENDIX C

Characteristics of a Healthy Family

The following can help women to define what a healthy family is and prevent unhealthy family characteristics from being passed on to the next generation. Healthy families

1. Define, teach, and respect each other's boundaries.
2. Talk and share openly with each other.
3. Do not tease and cause intentional pain to other family members.
4. Understand that good humor is shared. They are able to laugh at situations and not at each other.
5. Express anger and disagreement without losing control or acting in a defensive manner.
6. Respect individual feelings and welcome the sharing of emotions without labeling what someone else is feeling.
7. Do not intrude on one another.
8. Delight in each other's differences while sharing the common bond of being in a family with a shared history.
9. Trust each other. They realize that when trust is broken, amends need to be made for trust to be regained.
10. Apologize and take responsibility for their behavior.
11. Share in the responsibilities of the family. Each member joins in and shares appropriate household duties.
12. Have parents who teach and model what being in a healthy family means.
13. Show courtesy to each other.
14. Have parents who grow in their own development as adults.
15. Recognize what children need in order to grow in self-esteem and self-confidence.
16. Devote time to play and fun. They recognize that leisure and hobbies are important for individual growth.

17. Show flexibility and consistency rather than adhering to arbitrary and authoritarian rules.
18. Seek and are open to new information. They are not threatened by change or new ideas.
19. Teach morals and values. They do so without judging and condemning each other or other people.
20. Share their spirituality and enhance each other's growth as spiritual people who believe in a divine influence in their lives.
21. Develop and practice positive and meaningful traditions that are passed on to each generation.
22. Respect privacy and model behavior that affirms the right to privacy in the home.
23. Help each other in a supportive and caring manner.
24. Admit to problems and seek help to solve problems when needed.
25. Promote outside friendships.
26. Strike a balance between joyful work and relaxing leisure.
27. Compliment each other and affirm the uniqueness of each family member.
28. Allow natural consequences to occur that teach through life experiences.
29. Do not punish in a harsh and destructive manner.
30. Seek new opportunities to promote diversity among family members.

APPENDIX D

Symptoms of Chronic Shock

The following are symptoms of chronic shock that can occur in relation to childhood sexual abuse as a traumatic experience:

Physical Symptoms	Mental Symptoms	Emotional Symptoms
A change in breathing pattern occurs; the breath is constricted and when it resumes it is shallow, ragged, and uneven.	The processes in the brain that help to form memory are disrupted; the child may not be able to access images of the abuse or they may not be sequential.	Fear and anxiety are experienced; feelings of terror often lead to a panic response. Obsessive thoughts may occur in response to fear and anxiety.
Muscles tense and there is increased tightness felt throughout the body; an inability to move occurs and a "frozen in place" response happens.	The processing of information related to the experience is interrupted. This interruption can affect her ability to recall the trauma later on in life or to put it into words.	The child feels overwhelmed and flooded with emotions brought on by the perpetrator's behavior. Compulsive acts occur to manage and control these emotions.
Face and skin lose color and feel cold and clammy, then hot flushes occur and the skin feels sweaty. The experience of the trauma may reoccur as aftershock symptoms.	The mind goes blank, and thoughts that occurred during the abuse seem to disappear. The child's ability to verbally tell about the sexual abuse is impaired.	Emotions are numbed and experienced later as an absence of feelings or the inability to feel. The child does not experience a full range of emotions, or emotions are restricted.

Physical Symptoms	Mental Symptoms	Emotional Symptoms
A look of vacancy and distance appears in the eyes, giving the appearance of not seeing or registering what is occurring.	Dissociation occurs and can be called upon to prevent the trauma from intruding on a daily basis; the mind disconnects from the trauma by blocking or forgetting memories.	Emotional suppression is related to a child's attempts to avoid remembering the trauma. Sensory impressions often remain intact but are fragmented and isolated from the visual image of the abuse.
Easily startled and does not like to be surprised by someone's sudden presence. Hypervigilant and may scan for danger.	Memories of the abuse are fragmented; isolated details may be recalled at various times; a loss of time and place can occur.	Depression occurs since the child is helpless to stop the abuse and realizes the perpetrator will not stop his behavior.
Difficulty falling asleep; easily awakened when sleeping; may not be able to stay asleep. Often wakes up during the time the abuse occurred.	Shortened attention span; inability to concentrate; disjointed and disorganized thought patterns about the abuse.	Intense anxiety feelings occur that can shift dramatically and seem to change from one moment to the next.
Hyperaroused when perceived danger or threat from others is determined to exist. Situations trigger this response.	May not process the emotional impact of the trauma; may deny the trauma and lack clarity about the traumatic event.	May isolate from others; intense reaction to invasion of privacy or may not know the concept of personal boundaries.
Speech is rapid, disjointed, or disrupted; may lose the ability to speak or be unable to express the traumatic experience in narrative form.	Trauma has a surreal or dreamlike quality; experienced as being unreal. Will doubt her perceptions and experiences confusion.	Low frustration tolerance. Can experience the loss of emotion or a lack of appropriate emotion in response to an event.

APPENDIX E

Managing Anxiety

The following are suggestions about what you can do to help manage symptoms of anxiety:

Physical Symptoms:	What You Can Do:
Flushing	Cool shower or bath
Sweating	Cool drink or shower
Dry mouth	Cool drink of water
Shallow, rapid breathing	10–20 deep breaths from the belly; repeat as needed
Chest constriction	Open your arms wide, stretch upward, and breathe deeply
Heart palpitations	10–20 deep breaths lying down; repeat as needed
Intestinal and gastric upsets	Chamomile tea, toast, or and crackers
Muscle tightness	Stretching, massage or a warm bath
Tremors	Warm bath, or blanket wrap
Easily startled	Deep breathing; state a boundary
Freezing or freezing up	Wrap yourself in a blanket; take deep breaths; repeat a mental affirmation that you are safe

Yoga, which combines deep breathing with stretching, meditation, and relaxation, is one of the best methods to decrease anxiety. Call your YMCA, look in the yellow pages, or contact your community center for a class schedule.

Emotional Symptoms:	What You Can Do:
Restless, agitated	Clean closets; organize or do yard work, do something physical.
Panic	Deep breathing, walks outside
Depression	Uplifting music, take walks
Irritability	Hit a punching bag, tear up magazines, punch a pillow

Cognitive (Mental) Symptoms	What You Can Do
Worry	Write down what is worrying you
Difficulty concentrating	Read passages in a book out loud to yourself, or talk into a tape recorder
Distractibility or forgetfulness	Repeat the word "focus" 2–3 times; use a calendar or small pad and write notes to yourself
Difficulty sleeping	Meditation; write in a journal; take a warm bath before bed; take a walk for 15 minutes an hour before bedtime; read something that relaxes you or makes you laugh
Nightmares or night terrors	Write them down; make drawings; share both in therapy; talk about your nightmares with someone you trust

Any combination of the above will work to help manage anxiety until it diminishes. Remember: anxiety passes. Give yourself time to practice the above suggestions or other methods you find helpful for the next thirty days, and be consistent.

Other contributing factors that can increase anxiety are:

_____Being a perfectionist
_____Excessive fear of failure
_____Problems with dependency
_____Problems with co-dependency
_____Not managing your finances
_____Overconcern for what others think of you
_____Fear of rejection, abandonment, or disapproval
_____Not having boundaries, or not keeping them
_____Being around the perpetrator
_____Not having control over decisions in your life
_____Engaging in catastrophic thinking

_____Marital problems
_____Abusive relationships
_____Sexual pressures
_____Loss of sexual pleasure
_____Problems with children
_____Problems with in-laws
_____A stressful job
_____Not enough—or too much—solitude
_____Not making yourself a priority

What would you add?

APPENDIX F

Dissolving the Rage and Anger

Childhood sexual abuse precedes the emotions of outrage or intense anger that women experience. The following can help to dissolve the outrage that women feel so that it no longer affects their lives. Remember to go through this process gradually as you would any other in your recovery.

1. Write down how the sexual abuse caused you to experience feelings of outrage and anger.
2. Talk through the angry feelings that you have about the sexual abuse with someone you trust to listen and understand.
3. Write a private letter to the perpetrator expressing the feelings of betrayal and sense of helplessness you experienced because of his abuse of you.
4. Write a private letter to family members you view as having a role in not protecting you and keeping you safe.
5. Identify any myths that you hold about a woman's right to express anger. Rewrite these myths into a personal statement of your right to express your feelings of anger.
6. Find a physical activity that helps you to release the energy that often goes with feelings and thoughts of anger. Be sure that this activity does not cause you or another person harm.
7. Identify the beliefs in your family that prevented the expression of anger, sadness, or disappointment.
8. Identify what causes you to feel intense anger today.
9. Identify how your anger motivates you to set and keep boundaries with people in your life today.
10. Describe the difference between expressing yourself assertively to someone and expressing yourself in an aggressive or passive way.
11. Pay attention to how you speak to others. Notice when you are speaking assertively versus speaking aggressively or passively. This way,

you can provide yourself feedback to consider how you want to approach someone in the future or restate what you have said.

12. Write down a critical thought you have about yourself and then write down a positive thought that contradicts and replaces the critical one.

13. How do you continue to allow family members to control you?

14. What decisions that you are making about your life today dissolve angry feelings rather than maintain them?

15. Take time each day or each week to regenerate your inner life and restore a sense of calm and quiet.

16. Write an affirmation that you can use daily to remind you that the life you have today is free of childhood sexual abuse. It can be as simple as "All is well."

17. As you come to a path of forgiveness, write down what you forgive yourself for, what you can forgive your family for, and what you hope forgiveness can bring to your life.

18. What connection do you find between the experiences of depression and unresolved outrage?

19. What connection do you find between the experiences of anxiety and unresolved outrage?

20. Who in the family are you closest to in terms of expressing anger? How did the person come to be a role model for you? How effective of a role model is this person?

21. Review the characteristics of a healthy family in Appendix C and identify the ones you practice in your family today. Among the ones you practice, identify those that increase your self-esteem.

22. Practice assertive body language: direct eye contact, good body posture, speaking clearly and forthright, a moderate tone of voice, and the use of facial gestures to add emphasis.

23. How do you respond to other people's anger? How is your response similar to or different from how you responded to anger in your childhood?

24. Do you hide your anger through procrastination, habitual lateness, sarcasm, overpoliteness, constant cheerfulness, smiling while hurting, or excessive irritability? Do you have difficulty sleeping or sleep excessively? Do you ruminate on thoughts and worries, use anger as a weapon or as a defense, or avoid confrontation? Do you experience fist clenching, jaw tightening, grinding of teeth, chronic stiff neck or shoulder muscles, or ulcers or irritable bowel syndrome?

25. Remember, childhood sexual abuse is a justified reason for outrage and anger. However, if this intense emotion is not dissipated, released, and allowed to diminish, it will continue to control your responses in the present, affect your relationships, and diminish your self-worth.

APPENDIX G

Boundaries

Establishing boundaries is a knowledge-based process that comes with reestablishing your personal right to live life on your terms. Boundaries can be physical, emotional, mental, and sexual. They allow women to feel safe and protected, exercise healthy control over their lives, and prevent revictimization from occurring.

The first step is to identify what boundaries you need for your life today. Practice stating them to other people and then following through by not allowing the ones you establish to be crossed. Remember: Nice people have boundaries! The following boundaries are ones that women in this treatment approach established for their lives. They are shared here to help with ideas and serve as examples of the kind of boundaries women find helpful.

1. No one touches me without my permission and consent, and I do not touch other people without their permission and consent.
2. I choose whom I am sexual with, and I am sexual only with someone who is safe. I need to feel comfortable with the person and have a reciprocal commitment of respect, love, and caring.
3. Trust is conditional; people earn my trust, and I earn theirs as well. I can give my trust to different people in different areas of my life.
4. I will not tolerate disrespectful behavior and will speak up when it happens to me.
5. I honor my feelings and the feelings of others.
6. I stand up for myself and what I believe is right for me.
7. I give myself permission to be who I am and to try new experiences.
8. I give myself and other people permission not to be perfect.
9. I affirm my life at least once a day and acknowledge the good that exists in my life today.
10. I will take time for myself and not allow other people to intrude on my time for me. I can say no and not feel guilt.

11. I will not lend money to family or friends, and I will not allow guilt to make me cross this boundary with myself.
12. I will spend money on myself when I can afford it.
13. I will not spend compulsively or save compulsively.
14. I will not live in fear of not having enough money to provide for me.
15. I will not use credit cards to excess or accumulate debt.
16. I will not have sex with my partner unless I want to, and I will give the same respect to my partner.
17. I will do work that gives me pleasure and enjoyment.
18. I will not do the work of other people.
19. I will say no, as it is my right to do so. I can also say yes or wait to give an answer when I am asked to make a commitment to someone or something.
20. I will be kind and compassionate to myself.
21. I will not be around the perpetrator.
22. I will not allow my mother/father to make me feel guilty.
23. I will not answer questions I do not want to answer or I view as an invasion of my right to privacy.
24. I will not keep friends who are not friends to me.
25. I will seek approval from myself and not from others.
26. I will create a life that brings me satisfaction.
27. I will ask for raises and promotions and believe in my own abilities to succeed. I deserve to be recognized for the work that I do and the accomplishments that I achieve.
28. I will let others solve their own problems, as they are competent and capable of doing so.
29. I will not give advice unless asked to do so.
30. I will not use alcohol and other addictive substances to numb my pain; this includes addictive relationships.
31. I will rest and take care of myself physically.
32. I will not purge food or binge on food to avoid what is troubling me in my life.
33. I will no longer allow my compulsions to control my life or the people I love and care for.
34. I will not hit my children.
35. I will develop a spiritual belief and attitude.
36. I will pray daily rather than criticize myself.
37. I will not judge myself for the past.
38. I will praise myself often.
39. For each negative thought, I will think two positive thoughts and write them down.
40. I will tell those around me that I love them.
41. I will thank others for their support and ask them for what I need.

42. I will take more time for my recovery.
43. I will be patient with myself during my recovery.

Answer the following questions:

1. How would you define a boundary?
2. What boundaries do you have in your life today?
3. What do they allow you to accomplish?
4. What boundaries do you struggle with keeping?
5. What boundaries are carried out with ease and comfort?
6. What has been the reaction of other people to your boundaries?
7. Have the reactions of other people influenced your boundaries either positively or negatively?
8. What boundaries are the most important for you right now?
9. How are you with accepting other people's boundaries?
10. Who in your life supports the changes you are making or have already made through your healing?

APPENDIX H

Suggestions for Family Members

Family members who have detached from the harmful belief system that perpetuates childhood sexual abuse can be of particular support to women during their healing. Families can seek help and support as well from a professional therapist who has specialized experience and knowledge in this specific trauma.

Family members need to acknowledge that even though this trauma happened in childhood, it is only now being healed. Consider that women need the same compassionate approach *today* that they would have needed as children if they had disclosed the sexual abuse then.

PARTNERS

The book *Partners in Recovery: How Mates, Lovers and Other Prosurvivors Can Learn to Support and Cope with Adult Survivors of Childhood Sexual Abuse,* by Beverly Engel, is good support for you and your partner. You can also

1. Encourage her therapy by not complaining about the time or financial investment in her healing.
2. Show her that she can trust you by not confiding to anyone else what is private to her unless you discuss with her the person you want to confide in and your reason.
3. Hold her hand, ask to give her a hug, comfort her when she cries, have fun with her when she needs to be encouraged to have fun, listen with an open mind and open heart, and allow her the amount of time she needs to heal. Let her know that her needs come first right now.
4. Ask her directly what she needs from you to support her through this stage of her life.
5. Tell her how you view her recovery as a positive outcome for the relationship.

6. Identify how you are willing to change in order to have a more meaningful relationship with her.

7. Identify when you need to take over some of her responsibilities in the home or with the children.

8. Treat her as though she is recovering from a long illness; send flowers and/or cards, encourage her to nap or rest.

9. If she is working outside the home and a medical leave is recommended, encourage her to act on this recommendation.

10. If she is working from the home or is a woman who is wife and mother in the traditional way and a medical leave is recommended, encourage her to act on this recommendation.

11. Together, agree that during her medical leave she is not to take on more responsibilities around the house.

12. Believe what she tells you about the sexual abuse, but do not ask intrusive questions. Intrusive questions are those that seek details about the abusive acts. Do not ask too many questions all at once. If you ask questions that she would rather not answer, then respect her privacy.

13. Do not make decisions for her. This is especially true with disclosing to anyone else about the sexual abuse. It is also true with regard to confronting the perpetrator or any other family member about the sexual abuse.

14. Listen to her more than you ask questions of her. It is okay to give suggestions to her about how she can take care of herself when you see she is not doing so. A gentle reminder is often well received.

15. Do not minimize, negate, or become critical of what she has to share regarding her needs at this time or what she is going through.

16. Always affirm for her that she is not to blame for the perpetrator's abuse or how it affected her.

17. When you feel angry, express your anger safely about the perpetrator and the abuse, not her.

18. Consider seeing a therapist on your own to ask questions, discuss your feelings, and gain support outside of the relationship.

19. Take time for yourself and maintain activities that help you manage your stress.

20. If you have children, communicate to her what your expectations are for your children and their contact or relationship with the perpetrator.

EXTENDED FAMILY MEMBERS

The book *When Your Child Has Been Molested: A Parent's Guide to Healing and Recovery,* by Kathryn B. Hagans and Joyce Case, is a good resource for parents. It answers questions and provides information across a variety of topics. For siblings, I recommend reading this book and others that can be found at their local libraries or bookstores.

In general, parents and siblings are in a unique position to support their daughter or sister who was sexually abused. Parents and siblings can share what they know about the family history. They can provide information, complete the history, believe in her, encourage her, and support her partner and children.

A daughter needs for her parents to believe her and not blame her or be angry with her about the sexual abuse. She needs support regarding her choice to disclose this trauma within the family. A daughter is not asking that parents who are not perpetrators take the blame for the abuse. She does need her parents to acknowledge the family history, her lack of being protected, and the belief system that allowed the abuse to occur and remain a secret.

If either of her parents was also a victim of sexual abuse, or other types of abuse, letting her know this can help her in her recovery and help her to understand her parents better. Do not deny what you know to be true. If the perpetrator is from either of your families, then you will need to decide if you will confront this person or support your daughter in her disclosure with him. Discuss this decision with your daughter before you take action.

For Parents Who Are Not the Perpetrator

1. Believe your daughter, accept that the abuse occurred, do not blame her, do not ask her to keep it a secret, and do not express anger that she has told.
2. Be proud of the courage and perseverance she has shown throughout the years since the trauma.
3. She does not expect you to take sides. She needs you to support her and to give her a healthy loyalty.
4. Ask her how the abuse has affected her. Listen to her without interrupting so that you can understand.
5. Do not ask intrusive questions or details about the abusive acts. When you ask a question, preface it by acknowledging that the decision to answer your question is hers. Realize that she will not want to answer some questions because of privacy issues she has.
6. If you experience a sense of disbelief, affirm for her that this feeling is about not wanting to believe this trauma happened to her and not that you do not believe her. Acknowledging that you believe her and that you believe it happened to her is important.
7. Parents can benefit from seeing a therapist with whom they can discuss their feelings, thoughts, and experience. Fortunately, there are professionals who have knowledge and experience working with families through this trauma.

8. If she thought you knew about the sexual abuse, explain to her what you knew and what you did not know. Help her to understand how you did not keep her safe or protect her from harm.

9. Parents need to support their daughter's decision about her children. Do not expect your daughter to visit if the perpetrator is in your home.

10. Expect relationships to change. The changes that occur will be for the better and will be based on openness and honesty within the family.

11. Give yourself time to accept the truth of what you learn.

12. Expect several discussions to take place over a period of time rather than all at once.

SIBLINGS

Believe what your sister has to tell you and do not make excuses for the perpetrator. She is not asking you to take sides. She is telling you about the abuse and the perpetrator. She needs your support to do so and perhaps to protect your children from the perpetrator as well. Your sister's disclosure will help you to understand problems that you have experienced in the family.

1. Discuss with your sister what you remember about the perpetrator and the family history. Siblings can share memories and provide meaningful accounts of events.

2. If you were a victim, it is your decision whether to disclose this to your sibling.

3. Allow time to help you accept what you are learning.

4. Recognize that if this is the first disclosure of sexual abuse in your family, neither you nor your parents have experience regarding how to get through this trauma. Seek professional help even if it is for a limited time.

5. Do not blame yourself. You were a child as well and could not have stopped or prevented the sexual abuse from happening.

For All Family Members

1. Call and ask how she and her family are doing.

2. Ask if they need anything from you. Send cards and/or flowers, visit, and encourage her recovery.

3. Let her know that you love her and care about her.

4. Stay in touch with her partner. Give him support.

5. Be near without being intrusive.

6. Do not talk about the abuse unless she brings it up or you ask her if it is all right to discuss it.

7. Do not share your memories all at once if you were also a victim of sexual abuse. Depending on her stage of recovery, your memories may overwhelm her. Ask before you share about the sexual abuse that occurred to you.
8. Do not disclose to other people in the family unless you first discuss this decision with her.
9. When disclosure occurs, the focus is on the perpetrator's behavior, not on the victim's behavior during the abuse.
10. Respect her boundaries and the decisions she makes during her recovery and into her life.

APPENDIX I

Forgiveness

The following is meant to help women either begin or continue learning about the healing process of forgiveness. The benefits of forgiveness can include the experience of positive emotions, a greater sense of control over our lives, and less physiological stress. Forgiveness is not about forgetting, condoning, or accepting what is wrong; it is about letting go of the hurt and pain that cause you not to feel well.

Do not rush into forgiveness. Forgiving the person who sexually abused you takes time. Forgiveness does not always mean that reconciliation occurs with the person who harmed you. Forgiveness can involve empathy, relinquishing revenge, and adopting merciful feelings.

1. Write down the name of the perpetrator.
2. What specifically did this person do to you that you need or want to forgive?
3. What do you want forgiveness to bring to you?
4. What do you want forgiveness to bring to this person?
5. What emotions would you be letting go of and releasing with forgiveness?
6. What painful memories would be released and diminished?
7. What do you need to forgive within yourself?

Repeat this process as many times as necessary. You can use the same process with other people who have harmed you or mistreated you. You can also use this process to identify how you have harmed other people. For example, you would

1. Write down the name of the person you have harmed.
2. What specifically did you do to this person to cause them harm?
3. What do you want their forgiveness to bring to you?

4. What would forgiving you bring to this person?
5. What prevents you from asking for forgiveness?
6. What emotions would you be letting go of if you asked for forgiveness?
7. What will you feel if you are not forgiven?
8. What will you feel if you are forgiven?
9. What painful memories would you be releasing?

MEDITATIONS

When we meditate, we focus inward and concentrate our minds to find a place of peace and surrender. Meditation is similar to prayer as we open ourselves to its healing power of quiet contemplation.

May I be happy. May I be healthy. May I know peace of mind. May the light of my spirit be a blessing to those I meet.

All that has offended, I forgive. Whatever has made me bitter, resentful, and unhappy, I forgive. Within and Without, I forgive. Things past, things present, things future, I forgive.

Post-Traumatic Stress Disorder (PTSD)

A. The person has been exposed to a traumatic event in which both of the following were present:
  1. The person experienced, witnessed, or was confronted with an event or events that involved actual or threatened death or serious injury, or a threat to the physical integrity of self or others.
  2. The person's response involved intense fear, helplessness, or horror. Note: In children, this may be expressed instead by disorganized or agitated behavior.

B. The traumatic event is persistently reexperienced in one (or more) of the following ways:
  1. Recurrent and intrusive distressing recollections of the event, including images, thoughts, or perceptions. Note: In young children, repetitive play may occur in which themes or aspects of the trauma are expressed.
  2. Recurrent distressing dreams of the event. Note: In children, there may be frightening dreams without recognizable content.
  3. Acting or feeling as if the traumatic event were recurring (includes a sense of reliving the experience, illusions, hallucinations, and dissociative flashback episodes, including those that occur on awakening or when intoxicated). Note: In young children, trauma-specific reenactment may occur.
  4. Intense psychological distress at exposure to internal or external cues that symbolize or resemble an aspect of the traumatic event.
  5. Physiological reactivity on exposure to internal or external cues that symbolize or resemble an aspect of the traumatic event.

C. Persistent avoidance of stimuli associated with the trauma and numbing of general responsiveness (not present before the trauma), as indicated by three (or more) of the following:
   1. Efforts to avoid thoughts, feelings, or conversation associated with the trauma
   2. Efforts to avoid activities, places, or people that arouse recollection of the trauma
   3. Inability to recall an important aspect of the trauma
   4. Markedly diminished interest or participation in significant activities
   5. Feelings of detachment or estrangement from others
   6. Restricted range of affect (e.g., unable to have loving feelings)
   7. Sense of a foreshortened future (e.g., does not expect to have a career, marriage, children, or a normal life span)

D. Persistent symptoms of increased arousal (not present before the trauma), as indicated by two (or more) of the following:
   1. Difficulty falling or staying asleep
   2. Irritability or outbursts of anger
   3. Difficulty concentrating
   4. Hypervigilance
   5. Exaggerated startle response

E. Duration of the disturbance (symptoms in Criteria B, C, and D) is more than one month.

F. The disturbance causes clinically significant distress or impairment in social, occupational, or other important areas of functioning.

Specify if:

Acute: Duration of symptoms is less than three months.
Chronic: Duration of symptoms is three months or more.

Specify if:

With Delayed Onset: Onset of symptoms is at least six months after the stressor.

Source: Diagnostic and Statistical Manual of Mental Disorders, 4th ed., Text Revision, American Psychiatric Association, 2000.

Author's Note: The *Diagnostic and Statistical Manual IV-TR* (DSM-IV-TR) that is used by mental health practitioners to classify the symptoms of problems individuals present for treatment does contain the diagnosis of Child Sexual Abuse. It is in the section "Other

Conditions That May Be a Focus of Clinical Attention," which follows the sections covering the sixteen major diagnostic classes of the DSM-IV. The code for Child Sexual Abuse is V61.21, which indicates that it is not included under the major classes. Here is the description: "V61.21 Sexual Abuse of Child. This category should be used when the focus of clinical attention is sexual abuse of a child. Coding note: Specify 995.52 if focus of clinical attention is on the victim" (DSM-IV-TR, 2000, American Psychiatric Association). As a clinician, I have continued to question the reason that Child Sexual Abuse as a trauma is not yet provided as a major classification of diagnosis when it is so prevalent in our society and is a major reason children and adults seek mental health services. Perhaps one day the authors of this prestigious and widely used classification system will give child sexual abuse the attention it deserves.

Notes

Preface

1. Joan Borysenko, *A Woman's Book of Life: The Biology, Psychology, and Spirituality of the Feminine Life Cycle* (New York: Riverhead Books, 1996), pp. 128–130.

2. "Female Population by Age, Race and Hispanic or Latino Origin for the United States: 2000," U.S. Census Bureau, Census 2000, Summary Table 1, October 3, 2001.

3. Bessel A. van der Kolk, Alexander C. McFarlane, and Onno van der Hart, "A General Approach to Treatment of Posttraumatic Stress Disorder," in *Traumatic Stress: The Effects of Overwhelming Experience on Mind, Body, and Society,* ed. Bessel A. van der Kolk, Alexander C. McFarlane, and Lars Weisaeth (New York: The Guilford Press, 1996), pp. 417–440. B. E. Saunders, L. Berliner, and R. F. Hanson, *Child Physical and Sexual Abuse: Guidelines for Treatment* (Charleston: National Crime Victims Research and Treatment Center, 2003), pp. 12–16, 104–108.

Introduction

1. Caroline Myss, *Why People Don't Heal and How They Can* (New York: Harmony Books, 1997), p. 8.

2. Bessel A. van der Kolk and Alexander C. McFarlane, "The Black Hole of Trauma," in *Traumatic Stress: The Effects of Overwhelming Experience on Mind, Body, and Society,* ed. Bessel A. van der Kolk, Alexander C. McFarlane, and Lars Weisaeth (New York: The Guilford Press, 1996), pp. 17–19.

3. Charles L. Whitfield, *Memory and Abuse: Remembering and Healing the Effects of Trauma* (Deerfield Beach, Fla.: Health Communications, 1995), p. 2.

4. Alexander C. McFarlane and Giovanni de Girolamo, "The Nature of Traumatic Stressors and the Epidemiology of Posttraumatic Reactions," in *Traumatic Stress,* p. 130.

5. Daniel J. Siegel, "An Interpersonal Neurobiology of Psychotherapy: The Developing Mind and the Resolution of Trauma," in *Healing Trauma: Attachment, Mind, Body, and Brain*, ed. Marion F. Solomon and Daniel J. Siegel (New York: W. W. Norton and Company, 2003), pp. 8–32.

6. Alice Miller, *Breaking Down the Wall of Silence: The Liberating Experience of Facing Painful Truth* (New York: Penguin Books, 1993), p. 3.

7. Ellen Bass and Laura Davis, *The Courage to Heal: A Guide for Women Survivors of Child Sexual Abuse* (New York: Harper & Row, 1988), pp. 92–93.

Chapter 1

1. Diana Sullivan Everstine and Louis Everstine, *Sexual Trauma in Children and Adolescents: Dynamics and Treatment* (New York: Brunner/Mazel Publishers, 1989), pp. 2–3.

2. Bessel A. van der Kolk, "Posttraumatic Stress Disorder and the Nature of Trauma," in *Healing Trauma: Attachment, Mind, Body, and Brain*, ed. Marion F. Solomon and Daniel J. Siegel (New York: W. W. Norton and Company, 2003), pp. 168–170. Amy Naugle, "Child Sexual Abuse Fact Sheet," National Violence Against Women Prevention Research Center, Medical University of South Carolina, n.d., http://www.vawprevention.org/research/factsheet.shtml.

3. B. E. Saunders, L. Berliner, and R. F. Hanson, *Child Physical and Sexual Abuse: Guidelines for Treatment* (Charleston: National Crime Victims Research and Treatment Center, 2003), pp. 5–8. David M. Heger, "Violence Against Women Policy Trends Report 19," National Violence Against Women Prevention Research Center, University of Missouri-St. Louis, July 5, 2001, http://www.vawprevention.org/policy/trends/trends19.shtml.

4. Virginia Sapiro, *Women in American Society: An Introduction to Women's Studies*, 4th ed. (Mountain View, Calif.: Mayfield Publishing Company, 1999), pp. 296–318. David M. Heger, review of Linda G. Mills, "Mandatory Arrest and Prosecution Policies for Domestic Violence: A Critical Literature Review and the Case for More Research to Test Victim Empowerment Approaches," *Criminal Justice & Behavior* 25(3) (Sept. 1998): 306–318, http://www.vawprevention.org/policy/mandarrest.shtml.

5. Howard N. Snyder, "Sexual Assault of Young Children as Reported to Law Enforcement: Victim, Incident, and Offender Characteristics," National Center for Juvenile Justice, U.S. Department of Justice, July 2000, pp. 8–10, http://www.ojp.usdoj.gov/bjs/pub/pdf/saycrle.pdf. Craig M. Allen, *Women and Men Who Sexually Abuse Children: A Comparative Analysis* (Brandon, Vt.: Safer Society Press, 1997), pp. 46–48. Marcia T. Turner and Tracy T. Turner, *Female Adolescent Sexual Abusers: An Exploratory Study of Mother-Daughter Dynamics with Implications for Treatment* (Brandon, Vt.: Safer Society Press, 1994), pp. 24–25.

6. Naugle, "Child Sexual Abuse Fact Sheet," pp. 1–5.

7. Ron Smith, Director, Indianapolis Counseling Center, interview by Karen A. Duncan, Indianapolis Counseling Center, Indianapolis, Indiana, April 29, 2003.

David Finkelhor and Richard Ormrod, "Characteristics of Crimes Against Juveniles," *Juvenile Justice Bulletin,* June 2000, p. 8. Lawrence A. Greenfield, "Sex Offenses and Offenders: An Analysis of Data on Rape and Sexual Assault," Bureau of Justice Statistics, U.S. Department of Justice, February 1997, p. 23.

8. David Finkelhor and Richard Ormrod, "Offenders Incarcerated for Crimes against Juveniles," *Juvenile Justice Bulletin,* December 2001, p. 9. Snyder, "Sexual Assault of Young Children," p. 8.

9. Allen, *Women and Men Who Sexually Abuse Children,* pp. 19 and 49–55.

10. Juliann Mitchell and Jill Morse, *From Victims to Survivors: Reclaimed Voices of Women Sexually Abused in Childhood by Females* (Bristol, Pa.: Accelerated Development, 1998), pp. 149–150.

11. Allen, *Women and Men Who Sexually Abuse Children,* pp. 12–13.

12. Finkelhor and Ormrod, "Characteristics of Crimes against Juveniles," p. 2; Snyder, "Sexual Assault of Young Children," pp. 4–8.

13. Rebecca Campbell and Sheela Raja, "The Secondary Victimization of Rape Victims: Insights from Mental Health Professionals Who Treat Survivors of Violence," *Violence and Victims* 14 (1999): 261–275.

14. Katherine B. Hagans and Joyce Case, *When Your Child Has Been Molested: A Parent's Guide to Healing and Recovery* (Lexington, Mass.: Lexington Books, 1990), pp. 29–31.

15. Campbell and Raja, "Secondary Victimization of Rape Victims," pp. 261–275. Charles L. Whitfield, *Memory and Abuse: Remembering and Healing the Effects of Trauma* (Deerfield Beach, Fla.: Health Communications, 1995), pp. 9–10. Rebecca Campbell, "Mental Health Services for Rape Survivors: Current Issues in Therapeutic Practice," *Violence Against Women Online Resources,* October 2001, http://www.vaw.umn.edu/documents/commissioned/campbell/campbell.html.

16. Whitfield, *Memory and Abuse,* pp. 215–216.

17. Finkelhor and Ormrod, "Characteristics of Crimes against Juveniles," p. 2. Ron Smith interview. Hagans and Case, *When Your Child Has Been Molested,* pp. 3–6.

18. Ron Smith interview.

19. William E. Prendergast, *Treating Sex Offenders: A Guide to Clinical Practice with Adults, Clerics, Children and Adolescents,* 2d ed. (New York: Haworth Press, 2004), pp. 3–17, 110–111, 141–143, and 190–194.

20. Allen, *Women and Men Who Sexually Abuse Children,* pp. 46–55.

21. Prendergast, *Treating Sex Offenders,* pp. 221–226.

22. Finkelhor and Ormrod, "Characteristics of Crimes against Juveniles," pp. 8–10.

23. E. Sue Blume, *Secret Survivors: Uncovering Incest and Its Aftereffects in Women,* 1st ed. (New York: John Wiley and Sons, 1990), pp. 230–232.

24. Priscilla Schulz, review of Klaas Wijma, Johan Soderquist, Ingela Bjorklund, and Barbro Wijma, "Prevalence of Posttraumatic Stress Disorder among Gynecological Patients with a History of Sexual and Physical Abuse," *Journal of Interpersonal Violence* 15 (September 2000), 1–2, http://www.vawprevention.org/research/prevalenceofptsd.shtml.

25. Allen, *Women and Men Who Sexually Abuse Children,* pp. 11–20.

26. Ibid.

27. Ibid., p. 55.

28. Catalina Arata, "Child Sexual Abuse and Sexual Revictimization," *Clinical Psychology: Science and Practice* 9(2) (2002): 135–164.

29. Terri L. Messman and Patricia J. Long, "Child Sexual Abuse and Its Relationship to Revictimization in Adult Women: A Review," *Clinical Psychology Review* 16 (1996): 397–420.

30. David M. Heger, "Violence Against Women Policy Trends Report 19," National Violence Against Women Prevention Research Center, University of Missouri—St. Louis, pp. 1–4.

31. Ron Smith interview. See also Michele Elliot, ed., *Female Sexual Abuse of Children* (New York: The Guilford Press, 1994), p. 97; Prendergast, *Treating Sex Offenders,* pp. 147–156.

32. Whitfield, *Trauma and Memory,* pp. 76–82. Allen, *Women and Men Who Sexually Abuse Children,* p. 56

33. Prendergast, *Treating Sex Offenders,* pp. 109–119.

34. Alice Miller, *Breaking Down the Wall of Silence: The Liberating Experience of Facing Painful Truth* (New York: Penguin Books, 1993), pp. 5–9.

35. Prendergast, *Treating Sex Offenders,* p. 225.

36. Miller, *Breaking Down the Wall of Silence,* pp. 129–144.

Chapter 2

1. Alice Miller, *Breaking Down the Wall of Silence: The Liberating Experience of Facing Painful Truth* (New York: Penguin Books, 1993), p. 1. Charles L. Whitfield, *Memory and Abuse: Remembering and Healing the Effects of Trauma* (Deerfield Beach, Fla.: Health Communications, 1995), p. 44, 70. Bessel A. van der Kolk, Alexander C. McFarlane, and Onno van der Hart, "A General Approach to Treatment of Posttraumatic Stress Disorder," in *Traumatic Stress: The Effects of Overwhelming Experience on Mind, Body, and Society,* ed. Bessel A. van der Kolk, Alexander C. McFarlane, and Lars Weisaeth (New York: The Guilford Press, 1996), pp. 425–428.

2. Bessel A. van der Kolk, and Alexander C. McFarlane, "The Black Hole of Trauma," in *Traumatic Stress,* pp. 6–9.

3. Renee Fredrickson, *Repressed Memories: A Journey to Recovery from Sexual Abuse* (New York: Simon and Schuster, 1992), pp. 88–97. Van der Kolk, McFarlane, and Hart, "General Approach," in *Traumatic Stress,* p. 421.

4. Bessel A. van der Kolk, "Posttraumatic Stress Disorder and the Nature of Trauma," in *Healing Trauma: Attachment, Mind, Body, and Brain,* ed. Marion F. Solomon and Daniel J. Siegel (New York: W. W. Norton and Company, 2003), pp. 183–186. Whitfield, *Memory and Abuse,* p. 40–46.

5. Joan Borysenko, *A Woman's Book of Life: The Biology, Psychology, and Spirituality of the Feminine Life Cycle* (New York: Riverhead Books, 1996), pp. 129–131. Bessel van

der Kolk, "Posttraumatic Stress Disorder and the Nature of Trauma," *Healing Trauma*, pp. 174–177.

6. Van der Kolk, "Trauma and Memory," in *Traumatic Stress*, p. 285.

7. Joan Borysenko, *Woman's Book of Life*, p. 128

8. Maryanna Eckberg, *Victims of Cruelty: Somatic Psychotherapy in the Treatment of Posttraumatic Stress Disorder* (Berkeley, Calif.: North Atlantic Books, 2000), pp. 7–9, 39–60.

9. Eckberg, *Victims of Cruelty*, p. 7.

10. Whitfield, *Memory and Abuse*, pp. xviii, 55–62. Alexander C. McFarlane and Bessel A. van der Kolk, "Trauma and Its Challenge to Society," in *Traumatic Stress*, pp. 36–39.

11. Whitfield, *Memory and Abuse*, pp. 67–74.

12. Susan Faludi, *Backlash: The Undeclared War against American Women* (New York: Anchor Books, 1991). Anne Wilson Schaef, *Women's Reality: An Emerging Female System in the White Male Society* (Minneapolis: Winston Press, 1981). Elizabeth Wurtzel, *BITCH: In Praise of Difficult Women*, 1st ed. (New York: Doubleday, 1998). Carol Gilligan, *In a Different Voice: Psychological Theory and Women's Development* (Cambridge: Harvard University Press, 1993).

13. Eckberg, *Victims of Cruelty*, pp. 7–8. Whitfield, *Memory and Abuse*, pp. 243–244. Candace Pert, Ph.D., former chief of brain biochemistry at the National Institute of Mental Health (NIMH), Jean Bolen, M.D., clinical professor of psychiatry, University of California School of Medicine, San Francisco and Bessel A. van der kolk, M.D., professor of psychiatry Harvard Medical School and director of the Trauma Clinic, all seem to agree that trauma is stored in the body and expressed as changes in the biological stress response; these researchers view the body as an organ of memory that, along with the brain, stores experience (45).

14. E. Sue Blume, *Secret Survivors: Uncovering Incest and Its Aftereffects in Women*, 1st ed. (New York: John Wiley and Sons, 1990), pp. 98–99.

Chapter 3

1. Juliann Mitchell and Jill Morse, *From Victims to Survivors: Reclaimed Voices of Women Sexually Abused in Childhood by Females* (Bristol, Pa.: Accelerated Development, 1998), pp. 7–10. Robert S. Pynoos, Alan M. Steinberg, and Armen Goenjian, "Traumatic Stress in Childhood and Adolescence: Recent Developments and Current Controversies," in *Traumatic Stress: The Effects of Overwhelming Experience on Mind, Body, and Society*, ed. Bessel A. van der Kolk, Alexander C. McFarlane, and Lars Weisaeth (New York: The Guilford Press, 1996), pp. 331–352.

2. Diana Sullivan Everstine and Louis Everstine, *Sexual Trauma in Children and Adolescents: Dynamics and Treatment* (New York: Brunner/Mazel Publishers, 1989), pp. 166–172. Terri L. Messman and Patricia J. Long, "Child Sexual Abuse and Its Relationship to Revictimization in Adult Women: A Review," *Clinical Psychology Review* 16 (1996): 397–420. Van der Kolk and McFarlane, "Black Hole of Trauma," in

Traumatic Stress, pp. 10–11. Catalina M. Avata, "Child Sexual Abuse and Sexual Revictimization," *Clinical Psychology: Science and Practice* 9(2) (2002): 135–164.

3. Charlotte Davis Kasl, *Women, Sex, and Addiction: A Search for Love and Power* (New York: Harper & Row, 1990), pp. 302–307.

Chapter 4

1. Wendy Maltz and Beverly Holman, *Incest and Sexuality: A Guide to Understanding and Healing* (Lexington, Mass.: Lexington Books, 1987), pp. 34–39.

2. Bessel A. van der Kolk, Alexander C. McFarlane, and Onno van der Hart, "A General Approach to Treatment of Posttraumatic Stress Disorder," in *Traumatic Stress: The Effects of Overwhelming Experience on Mind, Body, and Society*, ed. Bessel A. van der Kolk, Alexander C. McFarlane, and Lars Weisaeth (New York: The Guilford Press, 1996), pp. 422–425.

3. Wayne Kritsberg, *The Adult Children of Alcoholics Syndrome: A Step-by-Step Guide to Discovery and Recovery* (New York: Bantam Books, 1988). Gerald C. Davison and John M. Neale, *Abnormal Psychology*, 8th ed. (New York: John Wiley and Sons, Inc., 2001). Maryanna Eckberg, *Victims of Cruelty: Somatic Psychotherapy in the Treatment of Posttraumatic Stress Disorder* (Berkeley, Calif.: North Atlantic Books, 2000). Arieh Y. Shalev, "Stress Versus Traumatic Stress: from Acute Homeostatic Reactions to Chronic Psychotherapy," in *Traumatic Stress: The Effects of Overwhelming Experience on Mind, Body, and Society*, ed. Bessel A. van der Kolk, Alexander C. McFarlane, and Lars Weisaeth (New York: The Guilford Press, 1996).

4. Alexander C. McFarlane and Giovanni de Girolamo, "The Nature of Traumatic Stressors and the Epidemiology of Posttraumatic Reactions," in *Traumatic Stress*, pp. 131–132.

5. Kritsberg, *Adult Children of Alcoholics Syndrome*, pp. 49–56.

6. Eckberg, *Victims of Cruelty*, pp. 25–30.

7. Davison and Neale, *Abnormal Psychology*, pp. 184–193.

8. Ibid. Arieh Y. Shalev, "Stress Versus Traumatic Stress: from Acute Homeostatic Reactions to Chronic Psychotherapy," in *Traumatic Stress*, p. 89.

9. Eckberg, *Victims of Cruelty*, pp. 22–25

10. Juliann Mitchell and Jill Morse, *From Victims to Survivors: Reclaimed Voices of Women Sexually Abused in Childhood by Females* (Bristol, Pa.: Accelerated Development, 1998), pp. 18–19. Charles L. Whitfield, *Memory and Abuse: Remembering and Healing the Effects of Trauma* (Deerfield Beach, Fla.: Health Communications, 1995), p. 86. Linda Tschirhart Sanford and Mary Ellen Donovan, *Women and Self-Esteem: Understanding and Improving the Way We Think and Feel about Ourselves* (New York: Penguin Press, 1985), pp. 8–11.

11. Teresa Dunbar, "Women Who Sexually Molest Female Children," in *Female Sexual Abusers: Three Views*, ed. Euan Bear (Brandon, Vt.: Safer Society Press, 1999), pp. 352–354.

12. Bessel A. van der Kolk, Onno van der Hart, and Charles R. Marmar, "Dissociation and Information Processing in Posttraumatic Stress Disorder," in *Traumatic Stress*, pp. 303–319. Whitfield, *Memory and Abuse*, pp. 253–266.

13. Dusty Miller, *Women Who Hurt Themselves* (New York: Basic Books, 1994), pp. 8–10.

14. Ibid., pp. 15–16.

15. Ibid., p. 22.

16. Ibid., pp. 100–104.

17. Bessel A. van der Kolk, Onno van der Hart, and Charles R. Marmar, "Dissociation and Information Processing in Posttraumatic Stress Disorder," in *Traumatic Stress*, pp. 319–322.

18. Stuart W. Turner, Alexander C. McFarlane, and Bessel van der Kolk, "The Therapeutic Environment and New Explorations in the Treatment of Posttraumatic Stress Disorder," in *Traumatic Stress*, pp. 537–538.

Chapter 5

1. Bessel A. van der Kolk, Alexander C. McFarlane, and Onno van der Hart, "A General Approach to Treatment of Posttraumatic Stress Disorder," in *Traumatic Stress: The Effects of Overwhelming Experience on Mind, Body, and Society*, ed. Bessel A. van der Kolk, Alexander C. McFarlane, and Lars Weisaeth (New York: The Guilford Press, 1996) pp. 419–420.

2. Bessel A. van der Kolk, "The Complexity of Adaptation to Trauma Self-Regulation, Stimulus Discrimination, and Characterological Development," in *Traumatic Stress*, pp. 195–199. Robert S. Pynoos, Alan M. Steinberg, and Armen Goenjian, "Traumatic Stress in Childhood and Adolescence: Recent Developments and Current Controversies," in *Traumatic Stress*, pp. 332–336.

3. Wayne Kritsberg, *The Adult Children of Alcoholics Syndrome: A Step-by-Step Guide to Discovery and Recovery* (New York: Bantam Books, 1988), pp. 75–82.

4. Bessel A. van der Kolk, Alexander C. McFarlane, and Onno van der Hart, "A General Approach to Treatment of Posttraumatic Stress Disorder," in *Traumatic Stress*, pp. 417–436.

5. Bessel A. van der Kolk and Alexander C. McFarlane, "The Black Hole of Trauma," in *Traumatic Stress*, pp. 6–7. Robert S. Pynoos, Alan M. Steinberg, and Armen Goenjian, "Traumatic Stress in Childhood and Adolescence," in *Traumatic Stress*, pp. 331–336.

Chapter 6

1. Alexander C. McFarlane and Rachel Yehuda, "Resilience, Vulnerability, and the Course of Posttraumatic Reactions," in *Traumatic Stress: The Effects of Overwhelming*

Experience on Mind, Body, and Society, ed. Bessel A. van der Kolk, Alexander C. McFarlane, and Lars Weisaeth (New York: The Guilford Press, 1996), pp. 155–164.

2. Charles L. Whitfield, *Memory and Abuse: Remembering and Healing the Effects of Trauma* (Deerfield Beach, Fla.: Health Communications, 1995), pp. 137–138.

3. E. Sue Blume, *Secret Survivors: Uncovering Incest and Its Aftereffects in Women,* 1st ed. (New York: John Wiley and Sons, 1990), pp. xvii—xix. Whitfield, *Memory and Abuse,* pp. 150–152. Bessel A. van der Kolk, "The Complexity of Adaptation to Trauma Self-Regulation, Stimulus Discrimination, and Characterological Development," in *Traumatic Stress,* p. 184. Dusty Miller, *Women Who Hurt Themselves* (New York: Basic Books, 1994), pp. 3–6. Kristin A. Kunzman, *The Healing Way: Adult Recovery from Childhood Sexual Abuse* (San Francisco: Harper & Row, 1990), pp. 12–16.

4. *Diagnostic and Statistical Manual of Mental Disorders,* 4th ed., Text Revision (Washington, D.C.: American Psychiatric Association, 2000), pp. 463–468.

5. Alexander C. McFarlane and Giovanni de Girolamo, "The Nature of Traumatic Stressors and the Epidemiology of Posttraumatic Reactions," in *Traumatic Stress,* pp. 129–130, and Whitfield, *Memory and Abuse,* p. 152.

6. Alexander C. McFarlane, "Resilience, Vulnerability, and the Course of Posttraumatic Reactions," in *Traumatic Stress,* pp. 129–130.

7. Tony Bates, *Understanding and Overcoming Depression: A Common Sense Approach* (Freedom, Calif.: The Crossing Press, 2001), p. 16.

8. Ibid., p. 47. Arieh Y. Shalev, "Stress Versus Traumatic Stress: From Acute Homeostatic Reactions to Chronic Psychotherapy," in *Traumatic Stress,* pp. 89–91.

9. Jonathan R. T. Davidson and Bessel A. van der Kolk, "The Psychopharmacological Treatment of Posttraumatic Stress Disorder," in *Traumatic Stress,* pp. 511–524.

10. Carolyn Ainscough and Kay Toon, *Surviving Childhood Sexual Abuse: Practical Self-Help for Adults Who Were Sexually Abused as Children* (London: Fisher Books, 2000), p. 60. Whitfield, *Memory and Abuse,* pp. 150–154.

11. Ainscough and Toon, *Surviving Childhood Sexual Abuse,* p. 101.

12. Miller, *Women Who Hurt Themselves,* pp. 168–169.

13. Bessel A. van der Kolk and Alexander C. McFarlane, "The Black Hole of Trauma," in *Traumatic Stress,* pp. 13–14.

14. Jerilyn Ross, *Triumph Over Fear: A Book of Help and Hope for People with Anxiety, Panic Attacks, and Phobias* (New York: Bantam Books, 1994), p. 186.

15. Ibid., p. 17.

16. Miller, *Women Who Hurt Themselves,* pp. 154–155. Whitfield, *Memory and Abuse,* pp. 159.

17. Blume, *Secret Surivors,* pp. 128–129.

18. Van der Kolk, "Complexity in Adaptation," in *Traumatic Stress,* pp. 188–193.

19. Ainscough and Toon, *Surviving Childhood Sexual Abuse,* p. 132.

20. Van der Kolk, "Complexity in Adaptation," in *Traumatic Stress,* p. 190.

21. Barbara McFarland and Tyeis Baker-Baumann, *Shame and Body Image: Culture and the Compulsive Eater* (Deerfield Beach, Fla.: Health Communications, 1990), pp. 86–90.

22. Susie Orbach, *Fat Is a Feminist Issue: A Self-Help Guide for Compulsive Eaters* (New York: The Berkeley Publishing Group, 1988), pp. 69–90.

23. Kathleen Zraly and David Swift, *Anorexia, Bulimia, and Compulsive Overeating: A Practical Guide for Counselors and Families* (New York: The Continuum Publishing Company, 1990), pp. 111–119.

24. Orbach, *Fat Is a Feminist Issue* pp. 107–119.

25. Ibid., pp. 183–193. Margo Maine, *Body Wars: Making Peace with Women's Bodies* (Carlsbad, Calif.: Gürze Books, 2000), pp. 149–153.

26. Maine, *Body Wars*, pp. 45–55.

27. Miller, *Women Who Hurt Themselves*, pp. 7–15, 27–29, 108–109.

28. James N. Dillard with Leigh Ann Hirschman, *The Chronic Pain Solution: Your Personal Path to Pain Relief—The Comprehensive, Step-by-Step Guide to Choosing the Best of Alternative and Conventional Medicine* (New York: Bantam Books, 2002), p. xvi.

29. Whitfield, *Memory and Abuse*, p. 154.

30. Van der Kolk, "Complexity of Adaptation," in *Traumatic Stress*, pp. 193–194.

31. Ibid., pp. 194–195.

32. Dillard with Hirschman, *Chronic Pain Solution*, pp. 333–336.

33. Ibid., p. 334.

34. Ibid., pp. 3–8.

35. Ainscough and Toon, *Surviving Childhood Sexual Abuse*, p. 90.

36. Miller, *Women Who Hurt Themselves*, p. 100.

37. Bessel A. van der Kolk and Alexander C. McFarlane, "The Black Hole of Trauma," in *Traumatic Stress*, p. 11.

38. Van der Kolk, "Complexity of Adaptation," in *Traumatic Stress*, pp. 196–200.

Chapter 7

1. Bessel A. van der Kolk, *Traumatic Stress: The Effects of Overwhelming Experience on Mind, Body, and Society*, ed. Bessel A. van der Kolk, Alexander C. McFarlane, and Lars Weisaeth (New York: The Guilford Press, 1996), p. xxi.

2. Ibid.

3. Charles L. Whitfield, *Memory and Abuse: Remembering and Healing the Effects of Trauma* (Deerfield Beach, Fla.: Health Communications, 1995), pp. 138–139.

4. Ibid., pp. 138–143.

5. Kristin A. Kunzman, *The Healing Way: Adult Recovery from Childhood Sexual Abuse* (San Francisco: Harper & Row, 1990), pp. 115–126.

Chapter 8

1. Jacob Wetterling Crimes Against Children and Sexually Violent Offender Registration Program, Sec. 14071, Legal Information Institute, Cornell Law School http://www4.law.cornell.edu/uscode/42/14071.html.

2. Megan's Law Part I: Federal and State Legislation, http://members .tripod.com/~Parents_United/Megan1.htm.

3. The Jacob Wetterling Foundation, "Jacob Wetterling Act," http://www .jwf.org/www-source/jwf_legislation.html.

4. "High Court Agrees to Hear Challenge to Sex-Offender List," May 20, 2003, http://www.freedomforum.org/templates/document.asp?documentID=16278, and "Supreme Court Debates Merits of Megan's Laws," November 14, 2002, http://www.freedomforum.org/templates/document.asp?documentID=17253.

5. "Supreme Court to Examine Megan's Law," November 11, 2002, http://www. freedomforum.org/templates/document.asp?documentID=17237.

6. "U.S. Rep. Jennifer Dunn Responds to Supreme Court Decision on Megan's Law," March 6, 2003, http://www.house.gov/dunn/pr/PR_03/March03/ meganslawsc.htm.

7. Charles L. Whitfield, *Memory and Abuse: Remembering and Healing the Effects of Trauma* (Deerfield Beach, Fla.: Health Communications, 1995), p. 140.

8. Ibid., p. 145.

9. Ibid., pp. 2, 316.

10. Gloria Steinem, *Revolution from Within*, 1st ed. (Boston: Little, Brown and Company, 1991), p. 80.

11. Ibid., p. 81.

12. Carol Gilligan, *In a Different Voice: Psychological Theory and Women's Development* (Cambridge: Harvard University Press, 2003), pp. 69–71.

13. Steinem, *Revolution from Within*, pp. 80, 102.

14. Whitfield, *Memory and Abuse*, p. 5. Daylon Welliver, Johnson County Deputy Prosecuting Attorney, Johnson County Prosecutor's Office, interview by Karen A. Duncan, Oren Wright Building, Franklin, Indiana, August 5, 2003.

15. Welliver interview.

16. Carolyn Ainscough and Kay Toon, *Surviving Childhood Sexual Abuse: Practical Self-Help for Adults Who Were Sexually Abused as Children* (London: Fisher Books, 2000), pp. 258–259.

17. Daniel J. Wakin, "Public Lives: A Dispassionate Look at the Wolf in Priest's Clothing," *New York Times*, March 5, 2004, late edition, sec. B. Pam Belluck, "Boston Study Traces Patterns of Sexual Abuse by Priests," *New York Times*, February 27, 2004, late edition, sec. A.

Chapter 9

1. Stuart W. Turner, Alexander C. McFarlane, and Bessel van der Kolk, "The Therapeutic Environment and New Explorations in the Treatment of Posttraumatic Stress Disorder," in *Traumatic Stress: The Effects of Overwhelming Experience on Mind, Body, and Society*, ed. Bessel A. van der Kolk, Alexander C. McFarlane, and Lars Weisaeth (New York: The Guilford Press, 1996), p. 542.

2. Alexander C. McFarlane and Giovanni de Girolamo, "The Nature of Traumatic Stressors and the Epidemiology of Posttraumatic Reactions," in *Traumatic Stress,* p. 131. Turner, McFarlane, and van der Kolk, "Therapeutic Environment," in *Traumatic Stress,* p. 535.

3. Susan Faludi, *Backlash: The Undeclared War against American Women* (New York: Anchor Books, 1991), p. 335.

4. Van der Kolk, "Complexity of Adaptation," in *Traumatic Stress,* pp. 183–184.

5. Bessel A. van der Kolk and Alexander C. McFarlane, "The Black Hole of Trauma," in *Traumatic Stress,* p. 5.

6. *Diagnostic and Statistical Manual of Mental Disorders,* 4th ed., Text Revision (Washington, D.C.: American Psychiatric Association, 2000), p. 467.

7. Elizabeth A. Brett, "The Classification of Posttraumatic Stress Disorder," in *Traumatic Stress,* pp. 124–125. Faludi, *Backlash,* p. 349.

8. Turner, McFarlane, and van der Kolk, "Therapeutic Environment," in *Traumatic Stress,* p. 546.

9. Ibid., p. 538.

10. Rebecca Campbell and Sheela Raja, "Secondary Victimization of Rape Victims: Insights from Mental Health Professionals Who Treat Survivors of Violence," *Violence and Victims,* 14(3) (1999): 261–275.

11. David Finkelhor and Richard Ormrod, "Offenders Incarcerated for Crimes against Juveniles," *Juvenile Justice Bulletin,* December 2001, Washington, D.C.: U.S. Department of Justice, Office of Justice Programs, Office of the Juvenile Justice and Delinquency Prevention.

Chapter 10

1. William E. Prendergast, *Treating Sex Offenders: A Guide to Clinical Practice with Adults, Clerics, Children and Adolescents,* 2d ed. (New York: Haworth Press, 2004), p. 98.

Suggested Resources

All These Years
Tori Amos Inspired Site for Survivors of Sexual Abuse
http://www.alltheseyears.net/resources.htm

The Anxiety Disorders Education Program, National Institute of Mental Health (NIMH)
Phone: (301) 443–4536
1–888-269–1389 for publications
http://www.nimh.nih.gov/publicat/anxiety.cfm

The Association for the Treatment of Sexual Abuse
http://atsa.com

Center for Sex Offender Management
http://www.csom.org

Freedom Forum
http://www.freedomforum.org

Incest Survivors Resource Network International
P.O. Box 7375
Las Cruces, NM 88006
Phone: (505) 521–4260
http://www.soc-um.org/survivors/links/resources.htm

Information Resources and Inquiries Branch
6001 Executive Blvd.
Room 8184, MSC 9663
Bethesda, MD 20892–9663
Phone: (301) 443–4513
Fax: (301) 443–4297
Mental Health FAX4U: (301) 443–5158
Email: nimhinfo@nih.gov
http://www.nimh.nih.gov

International Society for Traumatic Stress Studies (ISTSS)
60 Revere Drive, Suite 500
Northbrook, IL 60062
Phone: (847) 480–9028
http://www.istss.org

Jennifer Dunn, U.S. House of Representatives (R-WA)
http://www.house.gov/dunn

Klaas Kids Foundation
http://www.klaaskids.org

Men Can Stop Rape
P.O. Box 57144
Washington, DC 20037
Phone: (202) 265–6530
Email: info@mencanstoprape.org
http://www.mencanstoprape.org

National Center for PTSD
215 N. Main Street
White River Junction, VT 05009
Phone: (802) 296–5132
http://www.dartmouth.edu/dms/ptsd

National Center on Child Abuse and Neglect
U.S. Department of Health and Human Services
P.O. Box 1182
Washington, DC 20013
Phone: (800) 841–3366
http://nccanch.acf.hhs.gov

National Committee to Prevent Child Abuse (NCPCA)
332 South Michigan Avenue, Suite 1600
Chicago, IL 60604–4357
Phone: (312) 663–3520
TDD: (312) 663–3540
Fax: (312) 939–8962
Email: ncpca@childabuse.org
http://www.childabuse.org

Office of Juvenile Justice and Delinquency Prevention
Phone: (800) 638–8736
http://www.ojjdp.ncjrs.org

Office for Victims of Crime Resource Center
National Criminal Justice Reference Service
P.O. Box 6000
Rockville, MD 20850
Phone: (800) 627–6872
http://www.ncjrs.org

Parents and Loved Ones of Sexual Abuse and Rape Victims
http://www.geocities.com/HotSprings/2656/dozhelp.html

Prevent Child Abuse America
P.O. Box 2866
Chicago, IL 60609
Phone: (312) 663–3520
http://www.preventchildabuse.org

Rape, Abuse & Incest National Network (RAINN)
635-B Pennsylvania Ave., SE
Washington, DC 20003
Phone: (800) 656–4073
http://www.rainn.org

Strength Campaign
Men Can Stop Rape
P.O. Box 57144
Washington, DC 20037
Phone: (202) 265–6530
Email: info@mencanstoprape.org
http://www.mencanstoprape.org/info-url2698/info-url.htm

Voices in Action
P.O. Box 148309
Chicago, IL 60614
Phone: (800) 786–4338
http://www.voices-action.org/index.htm

Selected Bibliography

The books and articles included in the bibliography are those that I believe will be of particular interest and help to women. Additional resources consulted and cited in the writing of this book appear in the endnotes.

Barney, Paul. *Clinical Applications of Herbal Medicine.* Pleasant Grove, Utah: Woodland Publishing, 1996.

Benson, Herbert. *The Relaxation Response.* New York: Avon Books, 1976.

Bent, Robert Freeman. *Forgiving Your Parents: A Day-by-Day Plan to Break the Bonds of the Past—For New Energy, New Freedom, and New Love.* New York: Warner Books, 1990.

Black, Claudia. *Changing Course: Healing from Loss, Abandonment, and Fear,* 2d ed. Center City, Minn.: Hazelden, 2002.

Bloomfield, Harold H., and Peter McWilliams. *How to Heal Depression.* Los Angeles: Prelude Press, 1996.

Bradshaw, John. *Bradshaw on The Family: A Revolutionary Way of Self Discovery.* Deerfield Beach, Fla.: Health Communications, 1988.

Campbell, Rebecca. "Mental Health Services for Rape Survivors: Current Issues in Therapeutic Practice." *Violence Against Women Online Resources,* October 2001, http://www.vaw.umn.edu/documents/commissioned/campbell/campbell.html.

Carter, Les, and Frank Minirth. *The Anger Workbook: A 13-Step Interactive Plan to Help You. . . .* Nashville: Thomas Nelson, 1993.

Daugherty, Lynn B. *Why Me? Help for Victims of Child Sexual Abuse (Even If They Are Adults Now).* Racine, Wis.: Mother Courage Press, 1984.

Davin, Patricia A. "Secrets Revealed: A Study of Female Sex Offenders," in *Female Sexual Abusers: Three Views*, ed. Euan Bear. Brandon, Vt.: Safer Society Press, 1999.

Davison, Gerald C., and John M. Neale. *Abnormal Psychology*, 8th ed. New York: John Wiley and Sons, 2001.

Demar, Alice D., and Henry Dreher. *Healing Mind, Healthy Woman: Using the Mind-Body Connection to Manage Stress and Take Control of Your Life*. New York: Henry Holt and Company, 1996.

Dunbar, Teresa. "Women Who Sexually Molest Female Children," in *Female Sexual Abusers: Three Views*, ed. Euan Bear. Brandon, Vt.: Safer Society Press, 1999.

Eckberg, Maryanna. *Victims of Cruelty: Somatic Psychotherapy in the Treatment of Post-traumatic Stress Disorder*. Berkeley, Calif.: North Atlantic Books, 2000.

Elliot, Michele. "What Survivors Tell Us—An Overview," in *Female Sexual Abuse of Children*, ed. Michele Elliot. New York: The Guilford Press, 1994.

Emery, Gary, and James Campbell. *Rapid Relief from Emotional Distress: A New, Clinically Proven Method for Getting Over Depression and Other Emotional Problems Without Prolonged or Expensive Therapy*. New York: Rawson Associates, 1986.

Engel, Beverly. *Partners in Recovery: How Mates, Lovers and Other Prosurvivors Can Learn to Support and Cope with Adult Survivors of Childhood Sexual Abuse*, 1st ed. Los Angeles: Lowell House, 1991.

Faludi, Susan. *Backlash: The Undeclared War Against American Women*. New York: Anchor Books, 1991.

Finkelhor, David, and Richard Ormrod. "Offenders Incarcerated for Crimes against Juveniles." *Juvenile Justice Bulletin*, December 2001, Washington, D.C.: U.S. Department of Justice, Office of Justice Programs, Office of the Juvenile Justice and Delinquency Prevention.

Foley, Denise, Eileen Nechas, and the Editors of *Prevention* Magazine. *Women's Encyclopedia of Health and Emotional Healing*. Emmaus, Pa.: Rodale Press, 1993.

Forward, Susan, and Craig Buck. *Betrayal of Innocence: Incest and Its Devastation*. New York: Penguin Books, 1987.

———. *Toxic Parents: Overcoming Their Hurtful Legacy and Reclaiming Your Life*. New York: Bantam Books, 1989.

Frankel, Lois P. *Women, Anger, and Depression: Strategies for Self Empowerment*. Deerfield Beach, Fla.: Health Communications, 1991.

Friedan, Betty. *The Feminine Mystique*. New York: Dell Publishing, 1962.

Gil, Eliana. *Outgrowing the Pain: A Book for and About Adults Abused as Children*. New York: Dell Publishing, 1988.

Gilligan, Carol. *In a Different Voice: Psychological Theory and Women's Development*. Cambridge: Harvard University Press, 1993.

Hislop, Julia R. C. "Female Child Molesters," in *Female Sexual Abusers: Three Views*. ed. Euan Bear. Brandon, Vt.: Safer Society Press, 1999.

Jennings, Kathryn T. "Female Child Molesters: A Review of the Literature," in *Female Sexual Abuse of Children*, ed. Michele Elliot. New York: The Guilford Press, 1994.

Kilpatrick, Dean G. "From the Mouths of Victims: What Victimization Surveys Tell Us about Sexual Assault and Sex Offenders." November 1996. Paper presented at the Association for the Treatment of Sexual Abuse Meeting, Chicago, Illinois.

———. "The Mental Health Impact of Rape." National Violence Against Women Prevention Research Center. Medical University of South Carolina. N.d. http://www.vawprevention.org/research/mentalimpact.shtml.

———. "Rape and Sexual Assault." National Violence Against Women Prevention Research Center. Medical University of South Carolina. N.d. http://www.vawprevention.org/research/sa.shtml.

Lerner, Harriet Goldhor. *The Dance of Anger: A Woman's Guide to Changing the Patterns of Intimate Relationships.* New York: Harper & Row, 1989.

Louden, Jennifer. *The Woman's Comfort Book: A Self-Nurturing Guide for Restoring Balance in Your Life.* San Francisco: HarperCollins, 1992.

Maltz, Wendy. *The Sexual Healing Journey: A Guide for Survivors of Sexual Abuse.* New York: HarperCollins, 2001.

McFarland, Barbara, and Tyeis Baker-Baumann. *Shame and Body Image: Culture and the Compulsive Eater.* Deerfield Beach, Fla.: Health Communications, 1990.

McKay, Matthew, Peter D. Rogers, and Judith McKay. *When Anger Hurts: Quieting the Storm Within.* Oakland, Calif.: New Harbinger Publications, 1989.

Miller, Jean Baker. *Toward a New Psychology of Women,* 2d ed. Boston: Beacon Press, 1986.

Mooney, Al J., Arlene Eisenberg, and Howard Eisenberg. *The Recovery Book.* New York: Workman Publishing, 1992.

Morrison, Andrew P. *The Culture of Shame,* 1st ed. New York: Ballantine Books, 1996.

Myss, Caroline. *Why People Don't Heal and How They Can.* New York: Harmony Books, 1997.

O'Leary, Virginia E. *Toward Understanding Women.* Monterey, Calif.: Brooks/Cole Publishing Company, 1977.

Orsborn, Carol. *The Art of Resilience: 100 Paths to Wisdom and Strength in an Uncertain World.* New York: Three Rivers Press, 1997.

Ratner, Ellen F. *The Other Side of the Family: A Book for Recovery from Abuse, Incest and Neglect.* Deerfield Beach, Fla.: Health Communications, 1990.

Roth, Geneen. *Breaking Free from Compulsive Eating.* New York: Signet, 1986.

———. *When Food Is Love: Exploring the Relationship between Eating and Intimacy.* New York: Penguin Books, 1992.

Rothbaum, Barbara Olasov, and Edna B. Foa. "Cognitive-Behavioral Therapy for Posttraumatic Stress Disorder," in *Traumatic Stress: The Effects of Overwhelming Experience on Mind, Body, and Society,* ed. Bessel A. van der Kolk, Alexander C. McFarlane, and Lars Weisaeth. New York: The Guilford Press, 1996.

Sanford, Linda Tschirhart, and Mary Ellen Donovan. *Women and Self-Esteem: Understanding and Improving the Way We Think and Feel about Ourselves.* New York: Penguin Books, 1985.

Sark. *The Bodacious Book of Succulence: Daring to Live Your Succulent Wild Life!* New York: Sark, 1998.

―――. *Succulent Wild Woman: Dancing with Your Wonder-Full Self!* New York: Sark, 1997.

Schaef, Anne Wilson. *Women's Reality: An Emerging Female System in the White Male Society.* Minneapolis: Winston Press, 1981.

Schulz, Priscilla. Review of Benjamin E. Saunders, Dean G. Kilpatrick, Rochelle F. Hanson, Heidi S. Resnick, and Michael E. Walker, "Prevalence, Case Characteristics, and Long-Term Psychological Correlates of Child Rape among Women: A National Survey," *Child Maltreatment* 4 (1999): 187–200, http://www.vawprevention.org/research/correlates.shtml.

―――. Review of Pallavi Nishith, Mindy B. Mechanic, and Patricia A. Resick, "Prior Interpersonal Trauma: The Contributions to Current PTSD Symptoms in Female Rape Victims," *Journal of Abnormal Psychology* (n.d.): n.p., http://www.vawprevention.org/research/priortrauma.shtml.

―――. Review of Patricia A. Resick and Monica K. Schnicke, "Cognitive Processing Therapy for Sexual Abuse Victims," *Journal of Consulting and Clinical Psychology* 60 (1992): 748–756, 1992, http://www.vawprevention.org/research/savictims .shtml.

Shore, Lesley Irene. *Healing the Feminine: Reclaiming Woman's Voice.* St. Paul, Minn.: Llewellyn Publications, 1995.

Smedes, Lewis B. *Forgive and Forget.* New York: Harper & Row, 1984.

State of California, Office of the Attorney General. "Protecting Yourself and Your Family." http://caag.state.ca.us/megan/protect.htm.

Van der Kolk, Bessel A., Alexander G. McFarlane, and Lars Weisaeth, eds. *Traumatic Stress: The Effects of Overwhelming Experience on Mind, Body, and Society.* New York: The Guilford Press, 1996.

U.S. Department of Justice. "Children As Victims," 1999 National Report Series, *Juvenile Justice Bulletin,* May 2000.

Walker, Alexandra. "Considering the Victim in the Implementation of Megan's Laws." N.d. Violence Against Women Online Resources. http://www.vaw.umn.edu/ documents/commissioned/meganslaw/meganslaw.html.

Warshaw, Robin. *I Never Called It Rape,* 2d ed. New York: HarperCollins Publishers, 1994.

Williams, Mary Jane. *Healing Hidden Memories: Recovery for Adult Survivors of Childhood Abuse.* Deerfield Beach, Fla.: Health Communications, 1991.

Woititz, Janet G. *Healing Your Sexual Self.* Deerfield Beach, Fla.: Health Communications, 1989.

Wurtzel, Elizabeth. *BITCH: In Praise of Difficult Women,* 1st ed. New York: Doubleday, 1998.

Young, Val. "Women Abusers—A Feminist View," in *Female Sexual Abuse of Children,* ed. Michele Elliot. New York: The Guilford Press, 1994.

INDEX

About the Author

KAREN A. DUNCAN is a marriage and family therapist and licensed social worker. She has 19 years of experience working with women and children recovering from childhood sexual abuse. She is in private practice in Indiana.